Proxy War of Pakistan

Proxy War of Pakistan

S.K. Sharma

PRASHANT PUBLISHING HOUSE
DELHI-110094

Published by :
Prashant Publishing House
C-34, 28 Foota Road, Gali-3,
West Karwal Nagar, Delhi-110094
Phone : 011-22963970, Mob. : 9810396373
e-mail.: prashantpublishinghouse@gmail.com

First Published 2016

ISBN 978-93-80565-76-7

PRINTED IN INDIA
Published by Mr. R.K. Jha M/s Prashant Publishing House and Published at H.S. Offset House Press, Delhi.

Contents

Preface

The proxy war that Pakistan has been engaging in to fight India's 'superior' military, a term that was also mentioned by Prime Minister Narendra Modi, the Pentagon has brought to the attention of the US Congress Pakistan's use of militant groups as proxies. "Afghan - and India - focused militants continue to operate from Pakistan territory to the detriment of Afghan and regional stability. Pakistan uses these proxy forces to hedge against the loss of influence in Afghanistan and to counter India's superior military".

A proxy war is a conflict between two nations where neither country directly engages the other. While this can encompass a breadth of armed confrontation, its core definition hinges on two separate powers utilizing external strife to somehow attack the interests or territorial holdings of the other. This frequently involves both countries fighting their opponent's allies, or assisting their allies in fighting their opponent.

"The neighbouring country has lost the strength to fight a conventional war, but continues to engage in the proxy war of terrorism," Modi said in August during his maiden trip to Leh, adding that more Indian armed forces have been succumbing to acts of terror than war.

India & Pakistan are once again engaged in war of words & bullets at Borders. After the aborted meeting between National security adviser of India & Pakistan's adviser to PM on foreign affairs pursuant to Modi - Nawaz Joint statement in Russian city of Uffa , both the Countries appear as distant as ever. Even after 68 years of their independence, neither nation has learnt to live in peace, leave alone harmony.Innocent civilians are increasingly becoming fodder to their guns.

A sad factor of the ever deteriorating relations is the leverage enjoyed by the spies & security experts of both countries in determining the 'Red lines' for politicians of their respective countries.Every step between the two countries is now being measured & evaluated through security prism. The relations get further strained by ultra-nationalist & jingoistic media driven by agencies, particularly on the Indian Side. Politics & diplomacy is not allowed a free run to instill & nurture a good neighborly relation between the two Countries.

This book presents an incisive analysis of the trends and prospects of Pakistan's proxy war and its wider ramifications. Specific recommendations focus on the pro-active military measures that are necessary to regain control over the vitiated security situation and restore normalcy, even as the civil administration concentrates on winning the battle of hearts and minds.

—Editor

1

Introduction to Proxy War

A proxy war is a conflict between two nations where neither country directly engages the other. While this can encompass a breadth of armed confrontation, its core definition hinges on two separate powers utilizing external strife to somehow attack the interests or territorial holdings of the other. This frequently involves both countries fighting their opponent's allies, or assisting their allies in fighting their opponent.

Proxy wars have been especially common since the close of World War II and the rise of theCold War, and were a defining aspect of global conflict during the latter half of the 20th century. Much of this was motivated by fears that direct conflict between the United States and Soviet Union would result in nuclear holocaust, rendering proxy wars an ostensibly safer way of exercising hostilities. There were also more immediate reasons for the emergence of proxy war on the global stage. During its later years, the USSR often found it less expensive to arm or otherwise prop up NATO-antagonistic parties in lieu of direct engagement. In addition, the proliferation of televised media and its impact on public perception made the U.S. public especially susceptible to war-weariness and skeptical of risking American life abroad. This led to the practice of arming insurgent forces, such as the funneling of supplies to theMujahideen during the Soviet-Afghan War.

Proxy wars can also emerge from independent conflicts escalating due to the intervention of external powers. For example, the Spanish Civil War began as a civil war between the pro-fascist revolutionary Nationalists and supporters of the Spanish Republic, calledRepublicans. However, it evolved into a proxy war as Nazi Germany and its allies began supporting the Nationalists, while the USSR,Mexico and various international volunteers supported the Republicans.

PROXY WARS AS ABSTRACT

A significant disparity in the belligerents' conventional military strength may motivate the weaker party to begin or continue a conflict through allied nations or non-state actors. Such a situation arose during the Arab-Israeli conflict, which continued as a series of proxy wars following Israel's decisive defeat of the Arab coalitions in the First Arab-Israeli War, the Six-Day War and the Yom Kippur War. The coalition members, upon failing to achieve military dominance via direct conventional warfare, have since resorted to funding armed insurgent and paramilitary organizations, such as Hezbollah, to engage in irregular combat against Israel.

Additionally, the governments of some nations, particularly liberal democracies, may choose to engage in proxy warfare (despite military superiority) when a majority of their citizens oppose declaring or entering a conventional war. This featured prominently in US strategy following the Vietnam War, due to the so-called "Vietnam Syndrome" of extreme war weariness among the American population. This was also a significant factor in motivating the US to enter conflicts such as the Syrian Civil War via proxy actors, after a series of costly, drawn-out direct engagements in the Middle East spurred a recurrence of war weariness, a so-called "War on Terror syndrome".

Nations may also resort to proxy warfare to avoid potential negative international reactions from allied nations, profitable trading partners, or intergovernmental organizations such as the United Nations. This is especially significant when standing peace treaties, acts of alliance, or other international agreements ostensibly forbid direct warfare: breaking such agreements could lead to a variety of negative consequences due to either negative international reaction, punitive provisions listed in the prior agreement, or retaliatory action by the other parties and their allies. In some cases, nations may be motivated to engage in proxy warfare due to financial concerns: supporting irregular troops, insurgents, non-state actors, or less-advanced allied militaries (often with obsolete or surplus equipment) can be significantly cheaper than deploying national armed forces, and the proxies usually bear the brunt of casualties and economic damage resulting from prolonged conflict.

Another common motivating factor is the existence of a security dilemma. Leaders that feel threatened by a rival nation's military power may respond aggressively to perceived efforts by the rival to strengthen their position, such as military intervention to install a more favorable government in a third-party state. They may respond by attempting to undermine such efforts, often by backing parties favorable to their own interests (such as those directly or indirectly under their control, sympathetic to their cause, or ideologically aligned). In this case, if one or both rivals come to believe that their favored faction is at a disadvantage, they will often respond by escalating military and/or financial support. If their counterpart(s), perceiving a material threat or desiring to avoid the appearance of weakness or defeat, follow suit, a proxy war ensues between the two powers. This was a major factor in many of the proxy wars during the Cold War between the USand USSR, as well as in the ongoing series of conflicts between Saudi Arabia and Iran, especially in Yemen and Syria.

EFFECTS OF PROXY WARS

Proxy wars can have a huge impact, especially on the local area. A proxy war with significant effects was the Vietnam War between theUSA and the USSR. In particular, the bombing campaign Operation Rolling Thunder destroyed lots of infrastructure, making life more difficult for North Vietnamese citizens. In addition, unexploded bombs dropped during the campaign have killed tens of thousands since the war ended, not only in Vietnam, but in Cambodia and Laos too. Also significant was the Soviet-Afghan War, which cost millions of lives and billions of dollars, bankrupting the Soviet Union and contributing to its collapse.

Proxy wars generally have a destabilizing effect. For example, in the Middle East, proxy wars between Saudi Arabia and Iran and betweenIsrael and Palestine have destroyed the region. These conflicts have resulted in, among other things, the Syrian Civil War, the rise of ISIL, the current civil war in Yemen, and the reemergence of the Taliban. Since 2003, more than 500,000 have died in Iraq. Since 2011, more than 220,000 have died in Syria. In Yemen, over 1,000 have died in just one month. In Israel, more than 8,000 have died since 2000. In Afghanistan, more than 17,000 have been killed since 2009. In Pakistan, more than 57,000 have been killed since 2003.

In general, the lengths, intensities, and scales of existing armed conflicts are often greatly increased when belligerents' capabilities are augmented by external support. Belligerents are often less likely to engage in diplomatic negotiations, peace talks are less likely to bear fruit, and damage to infrastructure can be many times greater.

INDO-PAKISTANI WAR OF 1947

The Indo-Pakistani War of 1947–1948, sometimes known as the First Kashmir War, was fought between India andPakistan over the princely state of Kashmir and Jammu from 1947 to 1948. It was the first of four wars fought between the two newly independent nations. Pakistan precipitated the War a few weeks after independence by launching tribal*lashkar* (militia) from Waziristan, in an effort to secure Kashmir, the future of which hung in the balance. The inconclusive result of the war still affects the geopolitics of both countries.

On 22 October 1947, Muslim tribal militias crossed the border of the state, claiming that they were needed to suppress a rebellion in the southeast of the kingdom. These local tribal militias and irregular Pakistani forces moved to takeSrinagar, but on reaching Uri they encountered resistance. Hari Singh made a plea to India for assistance, and help was offered, but it was subject to his signing an Instrument of Accession to India. British officers in the sub-continent also took part in stopping the Pakistani Army from advancing.

The war was initially fought by the forces of the princely state and by tribal militias from the North-West Frontier Province (now Khyber Pakhtunkhwa) and the Federally Administered Tribal Areas. Facing the assault and a Muslim revolution in the Poonch and Mirpur area of Kashmir, the ruler of the princely state of Kashmir and Jammu, who was a Hindu, signed an Instrument of Accession to the Union of India. The Indian and Pakistani armies entered the war after this. The fronts solidified gradually along what came to be known as the Line of Control. A formal cease-fire was declared at 23:59 on the night of 1/2 January 1949.

Background

Prior to 1815, the area now known as "Jammu and Kashmir" comprised 22 small independent states (16 Hindu and 6 Muslim) carved out of territories controlled by the Amir (King) of Afghanistan, combined with those of local small rulers. These were collectively referred to as the "Punjab Hill States". These small states, ruled by Rajput kings, were variously independent, vassals of the Mughal Empire since the time of Emperor Akbar or sometimes controlled fromKangra state in the Himachal area. Following the decline of the Mughals, turbulence in Kangra and Gorkha invasions, the hill states fell successively under the control of the Sikhs under Ranjit Singh.

The First Anglo-Sikh War (1845–46) was fought between the Sikh Empire, which asserted sovereignty over Kashmir, and the East India Company.

In the Treaty of Lahore of 1846, the Sikhs were made to surrender the valuable region (the Jullundur Doab) between the Beas River and the Sutlej River and required to pay an indemnity of 1.2 million rupees. Because they could not readily raise this sum, the East India Company allowed the Dogra ruler Gulab Singh to acquire Kashmir from the Sikh kingdom in exchange for making a payment of 750,000 rupees to the Company. Gulab Singh became the first Maharaja of the newly formed princely state of Jammu and Kashmir, founding a dynasty, that was to rule the state, the second-largest principality during the British Raj, until India gained its independence in 1947.

PARTITION OF INDIA

The partition of British India and the independence of the new dominions of India and Pakistan was the result of the Indian Independence Act 1947. Article 2 (4) of the Act provided for the termination of British suzerainty over the princely states with effect from 15 August 1947, and recognised the right of the states to choose whether to accede to India or to Pakistan or to remain outside them. Before and after the withdrawal of the British from India, the ruler of the princely state of Kashmir and Jammu came under pressure from both India and Pakistan to agree to accede to one of the newly independent countries. Faced with painful choices, the Maharaja of Kashmir, Hari Singh, decided to avoid accession to either country. Following a Muslim revolution in the Poonch and Mirpur area and an allegedly Pakistani backed Pashtun tribal intervention from the Khyber Pakhtunkhwa aimed at supporting the revolution, the Maharaja asked for Indian military assistance. India set a condition that Kashmir must accede to India for it to receive assistance. The Maharaja complied, and the Government of India recognised the accession of the princely state to India. Indian troops were sent to the state to defend it. The Jammu & Kashmir National Conference volunteers aided the Indian Army in its campaign to drive out the Pathan invaders.

Pakistan was of the view that the Maharaja of Kashmir had no right to call in the Indian Army, because it held that the Maharaja of Kashmir was not a hereditary ruler and was merely a British appointee, after the British defeated Ranjit Singh who ruled the area before the British conquest. There had been no such position as the "Maharaja of Kashmir" before that. Hence, Pakistan decided to take action, but the Army Chief of Pakistan General Sir Douglas Gracey, would not send troops to the Kashmir front, refusing to obey the order to do so given by Muhammad Ali Jinnah, Governor-General of Pakistan. Gracey justified his insubordination by arguing that Indian forces occupying Kashmir, like those of Pakistan, had taken an Oath of Allegiance to King George VI —in his roles of King of India and King of Pakistan— and hence he could not engage in a military conflict with Indian forces. Pakistan finally did manage to send troops to Kashmir, but by then the Indian forces had taken control of approximately two thirds of the former principality. The Gilgit and Baltistan territories were secured for Pakistan by the Gilgit Scouts and the Chitral Scouts of the state of Chitral, one of the princely states of Pakistan, which had acceded to Pakistan on 6 October 1947.

STAGES OF THE WAR

The Rebellion in Poonch

In the Poonch region, there was a large number of ex-servicemen who had served in the British Indian Army and World War 2. Most of these ex-servicemen were of Sudhanorigin and had a long-standing dissident relations with the Dorga regime. On April 21, 1947, Hari Singh was invited to Rawalakot, where a large number of ex-servicemen turned up and paraded with their weapons. This triggered a series of defensive maneavers by Hari Singh to unarm the locals and enforce stricter military control. The Poonch region had around 60,000 ex-servicemen were organising a 'Home Gauard' that would attack the Dogra army at the right time. During the war, this group formed a War Council in Murree and most of the ammunition was smuggled from Darra Adam Khel and a large number of fighters from Waziristan and FATA were also injected through local contacts and the Pakistan Army.

Initial invasion

The first clash occurred at Thorar on October 3–4, 1947. On October 22 another attack was launched in the Muzaffarabad sector, The state forces stationed in the border regions around Muzaffarabad and Domel were quickly defeated by tribal forces (some Muslim state forces mutinied and joined them) and the way to the capital was open. Among the raiders, there were many active Pakistani Army soldiers disguised as tribals. They were also provided logistical help by the Pakistan Army. Rather than advancing toward Srinagar before state forces could regroup or be reinforced, the invading forces remained in the captured cities in the border region engaging in looting and other crimes against their inhabitants.In the Poonch valley, the state forces retreated into towns where they were besieged.

Indian operation in the Kashmir Valley

After the accession, India airlifted troops and equipment to Srinagar, where they reinforced the princely state forces, established a defence perimeter and defeated the tribal forces on the outskirts of the city. Initial defense operations included the notable defense of Badgam holding both the Capital and Airfield overnight against extreme odds. The successful defence included an outflanking manoeuvre by Indian armoured cars. during the Battle of Shalateng. The defeated tribal forces were pursued as far as Baramulla and Uri and these towns were recaptured.

In the Poonch valley, tribal forces continued to besiege state forces.

In Gilgit, the state paramilitary forces, called the Gilgit Scouts, joined the invading tribal forces, who thereby obtained control of this northern region of the state. The tribal forces were also joined by troops from Chitral, whose ruler, the Mehtar of Chitral, had acceded to Pakistan.

Attempted link-up at Poonch and fall of Mirpur

Indian forces ceased pursuit of tribal forces after recapturing Uri and Baramula, and sent a relief column southwards, in an attempt to relieve Poonch. Although the relief column eventually reached Poonch, the siege could not be lifted. A second relief column reached Kotli, and evacuated the garrisons of that town and others but were forced to abandon it being too weak to defend it. Meanwhile, Mirpur was captured by the tribal forces on 25 November 1947.

Fall of Jhanger and attacks on Naoshera and Uri

The tribal forces attacked and captured Jhanger. They then attacked Naoshera unsuccessfully, and made a series of unsuccessful attacks on Uri. In the south a minor Indian attack secured Chamb. By this stage of the war the front line began to stabilise as more Indian troops became available.

Operation Vijay: counterattack to Jhanger

The Indian forces launched a counterattack in the south recapturing Jhanger and Rajauri. In the Kashmir Valley the tribal forces continued attacking the Uri garrison. In the north Skardu was brought under siege by the Gilgit scouts.

Indian Spring Offensive

The Indians held onto Jhanger against numerous counterattacks, who were increasingly supported by regular Pakistani Forces. In the Kashmir Valley the Indians attacked, recapturing Tithwail. The Gilgit scouts made good progress in the High Himalayas sector, infiltrating troops to bring Leh under siege, capturing Kargil and defeating a relief column heading for Skardu.

Operations Gulab and Eraze

The Indians continued to attack in the Kashmir Valley sector driving north to capture Keran and Gurais (Operation Eraze). They also repelled a counterattack aimed at Tithwal. In the Jammu region, the forces besieged in Poonch broke out and temporarily linked up with the outside world again.

The Kashmir State army was able to defend Skardu from the Gilgit Scouts impeding their advance down the Indus valley towards Leh. In August the Chitral Forces under Mata-ul-Mulk besieged Skardu and with the help of artillery were able to take Skardu. This freed the Gilgit Scouts to push further into Ladakh.

Operation Bison

During this time the front began to settle down. The siege of Poonch continued. An unsuccessful attack was launched by 77 Parachute Brigade (Brig Atal) to capture Zoji La pass. Operation Duck, the earlier epithet for this assault, was renamed as Operation Bison by Cariappa.

M5 Stuart light tanks of 7 Cavalry were moved in dismantled conditions through Srinagar and winched across bridges while two field companies of the Madras Sappers converted the mule track across Zoji La into a jeep track. The surprise attack on 1 November by the brigade with armour supported by two regiments of 25 pounders and a regiment of 3.7-inch guns, forced the pass and pushed the tribal/Pakistani forces back to Matayan and later Dras. The brigade linked up on 24 November at Kargil with Indian troops advancing from Leh while their opponents eventually withdrew northwards toward Skardu.

Operation Easy; Poonch link-up

The Indians now started to get the upper hand in all sectors. Poonch was finally relieved after a siege of over a year. The Gilgit forces in the High Himalayas, who had previously made good progress, were finally defeated. The Indians pursued as far as Kargil before being forced to halt due to supply problems. The Zoji La pass was forced by using tanks (which had not been thought possible at that altitude) and Dras was recaptured.

Moves up to cease-fire

After protracted negotiations a cease-fire was agreed to by both countries, which came into effect. The terms of the cease-fire as laid out in a United Nations resolution of 13 August 1948, were adopted by the UN on 5 January 1949. This required Pakistan to withdraw its forces, both regular and irregular, while allowing India to maintain minimum strength of its forces in the state to preserve law and order. On compliance of these conditions a plebiscite was to be held to determine the future of the territory. In all, 1,500 soldiers died on each side during the war and Pakistan was able to acquire roughly two-fifths of Kashmir, including five of the fourteen eight thousanders peaks of the world, while India maintained the remaining three fifths of Kashmir, including the most populous and fertile regions.

2

The Real Victims of India and Pakistan Proxy War

Hostility between Afghanistan and Pakistan has been ongoing now for about four decades, whereas hostility between Pakistan and India has been present since 1947. The proxy war between between India and Pakistan lies in Afghanistan. It all started after the collapse of Dr. Najibullah's regime in 1992, which had been backed by the former USSR, which coincided with the establishment of Pakistan backed mujahideen government and then Taliban regime. The Afghan and Pakistan officials repeatedly talked about the proxy war and Pakistan confessed their involvement, but India accuses Pakistan only and refuses its involvement. The US-led war against terror has helped to conceal India's proxy war. Now is the right time for Afghans to debate, analyze and discuss this issue in depth, as well as to define their relationships based on mutual interest with both countries.

The Afghans, the US allies and Pakistan have paid a high price for this ongoing proxy war. But the Indian government is not willing to admit its responsibility. Over the last decade, every attempt at peace talks with the Taliban insurgents has been blocked by Pakistan due to a major a condition. The condition they try to impose is for Afghanistan to cut ties with India. The relationship and friendship with India has been costly for Afghanistan, it costs the lives of thousands of innocents Afghans and billions of dollars in damage and destruction. India has provided hundreds of low-quality scholarships and assisted in reconstruction projects, which is highly appreciated. But Pakistan has sent hundreds of suicide bombers and terrorists, which are dubbed"good militias" by Pakistan's leaders. Of course, the expectations regarding Pakistan's efforts are different, but still India has not contributed enough.

Besides the proxy war, Pakistan has repeatedly attacked Afghanistan, occupied strategic locations along the Durand Line, and killed dozens of Afghans with cross-border shelling. India has never shown a credible response to Pakistan's aggression. India's leaders have been ignoring the facts and have not even responded to Pakistan's political and military interventions in Afghanistan. Contrary to the Pakistanis' demands to cut ties with India, the Afghan government has given unprecedented access to India by welcoming its four consulates throughout Afghanistan. Indian companies have even been rewarded major mining contracts. In 2013, during the most difficult times, when Afghanistan was suffering from cross-border shelling from Pakistan and former Afghan president Hamid Karzai visited India and urged India's supportive efforts to stop those attacks, India did not even respond. Ultimately, President Karzai returned to Kabul empty handed.

Afghans are proud of their historic relationships with India and they would like to further grow and strengthen this relationship. But a friendly relationship between Afghanistan and India is not tolerated by Pakistan - and this has to be recognized by India. It's not a secret anymore that Afghanistan and Pakistan are at war, partially as a result of Indian relationships. It's wise for Afghanistan to sustain its partnership with India, but as an ally India should assist Afghanistan in the peace process. If required, it should not leave Afghanistan alone in this ongoing war. The war was defined by the Afghan president, Mohammad Ashraf Ghani as an "undeclared war." We equally need each other and only together can we stand stronger against our common enemies and their supporters. Only a self-sustaining and prosperous Afghanistan can be a strong ally of India and other partner countries. Thus, India should further support Afghanistan in an effort to arrive at a self-sufficient Afghanistan.

The long-lasting relationship and honest friendships of Afghans should not be misused. It is tactless for Afghanistan to remain a battleground for the two dangerous nuclear regional powers. India has not even taken a clear stance in support of the Afghan National Security Forces. India is privileged that the US and its allies as well have been fighting their proxy enemy in Afghanistan. If India truly wants to sustain its relationship with and presence in Afghanistan; the Afghan people deserve India's sincere support. The relationship with India should be clearly defined and India should not interfere in the peace process. If the Afghan leadership is not independent and strong enough to hold these two countries accountable, the Afghan nation has the right to hold them accountable through the UN Security Council for ending this proxy war.

THEATRES OF OPERATIONS

Any India-Pakistan conflict will take place in four major theatres, each varying in geography and, to a lesser extent climatically. The theatres of operations are:

1) Along the Line of Control - Northern Kashmir region
2) Southern Jammu & Kashmir and Punjab sectors
3) North and Central Rajasthan
4) South Rajasthan and Gujarat

When looking at these theatres of operations, it must be borne in mind that the Line of Control in the Northern Kashmir region is not an internationally recognized border. It should also be noted that Punjab and Kashmir are politically very sensitive areas for the political establishments in both countries. It is, therefore, hardly likely that any major loss of territory in either of these two areas would be acceptable.

In the Southern Jammu & Kashmir and Punjab sectors, stretching down into North and Central Rajasthan, there are a series of extremely formidable obstacle defences, which are called ditch-cum-bunds by the Indians, and canals by the Pakistanis. These defences, combined with the existing natural ground features make large-scale mechanized operations virtually impossible. These linear defences are extremely formidable, since the ditch-cum-bunds are liberally laced with diffused and well concealed concrete bunkers which have considerable defensive firepower and are difficult to locate, even with thermal imaging. This effectively limits operations to defensive positions with only local offensive capability.

The Rajasthan and Gujarat regions present an entirely different scenario. In the Northern/Central Rajasthan theatre, considerable scope exists for the large scale use of mechanised formations in the desert and semi-desert sectors. It is in these sectors, the Thar desert and the Rann of Kutch, that the major armoured battles of the next India-Pakistan war are likely to be fought. It is, therefore, not surprising that a complete Indian Strike Corps is earmarked for use primarily in this area.

The Thar Desert and Rann of Kutch also present the best possible place for tactical nuclear warfare. The barren desert areas are ideal in that so-called collateral damage could be reduced. Moreover, any meaningful Indian gains in this area, that is beyond the major river lines, would threaten the very existence of the Pakistani state, thus prompting Pakistan to actively consider using nuclear weapons in the event of a major Indian breakthrough.

On the other hand, since the Indian Strike Corps will be operating in this area, so will be the bulk of India's formidable Corps of Air Defence Artillery. This means that any Pakistani attack against a major Indian formation would be met with heavy resistance from extremely dense and sophisticated CADA assets - not to mention fighter squadrons from the Indian Air Force. Therefore, any Pakistani attack stands a good chance of being repelled without reaching their assigned target.

India could also reduce the risk of nuclear retaliation by limiting its advance to the major river lines, or to between 60-80 km in the North/Central Rajasthan sectors. This would mean that the existence of Pakistan would no longer be threatened while India would still occupy chunks of territory. Pakistan would probably be less willing to cross the nuclear threshold for such a limited Indian advance.

It is unlikely that either India or Pakistan would initiate nuclear warfare in either the Punjab or Kashmir regions purely for tactical gain. Indeed, for Pakistan the use of such weapons in Kashmir would almost certainly alienate the Muslim population of the

Kashmir Valley. In the case of Punjab, Pakistan's military and political elites are largely drawn from that Province and as such it is extremely unlikely that they would take a risk as large as this for limited tactical gains. From a purely military standpoint, it should also be pointed out that the ditch-cum-bund defences and their network of concrete bunkers would probably survive a nuclear attack. This would render a nuclear attack in this sector virtually useless.

Therefore, the only area in which nuclear weapons would be tactically useful is in Rajasthan and Gujarat - for reasons which have already been given. Yet that land, especially in Rajasthan, Thar Desert sector, is of virtually no strategic importance. Would any militarily sane nation risk revealing the full extent of its covert nuclear program unless its very existence was threatened ? The answer is clearly no. Therefore, if India limits its territorial gains in this area, Pakistan would have no reason to resort to nuclear weapons.

There is one wild card in this scenario - the Line of Control. If India were to launch a major assault along the LoC - would Pakistan use nuclear weapons ? An examination of a possible war scenario will perhaps illustrate Indian planning more clearly. War Scenario:

In 1987, the India army conducted a massive military exercise, 'Brasstacks', which outlined what was then a new tactical doctrine. No longer would the Indian army concentrate on operations in Punjab, as it had during the 1965 war, but would deploy massively powerful armoured formations in the Rajasthan sector with the aim of bisecting Pakistan at its weakest point in the Sindh Province.

This has been the model most often used and quoted by scholars in the literature available on possible war scenarios. Moreover, it has been further argued that thanks to Pakistan's nuclear capability, an Indian offensive in the Sindh that met with success would be answered by a Pakistani nuclear strike. Since the defences in the Punjab are strong, it was therefore argued that as India's military superiority was hardly overwhelming, the nuclear factor may be creating an environment where war was almost impossible.

This model is, however, obsolete and far from creating a certain conventional stalemate, has simply led to the Indian army re-thinking its tactical doctrine. No longer will the Indian army attempt to make major territorial gains, but it will concentrate on occupying a small stretch of territory, not enough to threaten Pakistan's existence, but enough to force Pakistan to commit its forces where they will be met by superior Indian firepower which will then inflict maximum attrition.

The reason for this in part lies in the risk of nuclear warfare, but the main reason lies in the fact that previous wars in 1965 and 1971 have shown that major territorial gains are unlikely in a short war.

If a major Indian offensive occurs, it will occur in Kashmir. Never before has the Indian army attempted any offensive in Kashmir, but this time, thanks to the massive influx of troops into the State, an Indian offensive along the Line of Control is very possible. It could be argued that these troops are primarily for counter-insurgency operations. However, this does not explain why the formations coming into Jammu and Kashmir are bringing their artillery with them. Any fighting will in Kashmir will centre around a clash of infantry and artillery and as such, the induction of substantial artillery assets into the region must be seen as significant.

At the outset one thing must be made clear. Neither India or Pakistan believes that anything would be decided in a war lasting less than four weeks. India bases its plans on a period of intense fighting lasting six to eight weeks followed by a period of major, but less intense fighting lasting up to four more weeks. War Wastage Reserves are calculated on this basis and so if a war lasts only two weeks or thereabouts, the most that can be hoped for is for heavy attrition of the enemy forces.

India has therefore moved away from the Brasstacks plan of bisecting Pakistan in the Sindh and threatening Islamabad with encirclement to a more modest objective of destroying as much of the Pakistani military as possible. Pakistan's nuclear weapons provide some deterrence against any Indian move to make deep thrusts into its territory and against any possible bisection of

Pakistan, they are of no use in a war aimed solely at inflicting maximum attrition against Pakistani military forces.

The Indian army has two Strike Corps, 2 Corps & 1 Corps, assigned to the Rajasthan and Punjab sectors respectively. The Strike Corps, but each is composed of one armoured division and several infantry divisions and supporting units. Each will also have an artillery division attached. There is another Strike Corps - 21 Corps which is not yet fully operational.

In the Brasstacks model, these were the two formations Pakistan was most concerned about and their continued presence in the Rajasthan and Punjab sectors will ensure that Pakistan cannot consider any major troop redeployments in either sector. Under current plans, India intends not to advance more than 60-80km in the North/Central Rajasthan sector and only up to the major river lines in South Rajasthan/Gujarat, Pakistan's existence would hardly be threatened.

However, it must be remembered that India and Pakistan will be fighting a political war as much as a military one and any loss of territory is considered a major political embarrassment. This means that Pakistan would invariably have to attempt a counterattack against Indian forces occupying any of its territory. Its forces would then be drawn into a battle of attrition against Indian forces, a battle that they would lose. If the current build up of air defence assets, upgrading of armour and anti-tank munitions and the increase in artillery within the India army is seen in light of this post-Brasstacks tactical doctrine, it is abundantly clear that India is building up its forces to ward off any Pakistani counterattack, inflicting devastating losses on the attackers.

In the Southern Jammu & Kashmir and Punjab sectors, the huge fixed fortifications described previouslyr effectively limit the scope of any Indian operation. India is highly unlikely to attempt a major offensive in this sector for two reasons. The first is the extent of the fortified defences in this sector, but the second is far more significant and goes to the core of Pakistan's vulnerability versus India.

The real vulnerability of Pakistan lies, not in a lack of 'strategic depth', but in the fact that so many of its major population centres and politically and military sensitive targets lie very close to the border with India. As was mentioned earlier, this negates the tactical use of nuclear weapons in the Punjab sector in particular. However, should India threaten Lahore, for example, Pakistan could be compelled to attempt a nuclear strike against an Indian civilian target. As such, it is hardly likely that India would want to risk a major advance in Punjab. Aims in this sector would be limited to holding Pakistani forces in a defensive deployment pattern while inflicting maximum attrition with 2 Corps and 21 Corps.

Along the Line of Control, however, the situation is very different. One of the consequences of the Kashmir insurgency is that India has transferred several divisions to the area to reinforce the troops already there and bringing total troop strength in this sector to over 250,000. The Indian divisions and brigades also brought their supporting artillery with them and this combination - which is far in excess of what is needed for defensive operations - enables Indian planners to contemplate a major offensive along the Line of Control with every chance of success. The importance of the term Line of Control cannot be understated. Pakistan clings to the illusion, in official pronouncements at any rate, that its part of Kashmir is not really part of Pakistan. As such, it has always refused to recognize the Line of Control as the international border with India. This is something that India intends to exploit to the fullest. Pakistan, on the other hand, appears to work to a different strategy. From the time of the 1965 and 1971 wars, up until India's Brasstacks exercise, emphasis was placed on the static defence of the Line of Control and the border. However, in light of India's substantially enhanced offensive capabilities, Pakistan realised that this 'stand and fight' doctrine would lead to serious Indian penetration of Pakistani territory with the Pakistani army being unable to manoeuvre to meet the threat. Counterattacking formations would then be destroyed piecemeal.

Pakistan has therefore adopted a new strategy - the Riposte. This is remarkably simple in concept in that Pakistan would accept the loss of territory in Indian penetrations, but would conduct a limited advance along narrow fronts with the aim of occupying territory near the border to a depth of 40-50km. Pakistan believes that this would give it a bargaining chip to be used in the aftermath of a ceasefire brought about by international pressure after 3-4 weeks of fighting.

The Pakistanis, to some extent, still assume that India will attempt deep penetrations into the territory. Moreover, it appears that though the Pakistani army is well prepared for this new doctrine, there is an inadequate appreciation of the threat posed by Indian air power to the attacking formations. Some planning has been based on the highly unrealistic assumption of local air superiority and as such these plans may go seriously awry.

So what will a future India-Pakistan war look like ? There are a number of good books on the 1965 and 1971 wars and some excellent accounts of the tactical thinking behind Exercise Brasstacks are available. These, however, are not of much use at present. However, perhaps the best and most realistic war scenario was painted by defence journalist Pravin Sawhney in the Asian Age newspaper in November 1994.

Holding formations in both India and Pakistan can man their forward defensive positions and fortifications in less than 24 hours. However, Corps level reserves with large stockpiles of munitions will take between 24 to 72 hours for mobilization after being given their orders. In this regard, both armies will be evenly matched in the first 24 hours since the Pakistani units have to travel a shorter distance to their forward positions.

Pakistan's Army Reserve North is based in the Kharian/Mangla complex and would need to travel only 200km to its forward concentration areas or even their assembly areas where regrouping before an offensive is done.

This could be done at extremely short notice and is consistent with Pakistan's pre-conceived offensive plans as outlined in the Riposte doctrine. Army Reserve South, which is based in the Multan area can also be available for operations in a similar time. While many of India's formations may take up to 72 hours to be fully deployed, two out of India's three Strike Corps, 1 Corps & 2 Corps, are so positioned as to match the mobilization timings of Army Reserve South. As of now, it is not known if the third

Strike Corps, 21 Corps, will be available at such short notice.

India could, in theory, disrupt the early deployment of Army Reserve North if the Indian Army's Northern Command denies deployment space with the pre-emptive mobilization and deployment of Northern Command's theatre reserves. In 1994, Sawhney was unconvinced that this was possible owing to the employment of so many units of the Indian army on internal security duties in Jammu & Kashmir. However, since 1994, the number of paramilitary units in Jammu & Kashmir has grown and the Indian army has deployed almost thirty thousand men from its Rashtriya Rifles battalions. These would take at least some pressure off the regular army in counter-insurgency operations. Moreover, the number of regular army troops in the state seems to have grown. These could provide the Indian army with sufficient troops in theatre to deny Pakistan's Army Reserve North deployment space, thus neutralizing any advantage Pakistan had in this regard.

The problem with assessing whether or not Indian troop strength is adequate to the task of neutralizing Army Reserve North's deployment is that the internal security situation in Jammu and Kashmir is very variable. It is possible that the paramilitary forces and the Rashtriya Rifles will free a large number of troops for conventional operations. Moreover, it is possible that up to three divisions, with over forty thousand men, could be moved from the China border without seriously degrading India's defences against a Chinese assault. These troops are held by Central and Eastern commands, and have actually been earmarked for out of theatre operations.

In the case of Army Reserve South, the Indian Air Force has the potential to cause havoc with their deployment by beginning an intensive interdiction campaign in the Gujrat (Punjab)-Sialkot-Gujranwala area. However, this would make India the aggressor in any conflict. Sawhney argues that this would make the Indian government reluctant to permit this, however, that is not at all certain. The Indian government may well engineer incidents to give an excuse, however flimsy, for the Indian Air Force to begin such an interdiction campaign.

In order to further reduce the risk of a Pakistani nuclear strike, it is possible that India, through the United Nations, might make certain pledges to Pakistan.

These might include a pledge not to deliberately attack a civilian target, to refrain from attacking civilian nuclear installations and a promise not to initiate the use of weapons of mass destruction unless attacked with such weapons. India could also make it clear that it would abide by these terms only if Pakistan agrees to do the same. Should Pakistan not agree, India would probably assume that a nuclear strike would be forthcoming.

Let us for the moment assume that India does not deny Army Reserve North deployment space and that the Indian government does not sanction the launching of preemptive air strikes. Both India and Pakistan will have a relative parity in manpower and combat formations at the start of any conflict. India will be able to bring up some very large combat formations from central and eastern India, but Pakistan would be almost fully committed. A force of three infantry divisions plus some independent brigades under 11 & 12 Corps would be transferable from the Peshawar and Quetta areas respectively, but with very little artillery and armour. Moreover, if there is any serious escalation of fighting in Afghanistan, Pakistan may be less willing to denude its Afghan border of all regular army formations.

The Indian objectives in the Northern sector, in Jammu & Kashmir, are somewhat unclear. The Indian Defence Review Research Team argued that the capture of Skardu to cut off the main glacier zone in Baltistan would be a major objective. Moreover, a strong offensive aimed at capturing Muzzafarabad from the North and the South of the Jhelum, and the neutralization of the Haji Pir (Bedori) Bulge would have to be undertaken. The Indian army would also attempt to capture the Mirpur-Mangla Complex with the view of presenting a clear and present threat to the Pakistani national capital region. Finally, to cope with the threat posed by Army Reserve North, Indian formations would make a penetration into the Sialkot sector with the sole aim of bottling up and denying deployment space to the Pakistani formations, thus ensuring its eventual destruction.

The scenario described above leads to the question as to whether Pakistan would launch a nuclear strike in response to the threat posed to its national capital. The Indian Defence Review Research Team does not answer this question in any way. Pravin Sawhney describes a far more detailed scenario which, while essentially similar in concept, seems to differ in some major details.

Sawhney, in his scenario, argues that the Indian army would have a choice - attacking into either Ladakh-Baltistan or into Pakistan Occupied Kashmir (***) and that the army would prefer an ingress into the latter along the Line of Control. He also argues that the main thrust would be in the Jammu division between Poonch and Chammb with a secondary thrust into the Tithwal-Keran sectors.

Northern Command might also suggest that a limited offensive be conducted to the west of Zojila in the Dras-Kargil sectors. The aim here would be to cut off the lines of communications of the Pakistani brigade based near the Shingo and Indus Rivers. These operations will call for troops specially trained and equipped for operations in mountainous and hilly terrain and to this end, the three divisions previously earmarked for use against China would be invaluable. Moreover, select formations from these forces already send divisional reconnaissance groups into Kashmir for terrain familiarization.

That these divisional reconnaissance groups have been conducting terrain familiarization for quite some time gives rise to the idea that India has been planning for a major offensive in the Jammu & Kashmir sector for a long time.

Pravin Sawhney assumes that the attack in Kashmir would be launched first with two mountain divisions concentrated to begin operations in the directions of Jhanghar-Mirpur and Nowshera-Bhimber with the ability to switch between the two. A third division would be allocated to the Mendhar-Kotli-Mirpur axis in two columns.

Pakistan would probably understand that some move was afoot at this stage to the sector defended by 19 Infantry Division. The Pakistanis would then move the 7 & 9 infantry divisions based at Peshawar to assist in their defence. However, it is not certain that these two divisions would be available entirely since the Afghan border is volatile at the best of times and the situation in Afghanistan is very fluid.

Nonetheless, assuming these formations begin an eastward movement, Pakistan's Army Reserve South would start mobilizing at Multan. At this stage, India's three Strike Corps would begin a forward movement. The plan as envisaged by Indian planners is for 1 Corps to face Army Reserve North and 2 & 21 Corps to face Army Reserve South.

The offensive would begin in the Ladakh sector with two brigades attacking from Kargil along with two brigades from the Northern Kashmir holding division tasked with straightening the Line of Control in the Tithwal-Bugina bulge sector.

The three mountain divisions mentioned earlier would then commence their offensive which would probably face extremely stiff resistance from the Pakistani infantry divisions facing them. Compared to the dashing manoeuvre warfare employed during the Brasstacks exercise, the current Indian army high command is fully convinced that their present offensive plans would be more akin to the 'meat-grinding' assaults of the Second World War.

As Pakistan's strategic depth was eroded around Islamabad and with its Army HQ at Rawalpindi fixed on the worsening situation at Mirpur, Army Reserve North would be committed to action. ARN would attempt an offensive aimed at the Jammu-Pathankot corridor while crossing the river Ravi aimed at threatening Gurdaspur-Pathankot.

These operations would be met by India's 1 Corps which would engage Army Reserve North in a savage battle of attrition, forcing Pakistan to move 9 division to the Mirpur sector, where the Indian offensive continues, while 7 division moved, along with 30 Corps, to reinforce Army Reserve North.

In the meantime, the Indian and Pakistani air forces would engage in their own battle of attrition, with the former waging a heavy counter-air offensive whilst engaging in a massive offensive-air-support operation for the Indian army.

THE INTRUSION IN KUTCH - OPERATION DESERT HAWK - APRIL 1965

The Rann of Kutch is a marshy area about 300 miles long and 50 miles wide on the western seaboard of India. The incident started in January 1965 with Pakistan claiming the entire Rann of Kutch on the grounds that Sind, one of Pakistan's provinces, used to exercise administrative control over the area during the British period. This was one of the many undemarcated areas pending since partition in 1947. Pakistan was keen to have at least the northern portion of the Rann, which it had earmarked for offshore drilling with the help of an American oil company. India asserted that Kanjarkot, Chadbet and Biarbet, which Pakistan claimed, belonged to India and not to Pakistan.

Operation Desert Hawk started with skirmishes between Indian police patrols and Pakistani border guards about an eighteen mile track, a mile and a half inside Indian territory where Pakistani forces established two posts. By early April, the fighting had spread to within 10 miles of the fort at Kanjarkot. On 9 April, Pakistan forces in brigade strength attacked the Central Reserve Police manned Sardar post near the old ruined fort of Kanjarkot. The CRPF contingent was forced to withdraw. The task of sanitising the area was then taken over by the Army. The Indian Army asked the Pakistan Army to vacate Kanjarkot. The Pakistan Army refused. On 16 April, Pakistan claimed Kanjarkot to be Pakistan territory. On 24 April, Pakistan launched a division size attack, using Patton tanks and field guns. The attack was contained with considerable casualties on both sides. When the incident had started, the British Prime Minister initiated moves to secure a cease-fire. During the Commonwealth Heads of Government conference in London, he succeeded in his efforts. A simple cease fire was declared on 29 April. On 15 June fighting erupted again. On 30 June, a formal cease fire was signed in London restoring India's police control over the disputed areas while allowing the Pakistan police the use of the disputed track.

Both the national and the international press commented adversely on the performance of the Indian troops. Though the Army did nor fare as badly as Pakistan claimed, Pakistan did make local gains. Logistics favoured Pakistan. It had an airfield at Badin where it had deployed F 86 Sabre fighter aircraft. And Pakistan had deployed its Army in force - an infantry division and two regiments of tanks, including the Patton tanks recently received from America. India protested to America against the use of these American supplied arms and America protested to Pakistan. Nothing much happened.

On the naval side, no encounter occurred. Early in 1965, the Indian Fleet had visited Bahrein and Kuwait as planned. The aircraft carrier VIKRANT had carried out a routine cooperation exercise with the Army in the Kutch area. When the skirmish occurred, some ships were on routine assignments on both coasts and in the Andamans. Most ships were in Bombay undergoing maintenance in preparation for the annual exercises in the Bay of Bengal for the duration of the southwest monsoon. The aircraft carrier had disembarked her air squadrons and was on her way back to Bombay for docking. When Pakistan intruded in Kutch, she was ordered to sail back and reembark her aircraft. By the time she had done so, the cease fire had been declared. This delay in her docking was to result in the carrier not being available for operations later in the year.

The official history of the Pakistan Navy titled 'Story Of The Pakistan Navy 1947 - 1972' states:

"In March 1965 the Indian Navy, having completed a series of exercises off Bombay and Cochin, sent their aircraft carrier and a number of destroyers and frigates on a goodwill visit to the Gulf ports. On their return they joined up with other units from Bombay and carried out extensive exercises off Kutch. These exercises included anti submarine, anti aircraft, strike and photo recce missions by carrier borne aircraft. This appears to have been a prelude to the Kutch operations in which the aircraft carrier played an important role in transporting men and material to the port of Kandla, which was being used as a support base for operations in the area.

"In Karachi, COMPAK arrived suddenly one afternoon and enquired how soon ships could proceed to sea. All available ships were made ready and proceeded to sea a few days later for the

Rann of Kutch operations which was a prelude to the September 1965 War.

"A notable feature of the 1965 war was that both its genesis and its outcome have remained largely unstated, but it was caused by frictions generated by the gradual change in India's stance over the Kashmir issue. In Pakistan it was becoming increasingly evident that India wanted to do a volte face on its commitment to a plebiscite in Kashmir. This was clear from the pronouncement of its leaders and by the practical steps initiated for the incorporation of the disputed territory in the Indian Union. The predominant view in Pakistan was that if nothing was done to thwart India's efforts, she would be emboldened to proceed ahead with her plans for the assimilation of the state into its territory. Lack of any response on Pakistan's part, it was feared, would enable the Indians to strengthen their claim over the State as time passed."

In June, a formal cease fire agreement was arrived at, effective from 1 July. It provided for ministerial level talks which, if they did not produce a compromise, would be followed by reference of the Kutch issue to a tribunal to demarcate the boundary. The ministerial meeting never took place - Pakistan did not reply to India's communications -so a tribunal was appointed. The tribunal upheld by 2 to 1 Pakistan's claim to the northern half of the Rann and awarded 10 percent of the disputed territory to Pakistan.

Mr Pradhan's memoirs state:

"After the cease-fire on the Rann of Kutch the Indian army had started moving troops to their battle locations with the object of restraining any Pakistani adventure in the Punjab or in Jammu and Kashmir. However for want of intelligence assessment the movement was considerably slow. During March and April 1965, the Kashmir valley was simmering with anti-India propaganda. In May 1965 the Indian government was forced to rearrest Sheikh Abdullah. There were pretests and agitations and the Pakistani hawks decided that the time was ripe to launch a guerrilla type operation in Jammu and Kashmir named `Operation Gibraltar'."

Pakistan's incursion into Kutch roused strong feelings amongst the people of India. They had vivid memories of the humiliation India had suffered at the hands of the Chinese in 1962. The opposition parties alleged that Prime Minister Shastri had not acted firmly enough. Several considerations appear to have weighed with the Prime Minister in handling the Kutch crisis. Mr C P Srivastava was the Private Secretary to the Prime Minister in 1965. His memoirs "Lal Bahadur Shastri", state:

"At the back of his mind was always the firm advice of the Army Chief that an escalation of fighting in the Rann of Kutch area was, tactically, not in the country's interest and that if there had to be a trial of strength between India and Pakistan, it should be elsewhere."

Mr L K Jha, the Principal Secretary to the Prime Minister in 1965, recalls:

"I was involved with some of the overall considerations which were guiding the war effort and meetings of the Emergency Committee of the Cabinet as well as the Secretaries where some aspects were viewed largely from the political point of view but equally from an operational point of view.

"Now, first of all, the attempt on our part was to keep the whole thing confined, territorially as well as otherwise, to a local conflict, rather than allow it to assume the character of an Indo -Pak War. This was the prime objective of our policy - it had been in the past also. But at the same time, we had come to realise that fighting on terrain chosen by the enemy would always leave you at a disadvantage. This came out very, very vividly during the Rann of Kutch affair when Pakistan had all the logistic advantage and we had a tremendous problem in getting men, material and supplies moving to the front.

"At that very time, a political decision had been taken that we would not fight with our hands tied behind our backs and therefore a plan for opening a second front in the Punjab by marching into Lahore had been drawn up and perfected. But it was not launched because a cease fire came into existence, and we naturally hoped that some peaceful way of resolving the Rann of Kutch dispute would be evolved and in fact it went to an international body to settle.

"But even when there was the state of uncertainty, a kind of simple cease fire without any formal agreement, the

Commonwealth Prime Minister's Conference was taking place in London. Shastriji went to London and I went with him. And when going, there was concern - supposing things hotted up in our absence, should the operation to march into Lahore be launched or not? The arrangement I made with Shri Y B Chavan, who was then the Defence Minister, was that if such a contingency arose, he would send me a message indicating the date by which the Prime Minister must get back because we were about to move forward. However the contingency did not arise.

"In fact I recall, and it might be useful for the record, a meeting between Prime Minister Shastri and President Ayub during the Commonwealth Conference session. It was a private meeting and I was there. Ayub said somewhat patronisingly " You know, your chaps tried to commit aggression on our territory, our chaps gave them a few knocks and they began to flee". Then Shastriji said "Mr President, you are a General. I have no military knowledge or experience. But do you think if I had to attack Pakistan, I would choose a terrain where we have no logistic support and you have all the advantages? Do you think I would make such a mistake or any of my Generals would allow me to make that mistake?" And one could see from the face of President Ayub that this thought startled him. Because quite obviously he had been led to believe, in my judgment by Bhutto, that the Indians had attacked in the Rann of Kutch. And he was firmly of that view until this question was posed by Shastriji. I could see him visibly pause and not pursue the point any further".

Mr C P Srivastava's memoirs state:

"Why was air power not deployed in the Rann of Kutch conflict? Air Chief Marshal Arjan Singh told me the reason. He said that soon after the commencement of hostilities in the Rann of Kutch region, he received a telephone call from Air Marshal Asghar Khan, his counterpart in Pakistan, suggesting an informal agreement that neither side should employ the Air Force in the conflict. Arjan Singh himself agreed on the wisdom of this proposal but he confirmed the arrangement after receiving political clearance from the Defence Minister and the Prime Minister. Arjan Singh was also of the opinion that the Rann of Kutch was not a suitable area for large-scale operations by India". "Shastri was a man of peace and he was determined to go to the farthest extent possible, consistent with national security and honour, to maintain peace with Pakistan."

Another consideration seems to have been Prime Minister Shastri's belief that it would be easier to make up with Pakistan, the people of which were of the same stock as Indians, than to make up with China. He was in favour of peace. And if war was forced upon India then, whilst reacting in whatever manner India thought fit, the conflict should be localised as far as possible.

Yet another consideration seems to have been the international political climate. After Russia's open clash with China, Russia began to be more friendly with her neighbors Turkey, Iran and Pakistan, who were still members of American led military alliances directed against Russia. In trying to woo Pakistan, Russia appears to have been influenced by the prospect of Pakistan getting closer to China. Russia invited President Ayub Khan. He visited Moscow in April 1965 during the Rann of Kutch conflict and India noticed that Russia tended to take a neutral position in the conflict. It was reluctant to say anything in public when it was trying to woo Pakistan. India also came to know that Russia was considering President Ayub Khan's request for arms. Prime Minister Shastri visited Russia soon after President Ayub Khan. Russian leaders reassured him that they were trying to wean Pakistan away from military pacts as well as from China and if they were successful, India would benefit more than Russia.

There was also the lurking threat from China. After the Sino Pakistan border treaty in 1963, China's Prime Minister Chou En Lai had made a state visit to Pakistan in 1964. This was followed by a state visit by President Ayub Khan to China in March 1965.

And there was Indonesia, whose relations with India had deteriorated after the Bandung Conference of 1955. The Communist Party of Indonesia had come to power and had close links with Communist China. In the end 1950's, the strength of the Indonesian Navy had increased substantially. Between 1959 and 1965, Russia gave Indonesia one cruiser, fourteen destroyers, fourteen submarines, eight anti submarine patrol vessels, twenty missile boats and several motor torpedo boats and gunboats. Indonesia had arrived at a mutual defence arrangement with Pakistan. Indonesian leaders started voicing claims to Great Nicobar which was closest to Sumatra and wanting the Indian Ocean to be renamed as the Indonesian Ocean. After China's attack on India's northern frontiers in 1962, the Army's hands were more than full and the Indian Navy had been charged with the garrisoning of the Andaman and Nicobar islands. In 1965, the Navy was responsible for the defence of these islands.

Not the least of Prime Minister Shastri's worries was the internal situation - the likelihood of Hindu - Muslim riots, the differences of opinion, between political parties and within the Cabinet, on how to deal with Pakistan's bellicosity and the no - confidence motions in Parliament at a time when there was a pressing need for greater unity.

3

Kashmir and India: Pakistan Proxy Wars

The 'unfinished agenda' of the subcontinent's partition in 1947, specifically the unresolved dispute on Jammu and Kashmir, keeps India and Pakistan locked in their historic enmity. While Pakistan calls Kashmir its "jugular vein," India labels it an "integral part." The latest border clashes, as well as accusations from both sides have heightened the possibility of non- state proxies exploiting each other's vulnerabilities, which may lead to a conventional conflict snowballing into a nuclear exchange.

Waking- up belatedly, Pakistan has been fighting its own battle against domestic terrorism since June 2014. Seeing Pakistan preoccupied with internal challenges, India has intensified pressure on its neighbour to facilitate its collapse or coerce it like other smaller South Asian states. Indian Prime Minister Narendra Modi doesn't miss any chance to accuse Pakistan for exporting terrorism, even as successive Indian governments moved away from the composite dialogue process after the Mumbai attacks of November 2008 – an architecture built in 1998to resolve bilateral disputes. Pressing Pakistan "to abide by its commitment to prevent its territory and territory under its control from being used for terrorism against India," India now demands the 'Four Ts' to be addressed before the talks could begin: Terrorism, Trade, (Afghan) Transit and Trial (of Mumbai attack suspects).

Historically, Indian leaders never approved the subcontinent's partition. Offended by the 'two- nation theory,' the seculars believed

Pakistan to be an artificial concept of a Muslim state, which eventually will have to rejoin India. Reflecting extreme Hindu ideologies, Thakur Prasad ofJana Sangh – the mother organization of the militant Rashtriya Swayamsevak Sangh and Bharatiya Janata Party (BJP) – stated in 1957, "We should not rest till Pakistan is destroyed and merged with Bharat."

Giving credence to Prime Minister Indira Gandhi's taunt about drowning "the Two- Nation Theory in the Bay of Bengal," Mr. Modi even admitted on his visit to Bangladesh in June 2015 that India conspired in the creation of Bangladesh out of former East Pakistan in December 1971 – establishing India's preoccupation with Pakistan's subjugation.

Other than the international boundary, both countries share a violent (i) 560 km long Line of Control (LOC) at Kashmir; (ii) 193 km long Working Boundary (WB) at Jammu; and (iii) a 60km long Line of Actual Control (LAC) at Siachen glacier, which keeps their hostilities perpetual. Despite the 1972 Simla Accord calling for the bilateral resolution of the Kashmir dispute, theUN Security Council Resolution 47/ 1948 of 21 April 1948 still demanded a plebiscite in the valley. The presence of the UN Military Observer Group in India and Pakistan (UNMOGIP) at the LOC establishes the UN's role in the dispute.

However, in order not to antagonize an emerging Indian market of 1.2 billion people (compared to Pakistan, said to be the 10th fragile state of the world), the international community has only been carrying- out conflict management between the two countries rather than conflict resolution. Stephen Cohen, in his book *Shooting for a Century*, notes the inability of international players in resolving the conflicts as a "tragic failure with hardly any prospects for normalization." Cohen records India's intransigence when in 2011 it denied entry to Richard Holbrook, President Obama's Special Representative for Afghanistan and Pakistan, for trying to mediate between the two countries.

Using state and non- state actors asymmetrically seems to be India's new strategy to weaken Pakistan. India is alleged to have supported Tehrik- e- Taliban Pakistan in the tribal areas as well as Baluch separatist leaders. The issue became a headline when it came up in a joint statement after a meeting between Indian and Pakistani leaders on 16 July 2009 at Sharm- al- Sheikh.

The BBC, in its damning report of 24 June 2015, further revealed that Indian intelligence agency, the Research and Analysis Wing (RAW) has been funding, training and arming Pakistan's Muttahida Qaumi Movement (MQM) – an urban Sindh's ethnic political party – for the past two decades. MQM's militant wing has been notorious for target- killings and other organized crime, as well as frequently shutting- down Karachi, Pakistan's biggest metropolis. Despite denying the serious allegations, neither MQM nor India has taken the BBC to court for defamation.

India's mindset was laid- out by its national security adviser, Ajit Doval. Proposing to adopt a "defensive- offense" strategy in February 2014, Doval dared Pakistan to "do one (more) Mumbai (type attack) and lose Baluchistan (province)." On 27 May 2015, Indian Defence Minister Manohar Parikar went a step further by suggesting a policy of "neutralizing" terrorists through terrorists, by which he means employing non- state proxies for counterterrorism purpose. The startling disclosure by former chief of RAW, Amarjit Singh Dulat in his book*Kashmir: The Vajpayee Years* that India had been paying militants and separatists thus comes as no surprise. Former Indian army chief, General V.K. Singh is also on record admitting that under his command, the army's spy unit (Technical Services Division) carried out several cross- border covert operations inside Pakistan.

Highlighting India's use of Afghan soil for proxy war, historian William Darymple quoted the Indian consul- general in Kandahar meeting with the dissident Baluch leaders in the presence ofRAW's agents, while former US Defense Secretary Chuck Hagel noted in 2011, "India has over the years financed problems for Pakistan on that (Afghan) side of the border."

Amid an upsurge in terrorist activities in Pakistan – especially in Baluchistan – its army set aside diplomatic norms to blame RAW behind Pakistan's destabilization. Reiterating the claim that Pakistan and Kashmir are inseparable, Pakistan's army chief General Raheel Sharifresolved on 3 June 2015, "not to allow any country [India] to use proxies against it [Pakistan]."

No doubt Pakistan practiced the policy of 'bleeding India by a thousand cuts' in Kashmir; it took an about- turn on supporting cross- border infiltration by Kashmiri jihadists under international pressure, proscribing the groups between January 2002 and November 2005. However, India's machinations may compel Pakistan to revert back to its old strategy of employing these so-called 'assets.' It must be remembered that if unleashed, Pakistan's 63jihadist outfits that have been involved in the liberation of Kashmir from Indian dominance will have the capability to inflame the valley, once again.

Although the BJP had failed in securing a majority in the 2014 Kashmir elections, with the goal of annulling Kashmir's 'special status' granted under the Indian constitution, its plan to resettle Hindus in the garb of displaced Kashmiri pundits through Israel-style exclusive townships has angered many, as it amounts to changing the demography of Kashmir, while a plebiscite is awaited. Meanwhile, the draconian Armed Forces Special Powers Act (AFSPA) that has been enforced since 6 July 1990 continues to allow the Indian army to use repression without any accountability – making Amnesty International criticize India in its report on 1 July 2015 for Indian security forces' human rights violations in the valley.

With state- sponsored jihadists turning their guns towards Pakistan after being proscribed, killing innocent citizens and bombing the cities, it is unlikely that Pakistan would patronize them again unless provoked. However, India needs to step back from its own belligerence and reckless proxy adventures, which is destabilizing the whole region. India should realize that the outstanding Kashmir resolutions lying in the archives of UN Security Council are the biggest impediment to its permanent membership to the world body. The international community also needs to play its role in the resolution of Indo- Pak disputes and proxy- wars rather than rushing every time when another conflict erupts between the two rival powers.

At the same time, India and Pakistan should remember that they cannot close their chapter of history by setting the book on fire.

THE RANN OF KACHCHH DISPUTE

Rann of Kachchh boundary was well defined according to Radcliffe award but Pakistan advocated that it was not properly delineated. That country argued that the Rann was not a marsh but a land-locked sea or lake and as such it should be equally divided between India and Pakistan. India countered Pakistani claim by presenting documentary proof that the Rann was a marsh which always remained a part of the Kachchh state. As this state merged with India after independence, the entire Rann of Kachchh should be given to India.

Pakistan claimed about 9,065 sq km out of a total area of 20,720 sq km of the Rann of Kachchh. During the 1965 Indo-Pakistan war, the Pakistan troops invaded this area and reached inside the Indian Territory.

The matter was referred to a boundary tribunal constituted by the International Court of Justice which awarded 906.5 sq km area of the Kachchh to Pakistan. After a number of protests and representations both India and Pakistan accepted the award and the demarcation of the boundary was completed in June 1969.

The Kashmir Problem

The former princely state (more precisely the state of Jammu and Kashmir), is undoubtedly the most complex and serious problem between India and Pakistan and is major stumbling block in normalising the relations between the two countries.

The Kashmir problem has led to bloody wars between the two countries in 1948, 1965, 1971 and more recently in 1999. Besides there had been skirmishes adding to bitterness between the two countries.

Both countries have large political, economic and strategic stakes in Kashmir and this state has become a symbol of national prestige and honour for either of the two countries. With an area of 2,22,236 sq km Jammu and Kashmir is the sixth largest state of India and represents heterogametic character with regard to geographic, economic, cultural and linguistic elements. The whole state of Jammu and Kashmir can be treated as conglomeration of six distinctive regions.

These regions (excepting for Hunza-Gilgit and Nagar) were brought as a united political unit by Maharaja Gulab Singh, who entered into a subsidiary alliance with the British within the Indian empire in 1849. The first is the beautiful Kashmir Valley.

It is the most important centre of tourist attraction and politically the seat of central authority. Until recent time, it was accessible from India by a single road. This road remained snowbound until the introduction of snowplows in 1948. A few roads connect it with Pakistan.

The nucleus of dispute in this valley is its overwhelmingly Muslim population. The minority of Kashmiri Brahmans have been holding high positions of economic, social and political significance, whereas the Muslim peasantry remained very poor.

The second is the Jammu region which lies in the southern part of the state. It covers only one-seventh of the total area of the state and is predominantly a Hindu region. More than half of the population of this region consists of Hindus. Jammu is the winter capital of the state and home of state's former rulers—the Dogra Rajputs.

The Third region is Gilgit. It lies in the northern part of the state. This region is marked by high mountains and is almost entirely inhabited by Muslims. Previously it used to be reached from Srinagar by crossing high mountains, plateaus and glaciers. Now it is well linked to Pakistan through Karakoram highway built by China-Pakistan in 1970.

The fourth region is that of Baltistan which lies in the extreme northern part of the state. Like Gilgit, it contains high mountains and is not easily accessible. It is reached by road along the Indus River in Pakistan. It is an overwhelmingly Muslim area.

The fifth region is that of Punch which lies to the north of the Jammu region and in the west of the Kashmir valley. It is near the Pakistan border and is inhabited by Muslims. Pakistan has easy access to this region.

The sixth is the Ladakh region which is also known as 'Little Tibet'. It lies in eastern part of the state and covers about one-third territory of the state. It is a vast, barren, high plateau which resembles Tibet in many respects.

As mentioned earlier, the state was ruled by a Hindu whereas about 77 per cent of the population of the consisted of Muslims before partition of the country. It is an extremely important state from the strategic point of view because of its contiguity to India, Pakistan, China and Afghanistan and proximity to Tajikistan (formerly a part of the U.S.S.R.).

The state was sought by Pakistan on the basis of its Muslim majority status. Moreover, major rivers of Pakistan namely Ravi, Chenab, Jhelum and Indus flow through Kashmir. Unlike most of the rulers of princely states who had acceded to either India or Pakistan before August 15, 1947, ruler of Kashmir did not make up his mind.

The Maharaja thought that any decision to accede to India or Pakistan may spark off chain reactions and disturb the peace of the state. Pakistan cut off the communications and stopped the supply of essentials to coerce Kashmir to accede to Pakistan. On October 22, 1947, fully armed tribesmen, supported by Pakistani armed forces, invaded Kashmir.

They indulged in large scale killing of Hindus and Muslims and committed large scale looting and arson. This forced the ruler to make a desperate appeal to the Indian government for military help. India promised to help the ruler but only after he decided to accede to the Indian Union.

The ruler agreed to this condition and the instrument of accession of Kashmir was signed by Maharaja Hari Singh on October 26, 1947. The accession was accepted by the Governor General of India on October 27, 1947. Thus, Kashmir became legally and constitutionally an integral part of the Indian Union.

Pakistan described the Maharaja's accession to India as based upon "fraud, deceit and Violence", and maintained that it was totally against the wishes of its long oppressed Muslim subject. Soon after, Pakistan rushed its own troops to support the invading tribesmen. India quickly moved its troops to halt the invaders and Indo-Pakistan war broke out in 1948.

India could have done much better, had it flushed out the invaders from the entire state. Instead, India took the case of aggression from Pakistan to the United Nations which immediately appointed a commission to investigate the dispute. The United Nations commission on India and Pakistan (UNCIP) proposed a plebiscite to ascertain the wishes of the people of the state. It also called on India and Pakistan to agree on a cease-fire line. A cease-fire line was delimited with areas of high altitude left un-delimited. The line was accepted by both India and Pakistan on January 1, 1949.

The cease-fire line left India in possession of two-thirds of the state including the Kashmir valley, lying south-east of the line, and one-third area in the north and west of the line remained under Pakistan's control.

The area is administered through the so-called Azad Kashmir government. The cease-fire line (adjusted under Shimla Agreement as Line of Actual Control) has crystallized into de facto boundary between areas controlled by India and Pakistan respectively.

Right from the beginning Pakistan has been insisting on plebiscite in the entire state in the hope that such an exercise will give clear mandate in its favour. That country argues that plebiscite has been recommended by the United Nations. India, on the other hand, held the position that Kashmir's accession had given India sovereignty over Kashmir.

Initially agreeing to the proposal of plebiscite, India rejected it on the ground that Pakistan had not withdrawn its invading forces from Kashmir. This condition was stipulated by the United Nation resolution, but had never been realised on the ground. India has been regularly stressing upon the illegality of Pakistani support of the raiders and the Azad Kashmir government.

Pakistan blames India for failing to withdraw its forces from the Indian- controlled territory, and for supporting a regime prejudicial to holding of a plebiscite. Since then the issue has been listing in the U.N. Security Council and the Cease Fire line or Line of Actual Control divides Kashmir between Indian and Pakistani occupied areas.

Ever since Kashmir's accession to India, the Kashmir government in Srinagar has maintained a close relationship with the Indian Union, and in 1952, negotiated a pact which has given it a special status within India. In 1956, arrangements were made for establishing an elected constituent assembly for Kashmir which voted to make it a regular state within India. Since then, India has treated Kashmir as a constituent unit of the country and the state is no longer open to a plebiscite.

Two major considerations have guided India's policy about Kashmir problem. First, India is secular state and surrender of Kashmir to Pakistan on religious grounds would amount to denial of the nation's essential principles.

Second, the strategic location of Kashmir is of great importance to India. China's occupation of Tibet and part of Ladakh and building a road through Aksai Chin to serve Tibet and Sinkiang, and full scale aggression on India in 1962 further lent urgency to the strategic aspect of Kashmir's location.

China helped Pakistan in building a new road across its occupied area to Sinkiang and Pakistan, in turn, ceded a large territory of 5,180 sq km to China.

This move by Pakistan has been termed as illegal; because India claimed that the entire state including the territory controlled by Pakistan, annexed by China and ceded by Pakistan to China belonged to India. Thus, out of a total area of 2, 22,236, a territory of 78,114 sq km is under illegal occupation of Pakistan, and 5,180 sq km illegally handed over by Pakistan to China and 37,555 sq km under illegal occupation of China in Ladakh district. Pakistan has so far made four abortive attempts to conquer Kashmir. Its forces had to trace back in 1947-48 war when Kashmir was legally acceded to India. Pakistan again invaded in 1965 and it was badly mauled by the Indian forces.

The 1971 India-Pakistan conflict led to the liberation of East Pakistan and emergence of a new country by the name of Bangladesh. This left Pakistan a truncated country and added much to already increasing bitterness between India and Pakistan.

In 1999, Pakistani troops stealthily occupied certain positions in the Kargil sector for which India had to use strong force. Unable to beat India in regular warfare, its forces are launching proxy war in Kashmir and sending foreign mercenaries and terrorists to disturb law and order in and incite communal tension in the state. Due to its link with Islamic terrorist organisations and ISI,

Pakistan has become the hot- bad of international terrorism and is posing a serious threat to world peace. Even after about six decades of Kashmir's accession to India, there seems no sign of resolving the Kashmir problem as both sides stick to their respective positions.

India is taking no chance to safeguard the integrity and sovereignty of the country, particularly of Jammu and Kashmir. There are an estimated 1,00,000 Indian troops ranged along 188 km International Border, the 788 km Line of Control (LoC) and 150 km Actual Ground Position Line (AGPL).

The Siachin Glacier Dispute

Siachin glacier is about 75 km long and 2 to 8 km wide. This glacier has the distinction of being the largest glacier outside the Polar or sub-Polar regions. It covers an area of about 450 sq km at an altitude of about 5,800 metre above sea level in Ladakh region near Karakoram Range.

The Karakoram highway between China and Pakistan is very close which enhances its strategic value. India occupies about two-third area of the glacier in its south-eastern part. Here Nubra river emerges from Karakoram glacier and meets the Shyok river which is a tributary of the Indus river. Indian troops use the Nubra valley to reach the glacier. The glacier has four passes. Of these Gasherbrum, Saltoro and Vilafondala are in India and Gyongla is in Pakistan.

It is worth mentioning that LoC demarcated in 1972 after the Shimla agreement stopped dead at the grid reference NJ. 9842, with no indication as to how it would run along the 70-odd km left to the Chinese border in the north.

While Pakistan decided to extend this line eastward to Karakoram Pass, thus claiming an area two-thirds the size of Sikkim, India's decision was to go by the wording of 1949 Karachi agreement that was superseded by LoC of 1972 which spoke of line "thence northwards joining the glaciers". Further, India wants Pakistan to officially recognise the Actual Ground Position Line (AGPL) begin NJ. 9892 grid point as a pre-requisite to de-militarisation of the Siachin glacier.

Pakistani troops established an observation post on Saltoro range. To counter this, India launched Operation Meghdoot on April 13, 1984. Since then both the countries are maintaining troops in this inhospitable environment at a very high altitude. A number of skirmishes have taken place making it the highest battlefield in the world.

Sending men and material in such an area is a very expensive affair. On an average India spends about Rs. 4 crore per day for maintaining troops in this hostile area. Pakistan also spends about Rs. 1 crore for the same purpose. Casualties on both sides of the border are also very high.

Even in normal circumstances, Indian troops suffer one casualty every second day while Pakistani troops suffer one casualty every fourth day. Besides there are psychological disorders, frostbite, high altitude pulmonary and cerebral edema and snow blindness. Such heavy losses can be avoided if both the countries start living in peace as friendly neighbouring countries.

Sir Creek

Sir Creek forms the boundary between Gujarat state of India and Sind Province of Pakistan. This creek is extremely rich in marine life and both the countries desire to include it in their respective territories. While India claims that the middle point of Sir Creek should be demarcated as the international boundary, Pakistan wants the eastern bank of the Creek as the border between India and Pakistan.

As such Sir Creek has become a contentious issue between the two countries as Pakistan has been claiming a 40 km region inside India's territory. Pakistan has responded positively to the goodwill gesture initiated by India since early 2004 to ease tension on the border. This can lead to friendly relations between the two countries if the concerned countries take necessary positive steps for normalisation of relations.

Some of the steps taken/proposed are:

(i) Srinagar-Muzaffrabad has survice.

(ii) Kargil-Skardu bus link and routes into Poonch-Rajouri sector.

(iii) Amritsar-Lahore bus and rail link.

(iv) Meeting points for divided families across LoC at Poonch, Mendhar,

(v) Suchetgarh, Uri, Tangdar and Kargil.

(vi) Rail link between Munnabao (Rajasthan) and Khokrapar (Sind).

(vii) Link between Ferozpur and Sahiwal.

(viii) Trade across the LoC/border.

(ix) Mechanisms to permit two-way religious pilgrims.

(x) Promotion of cultural interaction and cooperation.

(xi) Joint efforts to promote tourism.

CHANGE IN THE STATUS OF KASHMIR AND ITS ACCESSION TO PAKISTAN

Nobody has answered this better than the respected Indian statesman, the late Jayaprakash Narayan: "Few things have been said in the course of this controversy more silly than this one. The assumption behind the argument is that the states of India are held together by force and not by a sentiment of a common nationality. It is an assumption that makes a mockery of the Indian nation and a tyrant of the Indian state."

Contrary to the impression that has been created by the defenders of the status quo in Kashmir, it is the non-settlement of the Kashmir dispute, rather than its settlement, that threatens the territorial integrity of India, and it may be added, of Pakistan. A just and fair settlement of the dispute, in whatever form, would give to each country a mutually recognized and secure frontier and thus encourage their respect for each other's territorial integrity. It would strengthen internal cohesion in both countries. The only real safeguard against disintegration is peace and absence of external and internal conflict.

On the question of Kashmir becoming independent - regardless of whether the possibility is practical or theoretical - it has been argued that the emergence of another sovereign entity in the subcontinent would encourage secessionist tendencies in both India and Pakistan and lead to the collapse of their existing federal structures. What seems to be at work here is the notorious and now discarded falling dominoes theory. No area which is today part of India or Pakistan was dragged into a union against its will; all joined by a volition expressed or confirmed in a popular vote. The only exception is Kashmir, which has never been provided the opportunity to decide its own status or affiliation.

What, therefore, applies to Kashmir does not apply to Assam or Tamil Nadu in India or to Sind in Pakistan. This is also plain from the fact that both countries accepted an international obligation under the auspices of the United Nations regarding Kashmir which neither as a sovereign state would accept regarding any of its constituent units, namely the obligation to withdraw their forces from the territory and let the people decide its status.

The dispute over Kashmir is sue generis. The demilitarization of Kashmir and the holding of a plebiscite in it, in accordance with an international agreement, does not logically justify a bid for secession by other territories nor - what is more important - psychologically encourage it. Moreover another consideration that the Indian contention ignores is that part of Kashmir can emerge as independent and other parts join India or Pakistan. This would mean consolidation and common agreement rather than fission and dispute.

Finally, what is the common sense view of the matter? The Indian contention that the de-annexation of Kashmir would lead to the breakup of the Indian Union implies that the constituent units of that Union are only waiting for an example to be set in Kashmir, which they would follow and splinter off.

The reality, however, is that they are in the Indian Union because (a) they identify themselves as parts of a larger nation, and (b) it is in their perceived interest - economic, social and cultural - to be within the Union rather than face the hazards of a separate, independent existence. If and where the sense of identity and interest is lacking, the unit will secede in course of time regardless of what happens in Kashmir. The danger of the disintegration of the Kashmir dispute is thus only a specter raised to obstruct that settlement. The late Josef Korbel, who served as chairman of the UN Commission for India and Pakistan (incidentally father of the present United States ambassador to the United Nations, Ms. Madeline Albright), dealt with this Indian argument in an article he wrote for The New Leader, an American magazine, in its issue of 4 March 1957: "This is not true. Pakistan was not expected to withdraw her forces from Kashmir as long as there was no agreed-upon plan for simultaneous Indian withdrawal."

The withdrawal of Indian and Pakistani forces from Kashmir - i.e. demilitarization - as envisaged in UNCIP resolutions would not have been even a presentable proposition if it exposed one side to danger of attack from the other. Accordingly, while the resolution did require Pakistan to begin to withdraw its forces before India would begin the process on its side. They also required that the completion of the process be synchronized and simultaneous on both sides. This obviously required an agreed-upon plan. The Commission prepared such a plan - called the Truce Plan - and presented it to the two governments. India raised several issues. President Truman (US) and Prime Minister Attlee (UK) made a joint appeal to the two governments to accept the arbitration of the Plebiscite Administrator-designate on these points.

Pakistan promptly accepted the proposal, with no if's and but's; India rejected it. Later, two United Nations Representatives, Sir Own Dixon and Frank Graham (US) made intense efforts to secure India's agreement to a rational plan so that the Plebiscite Administrator would be inducted into office and would dispose of all the remaining forces - the residual Indian and the local - as he deemed fit. Sadly, they failed to overcome India's stubborn obstruction. This has been the cause of the stalemate in Kashmir ever since. The solution is there, only India is unwilling to implement it.

THE KASHMIR WAR AFTER KARGIL

The real war is the one in J&K: in this larger conflict, Kargil is just something of a footnote. But Kargil's impact on security in the rest of J&K might be mildly described as a calamity. 58 battalions of the Army engaged in counter-terrorist operations have been withdrawn for border deployment in the war's wake. 36 of these have been withdrawn from Kashmir and 22 from the Jammu Province. Just 14 Central Reserve Police Force (CRPF) and 6 BSF battalions have been moved in to take their place. A further six have been sent in for the Amarnath Yatra, and these may stay on until the 1999 Lok Sabha elections. With the prospect of a permanent manning of the LoC, no one has any cogent idea of just how the shortfall will be met in the long-run. During the 1998 Lok Sabha elections, moreover, 354 additional companies, each of approximately 125 men, had been deployed in J&K. This time round, at least 500 companies will have to be brought in to even meet the 1998 security levels. At least two significant elements of the war in J&K have already become evident. First, since last summer, the mountain heights of the State, areas of little political significance, have seen large concentrations of Pakistani and Afghan terrorists, as well as an assortment of other "freelance seekers of martyrdom". Received military wisdom has it that these groups lack the motivation or resources to fight a losing battle in the Kashmir Valley. But a more plausible possibility also exists. By building-up numbers on the heights dominating Doda, Banihal, the Rajouri-Poonch belt and Kupwara, terrorist groups will dominate the principal lines of access to the Kashmir Valley. Read in the context of recoveries of increasingly heavy weapons in recent months, ranging from mortar and anti-aircraft guns to a Grail anti-tank missile launcher, some argue that current deployment patterns suggest terrorist groups are preparing to support Pakistan troops in a conventional engagement.

The second key element of terrorist activity in months to come is certain to be the engineering of a deterioration in communal relations, pushing Muslims out of Hindu-dominated areas south of the Chenab river, and Hindus from the predominantly Muslim areas to its north. Such migrations will give a *de facto* demographic legitimacy to Pakistan's objective of securing some variant of the Owen Dixon plan. These processes have been in place at least since 1997, although they gathered momentum after the Pokhran II tests and Advani's promise of a "pro-active" policy in J&K. In a broader sense, revanchist groups in Pakistan believe the communal war they are engaged in is merely part of a larger struggle against supposedly-Hindu India. These faultlines, ironically but unsuprisingly, are precisely those that shape the *mentalité* of the Hindu Right.

Even as much of J&K finds itself without security cover, there is substantial evidence that cross-border infiltration of terrorists has been unusually high in summer 1999. Field intelligence officials in Kupwara and Baramulla estimate that at least six hundred terrorists have moved in since March, often occupying positions at heights above 4,000 metres. Anantnag, too, has seen sharp rise in the numbers of Pakistan and Afghan terrorists active in the district, with over two hundred reported to be based in the district. While most groups of terrorists have been avoiding frontal engagement with state forces, there is little doubt that the period since the Kargil conflict broke out has seen a marked escalation in violence in the State.

A secondary thrust of terrorist activity 1999 summer unveiled itself with the murder of Deputy Inspector General S.K. Chakravarty, Joint Director G-Branch Mahendra Raj, and Sub Inspector K. Bhaskar during a raid on the BSF's Sector Headquarters at Bandipore on July 13. Evidently, the increased targeting of security force personnel represents, at once, a shift in strategy as well as a radical enhancement in weapons capabilities and the proficiency of the foreign militants who have come to dominate the movement in J&K. This has been a progressive trend of the past three years, as the steadily worsening ratio of security force personnel to militants killed demonstrates. This ratio has declined from 1:5.79 in 1997, through 1:4.54 in 1988, to 1:3.20 in 1999. Worse, with the thinning out of security forces in the wake of Kargil and the escalation in Pak-backed militant activity, this ratio fell to 1:2 in June 1999 year, as compared to a ratio of 1:5 in June 1998. If the massacres and violent attacks this summer mark a vertical escalation in the conflict in J&K, there are also signs of a generalised horizontal escalation in the Leh region.

Last month's arrest of a twenty-five member terrorist cell from the Turtok area of Leh, led by local resident Ali Bhutto, has made it clear that conflict can be expected in this until-now quiet region. Bhutto's arrest, outside Leh, has been treated with little concern.

But terrorism had similar low-key origins elsewhere as well. In Poonch, the first sign of an offensive was the arrest of Ayub Shabnam in May 1990. Shabnam, who went on to spend five years in jail, was believed to be responsible for the training and distribution of weapons to several local operatives. But he, like Bhutto, had little knowledge of Pakistan's broader objectives. Few took the incident seriously, until Poonch went up in flames after 1993.

Bhutto was picked up along with his cell, which included two police constables, in a series of raids that began on June 7. The group had hidden 25 Kalashnikov assault rifles, one heavy machine gun, one general purpose machine gun, a sniper rifle, a rocket propelled grenade launcher and several kilogrammes of explosive material, brought in by Bhutto's Skardu-based brother, Ibrahim Sangsang. Sangsang, interrogators of the Turtok cell discovered, had made several trips accross the LoC in 1998, handing over weapons to relatives and associates in five villages. All the five villages, Turtok, Pachathang, Thakshi, Thang and Chalungpa were captured by India in the war of 1971. Bhutto's father had been instrumental in asking villagers, against Pakistan Army advice, to stay in India on the grounds that it was wrong to leave the land of their birth. Interestingly, dozens of villagers in nearby Bogdang village were issued rifles by the Pakistan Army in 1971 to wage a guerilla war against advancing Indian troops. Few complied, and the rifles were instead put to use poaching mountain goats.

Ibrahim Sangang's story illustrates the rich relationship between broad ideological factors and purely local issues in the emergence of terror. Sangsang had, by local accounts, been intimate with local officials and the military authorities, even having been sponsored to visit New Delhi for a Republic Day parade in 1987. But by 1994, Sangsang found himself embroiled in a series of legal disputes. Most emerged from a criminal assault on a police officer, the outcome of a violent dispute over the use of a diesel generator set that powered several villages. Under pressure from the criminal justice system, Sangpapa fled accross the LoC, where the ISI appears to have offered him a better deal as against several years in jail. But several larger factors appear to have been at play in the five villages. The *Noor Baksh* sect that historically dominated the region, an eclectic*Sufi*-inspired faith drawing both from *Sunni* and *Shia* custom, has been under sustained seige from ultra-conservative *Ahl-e-Hadis* prosletysers. The *Ahl-e-Hadis* have been closely associated with terrorist groups in J&K, notably the *Lashkar-e-Toiba* and the *Tehreek-ul-Mujaheddin*.

The near-unchallenged growth of revanchist religious groups both in Pakistan and in J&K is certain to prepare the real ideological agenda of events to come. In J&K, as the RAC Report illustrates, the National Conference has begun to tear away from its historic character as a secular, modernising force, and recast itself as a Muslim communal formation.

The tendency has been most marked in Jammu where, as I have pointed out earlier, leaders of the far-Right *Jamaat-e-Islami* have shared platforms with the National Conference. These trends will be reinforced from across the border as, most disturbingly, the future of Pakistan's establishment elite has never been more unsure than in recent years.

Back home, economic hardship and the inability of a corrupt government to bring relief has made Pakistan's Islamic fundamentalists more popular with ordinary folk and – crucially – with the military, which for decades has helped the Westernized elite to curb Islamic fervour. As Jamaat [e-Islami] leader Qazi Hussain Ahmad pointed out at a well-attended convention in Islamabad in October, the income gap between junior and senior officers has been widening as the economic crisis worsens.

In the first of his seminal articles on the Kargil War, Aijaz Ahmad had written, "The Pakistan we are dealing with was born not once but twice". He outlined the crisis of identity that emerged from the creation of Bangladesh, and the reinvention of Pakistan not as the home of sub-continental Muslims, but of a mythically pure Islam, subsidised by West Asian wealth. Nothing worked as magically in restoring the self-confidence of the Pakistani state and its privileged classes as the infusion of petrodollars. But this new sort of money brought with it a new and curiously effective commodity as well: petro-Islam. A hybrid thing, born of centuries of ferocious conservatism so characteristic of the desert, but also of the unprecedented levels of wealth that was newly gained but was the product neither of a settled history nor of accumulated labour but of chance, that the black gold flowed here rather than elsewhere. It was a curious kind of Islam, equally ferocious in its piety and in its consumerism.

To those who have noted the organic links between the emergence of a new middle class through the 1980s, and the rise of the Hindu Right through India, Ahmad's description of petro-Islam will be disturbingly familiar. In both India and Pakistan, the forces of reaction are far from spent, driven, as both now are by nuclear power. The end of the war on the Kargil heights, it is almost certain, is profoundly unlikely to mark the begining of peace.

THE KARGIL WAR TIMELINE

The 1999 Kargil conflict between India-Pakistan is the conflict that came the closest to a nuclear exchange than any other conflict in the post-Cold War period. Following the conflict in which Pakistan was perceived to have lost, Pakistani prime minister Nawaz Sharif is overthrown by the Army under Pervez Musharraf leading to a very tense period in bilateral relations between India and Pakistan.

- May 8th-15th 1999: Pakistani troops cross the Line of Control in Kashmir and occupy Indian positions in the disputed territory– Indian Army patrols detect intruders atop Kargil ridges. Army errs in saying 100 infiltrators are occupying 25 km of Indian Territory. India realises Pakistan plans to cut Leh from Srinagar by taking key highway.
- May 25th 1999: Indian Army acknowledges that 600-800 Pakistani infiltrators are lodged in remote Kargil-Drass-Batalik sectors. India surprises Pakistan, ups ante with air strikes. India launches air strikes against militants in Indian-administered Kashmir for the first time in 20 years.India promises further raids.
- May 26th 1999: India launches Kashmir air attack/ Indian Air Force MiG-27 flames out and Indian officer K. Nachiketa

is taken prisoner by Pakistan. MiG-21 on a rescue mission hovers over Line of Control, shot down. Squadron Leaderr Ajay Ahuja is killed in action. Srinagar airport closed. India mobilises its armed forces in response Operation Vijay puts 200,000 Indian troops on alert across the border almost overnight—sudden and massive escalation in tensions and military force available to both sides in the crisis/ Pakistani & Indian forces start exchanging fire/ quickly develops into brushfire war

- May 28th 1999: Mi-17 helicopter shot down. Four-man crew dead, Indian Army withdraws choppers. Fernandes goofs up, says Sharif and ISI have no hand in Kargil operations. Detecting the infiltrators by chance, the New Delhi admits it was caught unawares by intrusions

May 1999

India says it will continue to bomb militant infiltrators in Indian-administered Kashmir until it has driven them out.

- May 26th 1999: Pakistan army on high alert. Pakistan has called the Indian air strikes in Kashmir "very, very serious" and put its troops on high alert.
- May 27th 1999: India loses two jets over Kashmir. The Indian Government confirms that two of its aircraft are lost during a series of air strikes against militants in Kashmir.
- Pakistan proposes Delhi mission. Pakistan proposes sending foreign minister Sartaj Aziz to India to ease tensions in the disputed Kashmir region.
- May 30th 1999: Indian pilot 'killed in cold blood'. An Indian pilot whose plane was shot down by Pakistan forces died from bullet wounds suffered after he ejected, Indian officials say.
- May 31st 1999: Bid to defuse Kashmir tensions. India and Pakistan agree to hold talks over Kashmir in the first sign that the two sides might be trying to defuse escalating tensions.

June 1999

- 3rd June 1999: Kashmir peace hopes flounder. India slams 'dangerous' Kashmir claims. As India promises to continue ground and air strikes against infiltrators, a senior Indian minister warns there is little point in peace talks with Pakistan.
- 5th June 1999: India halts bombing. India hands over 'Pakistani bodies'. India announces a pause in bombing raids in Kashmir.
- 8th June 1999: Kashmir talks confirmed. Indian Prime Minister's address to the nation
- Pakistan and India fix a date for their first significant attempt to defuse the tension over Kashmir.
- 9th June 1999: New air strikes ahead of talks. India continues its assault on suspected infiltrators holed up in the Himalayas with fresh air strikes, ahead of talks with Pakistan.
- 11th June 1999: Pakistan denies mutilation claims. Pakistan strongly denies allegations that the bodies of six Indian soldiers in Kashmir were mutilated by its soldiers before being handed back.
- 13th June 1999: No deal at Kashmir talks. India and Pakistan end their talks on the fierce fighting in Kashmir without agreement on how to halt the conflict.
- 16th June 1999: India pushes on with offensive
- 17th June 1999: India claims successes in Kashmir. Thousands flee fighting. India presses ahead with its military offensive, a day after US President Clinton asked Pakistan to persuade them to pull out.
- 29th June 1999: Kashmir diplomacy hots up. Pakistan's Prime Minister Nawaz Sharif returns from China, as a flurry of diplomatic activity aimed at ending the ongoing Kashmir conflict gets underway in India and Pakistan.

July 1999

- 4th July 1999: Clinton urges India-Pakistan talks. Pakistan's

Prime Minister Nawaz Sharif and US President Bill Clinton that "concrete steps will be taken" to restore the fragile Line of Control between Indian and Pakistani forces in Kashmir. India seizes strategic peak.

- India announces it has taken the key Tiger Hill peak following an all-out assault, as it prepares to respond to a joint statement by Pakistan's prime minister. Nawaz Sharif and US President Bill Clinton agree that "concrete steps will be taken" to restore the Line of Control.
- 11th July 1999: Kashmir pull-out agreed. Islamic militants are reported to be leaving the mountains of Indian Kashmir as both Pakistan and India claim victory in the two-month conflict.
- 12th July 1999: The Pakistani Prime Minister, Nawaz Sharif, appeals for a permanent settlement of the Kashmir.

American Diplomacy

With India and Pakistan exchanging artillery fire and both sides suffering casualties in Kargil—Pakistan in particular suffering losses to the Indians army/ on July 4th 1999 Bill Clinton meets Pakistani president Nawaz Sharif at Blair House, Washington D.C. – US intelligence assets over Pakistan begin seeing movement concerning Pakistan's nuclear arsenal—

The deployment alarmed President Clinton due to two key areas that differed from the US-Soviet nuclear confrontations—firstly the move was alarming due to Pakistan and India's apparent unawareness of each other's doctrines relating to nuclear weapons—thus a nuclear war could have started by accident—secondly a questions and concerns over command and control in Pakistan—that the army in Pakistan may have circumvented the civilian leadership and deployed the weapons without Nawaz Sharif's prior knowledge—more dangerous than Soviet-US confrontations

The prospect of a nuclear exchange on the Indian-subcontinent represented one of the gravest threats at the end of the 20th Century— greater threat in the 1990s than the collapse of Yugoslavia and risking more lives lost than even the 2nd Congo War in central

Africa —a nuclear exchange would have been killed, injured and displaced millions of people—destroyed two great civilisations and forever damaged the Indo-Pacific as an economic area–

Indo-Pakistani relationship in Asia-Pacific: Long term effects

The Indo-Pakistani crises that occurred in the late 1990s & into 2000s represented a major threat to the economies and states of Asia-Pacific—key event in that Clinton diplomacy & dexterity with Pakistan & India prevented a crisis from escalating further—case of meeting at Blair House with Prime Minister Nawaz Sharif, India proved to be a key economic & security actor in the 2000s – providing large numbers of professionally trained troops to UN peacekeeping operations—the economic rise of India—creation of an Indian middle class– would have been forever halted if a nuclear exchange were to have had occurred—by 2050 India economy equal to US economy (Goldman Sachs figures) minimum larger than the United Kingdom, France and Japan.

India-Pakistan relations

India-Pakistan remains the most important flashpoint in Asia-Pacific in terms of danger to the region/ nuclear rivals that unlike the US-USSR have directly fought multiple conflicts/ every single one of these conflicts Pakistan has lost conventionally—hence the resort to violent non-state actors and a strategic nuclear deterrence/ Both the United States and China have a role to play in the Indian subcontinent—both command influence and hard power.

THE 1999 KARGIL WAR: NOT A GENERALS' VICTORY

Much has been written about the event, including by the Chief of Army Staff at that time, Gen V P Malik, as also by the then Home Minister L K Advani. There was an official inquiry by India's renowned strategic affairs analyst, K Subrahmanyam, but he has pointed out to this writer that he did not go into operational details and accordingly, could not comment on certain weaknesses some top Indian commanders displayed. The mid-level and younger officers and men though fought well, and even though many of them perished, the victory actually belonged to them.

The Pakistani military leadership as well as its Inter Services Intelligence (ISI) have always been indulging in nasty manoeuvers against India. But that they dared to infiltrate troops into India and tried to capture a part of Kashmir yet again was possible because we were negligent, partly because we generally are so by temperament and partly because the government of the day, led by Mr A B Vajpayee, had ordered the forces to be "soft" on Pakistan because of the "positive" talks between him and his Pakistani counterpart, Nawaz Sharif towards maintaining peace and building friendship.

While opportunities for peace must be seized by politicians, there was no reason for the armed forces – the Army in particular – to be lax. In fact, the Pakistani move as it happened had been debated in the Indian Army for years and had been taken up as a strong possibility in periodic exercises. Yet, when it was happening, we were blind to it.

In the foreword to Brig Gurmeet Kanwal's book, Indian Army Vision 2020, Gen Malik says: "The Fact is that even after 60 years of independence, knowledge and experience of defence and military issues is lacking in most of our political leaders and civilian bureaucrats."

But the General has not shared the lapses and neglect of responsibilities of the Army leadership, particularly of the sector commanders, and to an extent, his own. Some of these are by now, well known, including the mindset of the 15 Corps Commander, Lt Gen Krishan Pal, who insisted that there were only a handful of infiltrators – 60 to 80 – and that none of them was a Pakistani soldier. He committed troops without allowing them adequate weapons and strength, and if facts given by Lt Gen Y M Bammi in a book are taken into account, he punished an officer, Brig Devinder Singh, who wanted better preparations insisting that there were a large number of Pakistani soldiers inside the Indian territory.

The officer had eight battalions under his charge, and by all accounts, he fought very well, leading the troops from the front.

Gen Malik himself has been seen and heard praising this officer at various fora. Yet, Brig Devinder Singh's career was cut short to save those who were wrong.

To recall, the biggest players of the Kargil War were:

a. The Government at the highest echelon of the Political Leadership;
b. The top rung of the military leadership – The Army Chief, GOC-in-C Northern Command, 15 Corps Cdr , and the 3 Div Cdr;
c. The intelligence agencies, primarily the Intelligence Bureau (IB) and Research and Analysis Wing (RAW);
d. The Indian Air Force (IAF) and its exercise of Air Power.
e. The dedicated and committed soldiers and the middle and junior level officers.

The Role Of The Political Leadership

The NDA government was at its pinnacle in May 1998, having successfully conducted the nuclear test that month and having put India in the list of Nuclear Weapon States (NWS). The aim now was to resolve the Kashmir issue by seeking wellmeaning diplomatic and economic relations with Pakistan.

Mrs Indira Gandhi had also attempted that, after the 1971 Bangladesh Liberation War, by trying to tell the then Pakistani leader Z A Bhutto that only peace between the two neighbours would ensure their long-term economic prosperity and growth. In fact, she went out of the way to ensure a comfortable stay for Bhutto, personally choosing even the tapestry of the room he was to stay in Simla during the 1972 summit between them, and by telling Indian officers that the Pakistani leader must be given the respect due to a visiting head of government or state, and not that of a country which had lost war. She agreed to Bhutto's request to release nearly 96,000 Pakistani POWs, and Bhutto promised to work for peace with India.

Needless to say that he backed out. Mrs Gandhi did what was right in those circumstances. But the lesson for the Indian leadership was to understand that Pakistan is never to be trusted. Islamabad built a network of nuclear capability and missiles by smuggling and deceit, lying even to Washington which gave it liberal aid as a friend and mentor.

Prime Minister Vajpayee and his deputy, Advani, tried to establish a political dialogue with Pakistan. Coupled with the nuclear tests, a success with Islamabad would give them respect in the history books forever.

Intelligence organizations were told to be easy, and the armed forces stopped looking for periodic information from them. There was the February 1999 Bus Yatra (journey) by Vajpayee to Lahore to meet with his counterpart, Nawaz Sharif. It was a goodwill mission, seemingly wellresponded by Sharif.

But the fact that the then Pakistani Chief of Army Staff, Gen Parvez Musharraf, did not pay due respects to the visiting Indian leader during the visit, should have been an indication of the Pakistani army's intentions; that it had no intention to accommodate the rapprochement that the political leadership in Islamabad perhaps then wanted.

It may be noted that as a Brigadier on assignment with a think tank in London, Musharraf had written in a thesis that Pakistan must capture Kashmir to secure water from the Himalayan rivers for itself. As a Chief of Staff, he would certainly try to realize his thoughts.

It is a well known fact that the Srinagar-Leh axis runs closest to the Line of Control (LOC) in the Dras–Kargil Sector. Also, the terrain on the Indian side is hostile to defend, whereas the terrain on the Pakistan side is favorable to launch an offensive. Strategically, Pakistan has always intended to block, disrupt or permanently dislocate it.

My first posting after being commissioned into the IAF in 1963 was to Jammu in Squadron 43, flying Dakotas. The main task was to operate to Kargil and Thoise to provide logistic support to the troops deployed in forward areas. I was fortunate to be deputed as the Base Commander of Air Force clement at Kargil from Feb to May 1964, working along with 121 (Ind) Infantry Brigade.

It was an education. Brig Chopra, an Armoured Corps officer who was the Brigade Commander, always used to say that the

Dras-Kargil Sector was the most sensitive because of its close proximity to the LOC as well as the terrain factors.

Much later, during a course in 1980-81 at the Army's prestigious College of Combat at MHOW, now renamed Army War College, this lesson was repeated by none other than the Commandant, Lt Gen K Sunderji.

He became the Chief of Army Staff later, and had a sand-model exercise conducted, visualizing exactly what the Pakistanis did to occupy Kargil. A counteroffensive plan was discussed at the 15 Corps Headquarters. I was privy to that along with Lt Gen B C Nanda, Army Commander Northern Command, Air Marshal M M Singh, AOC-in-C Western Command and some other officers.

That in 1998 and 1999, the top brass in the same sector was oblivious to the risk from the Pakistani Army, is absolutely un-understanable.

Raw's Aviation Research Centre (ARC)

Till mid-1997, a user could approach ARC only through the RAW HQ for its operational tasks. This used to delay the process by a week. The legendary Billy Bedi, who headed ARC for several years, initiated userfriendly steps, and a required mission could be launched within hours. Analytical reports were delivered ASAP, within hours if required.

Top 3-star officers from the services were invited and informed of the ARC's capabilities in airborne electronic intelligence, and the then Chief of Air Staff, Air Chief Marshal A Y Tipnis, commended the ARC.

The Kargil Surprise

In May 1999, once reports of Pakistani infiltration had come in, Army's Directorate General of Military Intelligence (DGMI) sought Air Reconnaissance Mission in the Dras-Kargil sector. I personally flew missions beginning May 13 and soon, on May 18, we had pictures of six Pakistani Army MI-17 helicopters parked in the Mushok Valley area on the Indian side. These photographs were shown to the then Defence Minister George Fernandes, who was aghast and observed that this could have happened only after months of planning and preparation.

Gen Malik also praised ARC for the inputs but strangely, till some three weeks after this input, Lt Gen Krishan Pal still seemed to believe that there were only a few infiltrators on the Indian side. He himself said in a TV statement that he revised his opinion only after India lost many lives in the Battle of Tololing (June 13).

Did the Army HQ fail to convey him the confirmation of the Pakistani helicopters, and presence, inside India? Or he just insisted on ignoring reality?

Perhaps, the Army should come out with the truth after an honest introspection. For record, Gen Malik had told ARC that he had no hesitation in admitting that its inputs enabled the Army to correlate its operational plans and that otherwise the causality figures could have been much higher. The gap between this statement and Lt Gen Krishanpal's observation is glaring, and led to a tragic loss of lives.

The Indian Air Force

IAF does not have combat helicopters for high altitude offensive operations, and on May 25, it was decided to commit aircraft to neutralize the Pakistan-occupied positions on the Indian side. Initially, IAF lost two aircraft and one Mi 17 helicopter.

An IAF spokesman pointed out that the air operations in Kargil had taken place in an environment that was totally new in the history of world military aviation. The IAF had to unlearn what had been taught before, as it was operating with a new set of paradigms such as the ballistic trajectory of weapons in high altitude operations. A well-respected Air Marshal Vinod Patney, Air Officer Commanding in-Chief (AOC-in-C) Western Air Command, conducted the air operations after a short course to his officers in precision bombing.

The Subrahmanyam Committee

The Subrahmanyam Committee did not attribute any intelligence failures to RAW or ARC, but highlighted equipment inadequacies like the lack of high resolution, all-weather and sub-meter imaging capability. Lack of UAVs and better coordination between the security agencies was also mentioned but it acknowledged that the IB Director did convey certain inputs on activities in areas under the Gilgit-based FCNA (Force Commander orthern Areas) of Pakistan to the Prime Minister, the Home Minister, the Cabinet Secretary, the Home Secretary and the Director-General Military Operations (DGMO). There is apparently a general lack of awareness of the critical importance of, and the need for, assessed intelligence, at all levels. Joint Intelligence Committee (JIC) reports do not receive the attention they deserve at the political and higher bureaucratic levels. One officer in a listening post mentions that a senior bureaucrat asked him about some entertainment programmes only in a span of one year. It is clear that a Kargil-type situation could have been avoided either by plugging gaps as in Siachin, or by a credible declaratory policy of swiftly punishing wanton and willful violation of the sanctity of the LOC, as the Committee observed.

The Nuclear Tangle

Kargil was a stupid adventure for Pakistan. Threats from Islamabad about using nuclear weapons were considered but dismissed as Pakistan would not have been more stupid to invite destructive retaliation. The Kargil War has also helped strengthen India's doctrine that while India would not first use nuclear weapons, it would retaliate by inflicting massive destruction.

Conclusion

There is much evidence available to suggest that the intelligence agencies, RAW and IB, had in fact provided their political masters and military commanders with ample warning about Pakistani intentions and activities. In any case, lack of strategic intelligence could have been made up by the observation on the ground through scouts and patrolling. One did not have to get basic inputs about the Pakistani infiltration from shepherds, which as a matter fact, happened. After all, the Pakistani infiltration was spread over a large front. India deliberately limited its response to the eviction of Pakistani soldiers. But many of our officers and men died needlessly as we were neither prepared for the war nor ready to absorb the inputs towards efficient and better coordination between the security forces. The victory indeed belonged to those officers and men who fought, died or survived, but won.

4

India-Pakistan Proxy Wars

India & Pakistan are once again engaged in war of words & bullets at Borders. After the aborted meeting between National security adviser of India & Pakistan's adviser to PM on foreign affairs pursuant to Modi - Nawaz Joint statement in Russian city of Uffa , both the Countries appear as distant as ever. Even after 68 years of their independence, neither nation has learnt to live in peace, leave alone harmony.Innocent civilians are increasingly becoming fodder to their guns.

A sad factor of the ever deteriorating relations is the leverage enjoyed by the spies & security experts of both countries in determining the 'Red lines' for politicians of their respective countries.Every step between the two countries is now being measured & evaluated through security prism. The relations get further strained by ultra-nationalist & jingoistic media driven by agencies, particularly on the Indian Side. Politics & diplomacy is not allowed a free run to instill & nurture a good neighborly relation between the two Countries.

The security agencies are playing havoc in each other's country. Dismemberment of Pakistan in 1971 & Military Coup at Siachin in 1984 are two instances of India playing dirty games against Pakistan. Fear of an adversarial neighbor coupled with the unresolved issue of Kashmir, has lead Pakistan also to engage in secret operations against India. Training & arming of Sikh separatists in Eighties & Kargil intrusion in 1999 can be cited as Pakistani instances of covert operations against India. The resultant mess on ground is for all of us to see.

Graphic details of proxy wars between India & Pakistan , which intensified in 1987, are provided by writer & Historian Dilip Hiro in his book " The longest August". As per said details reproduced below, intelligence agencies of three Countries-RAW (India), KGB (Russia)& KHAD (Afghanistan), increased their training & arming of Baluchi separatists for subversive activities in Baluchistan. The separatists aim of establishing an independent Baluchistan would have meant reducing Pakistan by a hefty 43 percent and was, therefore resisted bitterly by Pakistani Govt. As part of the axis of three intelligence agencies, RAW's counter intelligence team –X in coordination with KHAD became an active participant in stoking subversion in Pakistan. The result was a low level but steady campaign of bombing s in Karachi, Lahore & Multan. According to US State Department, more than half of the 835 terrorist incidents worldwide in 1987 were in Pakistan (`Chicago Tribune 18th Jan. 1988)

On the Indian side Punjab remained on boil. Militants aided by ISI ,had started creeping into the Golden temple from the summer of 1986. Their takeover was complete in June 1987. Soon Delhi imposed president's rule which would eventually continue till 1992. In November 1986 Indian Army staged a biggest war game code named "Brasstracks" in Rajasthan, barely 30 miles from Pakistan border. It was the largest war game ever seen on the subcontinent involving four lakh troops from Nine Army divisions, Five independent armored brigades, 1300 tanks, 1000+ armored vehicles. Contrary to mutually accepted standard procedure, Indian Army chief didn't inform his Pakistani counterpart of the location, schedule and scale of the exercise. Pakistan thought this as an Indian attempt to launch a piercing strike to cut off northern Pakistan from the Southern Part. In defense Pakistan extended its army's winter exercises in Punjab and also mobilized the 5th Corps in Karachi as well as the Southern Air command while deploying mechanized divisions & artillery along the Indian border. Indians perceived this move as part of a pincer to squeeze Indian Punjab, where Sikh insurgency had revived following assassination of Indira Gandhi & Anti Sikh riots. On 18th January, Pakistani Foreign Minster Zain Noorani conveyed President Zia-ul-Haq's message to Indian ambassador

S.K.Singh that in the event of an Indian misadventure, Pakistan was capable of inflicting unacceptable damage on it. The underlying message of Zia-ul-Haq was clear that Pakistan possessed a nuclear weapon, notwithstanding the fact that few months earlier President Reagan of America, in order to enable him to continue military aid, had testified before the Senate that Pakistan was not pursuing a nuclear agenda.

While Pakistan's terse message created doubts in New-Delhi, it deployed veteran Journalist Kuldeep Nayyar to get some details. He arranged an interview with Pakistan's nuclear scientist Qadeer Khan who testified Pakistan's possession of bombs. Though publication of the interview was delayed by four weeks, but India got the message it wanted.

To reduce tensions between the two countries, Rajiv Gandhi used Cricket diplomacy and invited Zia-ul-Haq to witness a cricket match between India & Pakistan in Jaipur, who accepted the invitation. Sitting next to his host, Haq reportedly whispered to Gandhi-" If your forces cross our border by an inch, we are going to annihilate your cities" indicating that his military would not hesitate to make a first use of Atom bomb.(Nuclear Dangers in South Asia by S. A. Hashmi).Those sitting close to two leaders testify visible signs of nervousness in Rajiv Gandhi.

To ensure that Proxy wars played by two intelligence agencies in each other's country didn't escalate into a full fledged battle, Zia-ul- Haq conceived the idea of an unofficial meeting between two agencies. But he needed an intermediary with extraordinary skills to act as a go-between. For this he chose his Jordnain friend Crown Prince Hassan bin talal, whom he had met during his military assignment in Jordan. Talal was married to a Pakistani girl, Sarvath Ikramullah, the niece of H.S. Suharwardy, the former Prime Minster of Pakistan. The efforts fructified in a meeting of two intelligence chiefs- A.K.Verma of RAW & Lt. General Hamid Gul of ISI in Amman. The meeting resulted in phased handing over of nearly 3000 Sikh Militants by Pakistan who had crossed to Pakistan for training in lieu of RAW de-escalating bombing campaign in Pakistani cities in Stages (Ravi Shankar-spy wars).Another meeting between the two heads took place in Swiss city of Interlaken. This time resolving Siachen Glacier was on agenda-but no results were achieved.

It may be recalled that A. S. Dulat, former Raw chief has also testified to such meetings between the two intelligence chief in his recently released book-"Kashmir-the Vajpayee years" under the chapter Spy Vs. Spy at page 151.In a recent article published in 'the Hindu' of 28th August 2015,former RAW chief A.K.Verma has also confirmed such an agreement between the intelligence agencies of two Countries.

INDIA'S WAR AGAINST PAKISTAN IS NO PROXY WAR

At the last combined conference of the military commanders Prime Minister Narendra Modi showed an excellent grasp of India's security situation when he told them that the main threat to our country came not from a "war" but from the covert offensive of the adversary. While emphasising the importance of peace and security for economic development he went on to specially alert the defence forces against the "proxy war" that India was exposed to at the hands of a hostile neighbour.

The dastardly attack of Taliban on Peshawar Army Public School in which 132 students, among others, were massacred in cold blood has been followed by fresh intelligence alerts from Indian agencies about acts of cross-border terrorism in India. Already, Hafiz Saeed - the founder leader of LeT, has gone public in Pakistan blaming India for the Peshawar incident while Zakiur Rehman Lakhvi - the mastermind behind 26/11 - secured release from a Pakistan prison on bail.The whole issue of Pakistan-sponsored proxy war against India, has thus come alive again.

The hostile mindset of the Pakistan army against India remains unchanged in spite of the Peshawar killings. It wants to respond to the setback it has received in combating Islamic radicals, by stepping up its covert offensive against India. The strategy behind this is to tell the West that a disturbed eastern border would leave it with little time and resource to undertake the combat on the western front - unless it received greater patronage and policy support from the latter.

Pakistan army continues to believe that the US depends on it for protecting its interests in Afghanistan and would not take too much notice of the India-centric militants controlled by Pakistan's ISI like LeT's Hafiz Saeed beyond giving him the label of a terrorist.

In the post-Cold War era, terrorism has become the new weapon for conducting an "asymmetric warfare". India is perhaps the worst victim of proxy war in this era. Pakistan first instigated and sustained "Khalistan" movement in the '80s and then - having failed in its mischievous aim in Punjab - attempted to replicate the success of Afghan jihad in Kashmir in the '90s. Pakistan army and the ISI had become the blue-eyed boys for the US after the Soviet withdrawal from Afghanistan and it is no surprise that India came in pressure from the state department to heed Pakistan's demand on Kashmir at that point of time.

The Kargil intrusion itself was a war-like attack carried out in the proxy war mode as soldiers were sent in as Mujahideen. It had been planned by former Pakistani President Pervez Musharraf - an expert in commando operations. India had to conduct a full scale war to push back the intruders. Musharraf has now confirmed that Kargil was Pakistan's answer to India's action in Bangladesh.

Pakistan went on to take the proxy war against India to a new level of planning and bravado in staging 26/11 which has rightly been described as "India's 9/11". The weak-kneed response of the then government in accepting the unabashed denial by Pakistan of any responsibility for "the doings of non-state actors" only encouraged that country to keep up its cross border terrorism against India.

As the new government in India is being quite upfront on this issue-Union home minister having affirmed at the annual DGPs Conference in Guwahati on November 29 that there was Pakistan ISI's hand behind 26/11 - the Pakistan army has been keeping a tighter grip on the civilian rulers. This became evident at the recent SAARC summit at Kathmandu where the Pakistan prime minister blocked the passage of agreements on mutually beneficial initiatives and tried to sabotage the advance of an emerging regional forum. What the SAARC summit revealed even more significantly for India was the fact that there is a continuing shadow of Sino-

Pak axis on South Asia. This military compact now extends to China aiding the anti-India proxy war of Pakistan in return for the Pakistan advocacy of China's entry into the South Asian association. China wants to be a part of SAARC primarily to counter India's influence there and is likely to use its alliance with Pakistan for containing the rising profile of India in this part of the world under the leadership of Narendra Modi.

The Chinese have taken notice of the successful visits of the new Indian prime minister to Japan, US and Australia - not to forget Myanmar, Malaysia, Fiji and Nepal. The Sino-Pak collaboration against India is likely to become more pronounced in the days ahead.

Pakistan is effectively ruled by its army. The country has neither the willingness nor an external compulsion to abjure militancy and terrorism as an instrument of political power. The common man in Pakistan has no voice and the intelligentsia there does not want to buy trouble with the army - the real power centre in the country.

Only recently at a large rally held by Hafiz Saeed, under the total protection of the government, at Lahore, the LeT founder denounced the elections in J&K and reiterated the call for jihad in Kashmir. This indicates the shape of the monster in the times to come. Pakistan's ISI has been successful in exploiting the communal issues for fomenting militancy as is adequately established by the recent doings of SIMI and Indian Mujahideen. The internal security situation has to be closely monitored in the context of this added vulnerability.

We have to be fully geared to deal with the sponsors of the proxy war. If 26/11 is India's 9/11 Hafiz Saeed is our Osama bin Laden. India's right to get to him can not be questioned by the upholders of democracy in the world.

UNITED STATES' ROLE AND INFLUENCE ON THE INDIA-PAKISTAN CONFLICT

Although the Soviet Union played a critical role in formally ending the second India-Pakistan war in 1965—through the Tashkent Declaration—its close military and security relationships with Delhi during much of the Cold War years decreased its influence over Islamabad, which became increasingly linked to the United States for the supply of arms. China's discreet missile and nuclear linkages with Islamabad, along with memories of the India-China border war of 1962, precluded Beijing's influence over the India-Pakistan dispute. Despite an apparent shift in Beijing's position since 1996 (especially during the Kargil conflict in 1999 when it refrained from publicly supporting Pakistan, and due to its concerns over Islamist extremists in Xinjiang province), elements of future India-China competition make it difficult for Beijing to influence Delhi. While French, European Union or Japanese influence appear limited, a potential British role exists only alongside the United States, with the latter doing much of the 'heavy lifting'. Notwithstanding Washington's unprecedented and simultaneous influence over both Delhi and Islamabad, the nature and extent of its future engagement in the India-Pakistan conflict remains unclear.

Kashmir Dispute

In view of India's asymmetrical relationship with Pakistan—population, size, economic strength and relative military power—Delhi has invariably resisted the role of a third party or the United Nations in its conflict with Pakistan; it is precisely for these reasons that Islamabad has favoured such a role, with the hope that 'internationalization' would provide a favourable resolution of the Kashmir dispute. India's disillusionment with the international community over Kashmir began soon after Independence, when Prime Minister Jawaharlal Nehru took Pakistan's aggression against India in Kashmir to the United Nations on 1 January 1948.

Instead of being seen as the aggrieved party, losing Indian territory to an armed attack by Pakistan—following the signing of the Instrument of Accession by the Hindu ruler of the predominantly Muslim province of Jammu and Kashmir on 26 October 1947— India became a party to the dispute.

Subsequent UN Security Council resolutions advocating the future of Kashmir on the basis of a UN-mandated plebiscite—after the withdrawal of armed forces by both countries from divided Kashmir—were ignored by Delhi, as was the United Nations force, the UN Military Observer Group in India and Pakistan (UNMOGIP). Since the UN-sponsored ceasefire to the first India-Pakistan war over Kashmir on 1 January 1949, UNMOGIP has been deployed to monitor the ceasefire line—currently, the Line of Control (LoC) (the *de facto* border dividing Indianand Pakistan-administered Kashmir).

For Islamabad, however, the UN Security Council resolutions on Kashmir boosted its position on Kashmir, and justified its stance that it was a territorial dispute between the two sides. This contradicted Delhi's view that Kashmir was 'not a disputed territory', with the only point of contention being Pakistan's 'illegal occupation of a portion of the state', fortified by a Parliamentary resolution to this effect in the early 1990s. Even though it was clear that neither Pakistan nor India were inclined to withdraw forces from divided Kashmir, Islamabad was not averse to using UN Security Council resolutions on a plebiscite in Kashmir for political purposes.

However, Indian and Pakistani positions on a plebiscite and the status of Kashmir appeared to change in December 2003-January 2004. In an interview with Reuters in mid-December 2003, Pakistan's President Musharraf, in a bold move, publicly offered to drop Pakistan's traditional demand for a UN plebiscite in Kashmir, and meet India 'half-way' in a bid to resolve the Kashmir dispute. Musharraf reportedly stated, '... we are for the United Nations Security Council resolutions whatever it stands for. However, now we have left that aside'. Although this was subsequently denied by Pakistani officials, it was clear that this was simply a recognition that a UN plebiscite could never have been implemented, in view of Indian and Pakistani intransigence. Yet, it had been a major irritant to Delhi, which welcomed Musharraf's statement. Subsequently, in the joint press statement of 6 January 2004, following the meeting between Indian Prime Minister Vajpayee and Musharraf, on the sidelines of the twelfth South Asian Association for Regional Cooperation (SAARC) Summit in Islamabad, Delhi implicitly agreed that Kashmir was disputed territory, by explicitly agreeing that Kashmir was to be settled 'to the satisfaction of both sides'.

'Third Party' Involvement in War

Notwithstanding India's aversion to a 'third party' (including UN) role in its dispute over Kashmir, this did not apply to assistance in formally ending wars, or in the 1990s, preventing the outbreak of full-fledged conventional war. The second India-Pakistan war in 1965, for example, ended with a UN Security Council-sponsored ceasefire on 23 September 1965. Three months later, Indian Prime Minister Lal Bahadur Shastri and Pakistani President Mohammed Ayub Khan met in Tashkent and signed an agreement to formalize the end of the war and the withdrawal of their armed forces to positions held prior to 5 August 1965. The erstwhile Soviet-brokered 'Tashkent Agreement' of 10 January 1966 also pledged continued negotiations and the observation of ceasefire terms on the ceasefire line.

During this period, American policy towards South Asia remained fairly ambivalent, although an attempt at engagement on the Kashmir dispute had been made during the Eisenhower Administration in the 1950s. Although the Kennedy Administration was able to initiate direct negotiations between India and Pakistan—in the aftermath of the 1962 India-China war, the talks failed; by the mid-1960s the United States had virtually given up on Kashmir. During the 1971 India-Pakistan war, the United States 'tilt' towards Pakistan—through the deployment of an aircraft carrier task force in the Bay of Bengal in the midst of the war—whatever its intent or purpose—made it difficult for India, among other reasons, to develop a satisfactory 'comfort level' with the United States on security issues. Despite American economic and military sanctions on Pakistan in 1979 in an attempt to stem its covert nuclearweapons programme, Pakistan's role as a front-line state against the Soviet occupation of Afghanistan in the 1980s alleviated this situation. The demise of the former Soviet Union, along with India's economic liberalization in the aftermath of the 1991 economic crisis, began to lead to more favourable Indo-American relations.

In the late 1990s, high publicity American engagement with South Asia took place on nuclear issues, sparked off by multiple Indian and Pakistani nuclear tests in May 1998. On 11 and 13 May 1998, India carried out a series of five underground nuclear tests, twenty-four years after its first 'peaceful nuclear explosion' on 18 May 1974. This was promptly followed by six Pakistani nuclear tests on 28 and 30 May 1998.

Although the immediate American reaction was to impose economic and military-related sanctions on both India and Pakistan, their respective importance in United States foreign policy soon generated less coercive measures to counter proliferation. In a significant development, within the Lahore Memorandum of Understanding (MoU), both countries agreed to develop confidence-building measures (CBMs) in the nuclear and conventional fields aimed at the avoidance of conflict within nine months of the nuclear tests.

The Lahore documents—signed at the Summit between Vajpayee and Pakistani Prime Minister Nawaz Sharif in Lahore—appeared to provide the momentum towards enhanced and formalized nuclear stability in South Asia.

American Facilitation in the Kargil Conflict, 1999

Unfortunately, the Lahore framework remains unimplemented, with the single exception of advanced notification of ballistic missile flight tests on a unilateral basis—in the 'spirit' of the Lahore MoU—although this has generated its own share of controversy over the years. Pakistan's military intrusion across the LoC, allegedly at the time of the Lahore Summit, effectively ended all moves towards regional nuclear stability. Instead, India and Pakistan were involved in an armed conflict with each other for the first time after their nuclear tests; the Kargil conflict of May-July 1999 formally ended with United States facilitation.

In early 1999, Pakistan's regular and irregular forces crossed the LoC and occupied positions in the Kargil sector of Indian-administered Jammu and Kashmir, for reasons that are as yet unclear. When this was detected in early May 1999, Delhi's response was swift and comprehensive, involving the use of land and air forces to evict the intruders from the Indian side of the LoC.

After several weeks of increasingly bloody conflict, Indian forces captured the key heights of Tololing (14 June) and Tiger Hill (early morning on 4 July). With Pakistani forces suffering critical defeats, it was expected to be only a matter of time before they were pushed back across the LoC; but, undoubtedly this would have raised Indian casualties further.

Meanwhile, the United States was urging Pakistan to respect the LoC and withdraw its forces across the LoC, while at the same time, urging India to restrain itself from crossing the LoC to open another front in the conflict. Notwithstanding Delhi's public statements on not using force across the LoC, the potential for escalation into a full-scale conventional war raised fears in the international community of the risk of inadvertent nuclear escalation.

In early July, the Pakistani Prime Minister flew to Washington, concerned over Pakistan's increasing international isolation. At a hastily organized meeting with President Clinton on 4 July, Sharif requested American intervention to stop the fighting and resolve the Kashmir issue. But Clinton came down heavily on Sharif, and told him that a clear Pakistani withdrawal to the LoC was essential. Clinton also told Sharif that Pakistan was preparing its nuclear arsenal for possible deployment at the instructions of the Army Chief, General Musharraf, which was apparently taking place without Sharif's knowledge.

Amidst considerable American pressure, Sharif finally agreed 'to take concrete and immediate steps for the restoration of the LoC', which was accepted by Vajpayee when it was conveyed to him prior to its publicization.

In effect, the United States facilitated a formal end to the Kargil conflict, which shortly afterwards saw the withdrawal of all Pakistani forces to its own side of the LoC without many additional Indian casualties. American facilitation on the Kargil conflict—in Delhi's favour— came as quite an unexpected surprise to many in India's Ministries of External Affairs and Defence. This was, in effect, the first time in fifty years that the United States had sided with India against Pakistan 'openly and firmly'. This soon led to a greater 'comfort level' with the United States, followed by Clinton's successful visit to India in March 2000, followed by Vajpayee's visit to the United States in the final days of the Clinton Administration.

American Facilitation in the India-Pakistan Border Confrontation, 2001-2002

Even though the United States became involved in resolving the Kargil conflict, it is the Americanled war on terror in South Asia and the subsequent India-Pakistan border confrontation that has brought about a significant change in American engagement in South Asia. Following the American attack against Afghanistan in October 2001—targeting the terrorist Al-Qaeda leadership responsible for the attacks on the United States and their Taliban hosts—Pakistan became a frontline state for American logistics support and intelligence facilities in Afghanistan. A number of American military personnel and equipment also remain deployed in Pakistani military bases in support of the ongoing war on terror in Afghanistan.

However, the attack on the Indian Parliament on 13 December 2001—allegedly by Pakistanbased Jaish-e-Mohammed terrorists—threatened to disrupt the ongoing American-led military campaign in Afghanistan. As part of its 'coercive diplomacy' against Pakistan, Delhi launched 'Operation Parakram' ('valour') on 19 December 2001, which constituted the largest mobilization of the Indian armed forces. This was a deliberate move, taking place amidst the war on terror, to threaten military action against Pakistan if its demands to end alleged Pakistan-sponsored cross-border terrorism were not met. This included the deployment of India's three strike corps (comprising armoured and mechanized formations) at forward positions on the international border with Pakistan. With Pakistan's countermobilization, nearly one million armed personnel were deployed across the India-Pakistan borders. In view of the nuclear-armed status of both states, there appeared to be considerable risk of nuclear escalation—by misperception or miscalculation—following the break-out of a conventional war. On 20 March 2002, the Director of the Central Intelligence Agency (CIA), George Tenet, warned the United States Senate Armed Services Committee that the chances of a war in the region were the highest since 1971.

Having repeatedly stressed the sanctity of the LoC during the Kargil war, India's prospective actions—threatening the use of force across the LoC—set off alarm bells in Washington and London. Meanwhile, Pakistan appeared equally determined to counter an Indian military attack with conventional and nuclear forces. With the deliberate disruption of normal diplomatic communication, Delhi and Islamabad were communicating with each other on nuclear and conventional matters on a public basis during much of the ten months of the 2001–2002 border confrontation. These nuclear signals were multiple in nature, carried out at multiple levels, and addressed to multiple constituencies—internal, regional and international. For both India and Pakistan, the most important constituencies were the domestic public, each other and the United States, which had the most influence in the region. For Delhi, the United States could help put pressure on Pakistan to cease cross-border infiltration of militants into Indian-administered Kashmir; for Islamabad, the United States could restrain Delhi from military action.

With tensions heightening following the terrorist attack on an Indian Army residential camp in Kaluchak, Jammu, on 14 May 2002, and Delhi's subsequent nuclear signalling, a flurry of high-level American and British choreographed visits took place to Delhi and Islamabad. The contours of a possible easing of India-Pakistan tensions began to emerge from Jack Straw's visit at the end of May. On 28 May, Straw visited Islamabad, where he urged Musharraf to take action on the ground to counter cross-border 'terrorism' in Indian-administered Kashmir. In Delhi the next day, Straw urged India to exercise restraint and prevent its armed forces from using force across the LoC. He also told Delhi that Musharraf had promised to curb infiltration into India and to close down 'terrorist' camps in Pakistan-administered Kashmir by the time of Armitage's visit to the region in early June. On his return to London on 31 May, Straw publicly expressed his concern over the 'dangerous situation' in the region, 'when you have one million men under arms on either side of the LoC, all in a high state of alert and readiness, both countries have nuclear weapons, and one of them—Pakistan— has said they reserve the right to use them first'. This essentially signalled the issue of travel advisories on 1 June by the Governments of the United States, the United Kingdom, Canada, France, Japan, Australia, New Zealand and others, urging their citizens to leave India and Pakistan immediately, and warned others from travelling to either country. The travel advisories led to an exodus of business visitors, tourists, diplomatic personnel and their dependants, largely from India, as they had already pulled out from Pakistan earlier. Ostensibly ordered for fear of an outbreak of war, this unprecedented step caused much annoyance in Delhi, which perceived it as an attempt to pressure it against launching an attack across the LoC.

On 31 May, United States Secretary of State Colin Powell publicly criticized Pakistan for the 'continuing' infiltration across the LoC, despite Musharraf's assurances that it would be ended. The following day, in an interview with the BBC, Musharraf indicated that 'instructions' had been given by Pakistan to cease such activity. Although it was still too early to say that it had stopped, Powell emphasised that '... when, and if, it does stop, it must also stop permanently'. On 6 June, United States Deputy Secretary of State Richard Armitage arrived in Islamabad to build on Straw's visit, and hammer out a deal between India and Pakistan. After a tough meeting, Musharraf gave Armitage a commitment that he would end cross-border infiltration 'permanently'. This was a considerable improvement on his pledge to Straw a week earlier to curb infiltration into India. While Delhi formally welcomed this development, it expressed caution in terms of implementation. Consequently, Armitage described India-Pakistan tensions as 'a bit down on both sides'. Within days of Armitage's departure from Delhi, the thaw in India-Pakistan tensions was evident. In effect, American facilitation successfully eased India-Pakistan tensions, and ended the ten-month border confrontation—the longest period of military mobilization between the two countries.

India-Pakistan Joint Press Statement, 6 January 2004

In a dramatic development on the sidelines of the twelfth SAARC Summit in Islamabad in January 2004, India and Pakistan agreed to resume an official-level dialogue after a three-year hiatus. The Joint Statement of 6 January 2004 also noted that Delhi agreed to settle Kashmir 'to the satisfaction of both sides', and that Islamabad would not permit 'any territory under Pakistan's control to be used to support terrorism in any manner'. On 18 February 2004, after three days of official-level 'talks on talks' in Islamabad, India and Pakistan agreed to resume their bilateral 'composite dialogue' in May–June 2004, soon after the Indian general elections. This is to take the form of a 'composite dialogue' on eight issues, including two—on 'peace and security, including CBMs' and 'Jammu and Kashmir'— at the Foreign Secretary-level. The two foreign ministers are to meet in August 2004 to review progress. Both Delhi and Islamabad had strong motivations to reach an accord during the SAARC Summit. For Vajpayee, a personal desire for a stable bilateral relationship with Pakistan—his third and final peace effort—had been initiated with his 'hand of friendship' speech in Srinagar in April 2003, and buttressed by approaching general elections in April 2004; for Musharraf, two assassination attempts within eleven days in December 2003 had led to a renewed vigour to fight terrorism of all kinds, along with the increasing radicalization of domestic politics. Vajpayee's rising popularity, seen by the results of the Indian assembly elections in November 2003, also boosted Islamabad's view that it would be advisable to deal with Vajpayee himself.

In addition, American pressure on Islamabad to end cross-border infiltration into Indianadministered Kashmir, and to a lesser extent on India—to begin an official-level dialogue with Pakistan—may also have played a part in the success of bilateral diplomacy on the sidelines of the multilateral summit. Even if the United States had facilitated such a dialogue, it would have been advisable to have maintained this in a low-key manner, for fear of undermining the fledgling peace process.

THE INDIA-PAKISTAN CONFLICT - TOWARDS THE FAILURE OF NUCLEAR DETERRENCE

These are dismal times for peace. Since the tests of May 1998 and their overt nuclearization, Pakistan-India relations have visibly deteriorated. Crisis has followed crisis and nuclear weapons have played an increasingly prominent role. The massive military mobilisation and threat of war in spring of 2002 exposed several important features of the dynamics shaping nuclear South Asia, especially the repeated use of nuclear threats and the apparent fearlessness of policy makers and the public when faced with the prospect of nuclear war.

The context for these developments is a growing unwillingness among political and military leaders in South Asia to confront changed realties (but as Einstein famously remarked, the bomb has changed everything except our way of thinking). An arms race is growing, in fits and starts, as best as the two states can manage. Military doctrines are inter-linked in ways that lead inexorably to nuclear war. The poor are uneducated, uninformed and powerless. The well-to-do are uninformed or possessed by the religious fundamentalism - Islamic and Hindu - that is rapidly changing both countries. These forces are now being wedded to nationalism in ways that suggest restraints that were at work in previous India-Pakistan wars and crises may increasingly be over-ridden or suppressed. We are moving down a steep slippery slope whose bottom we have yet to see.

The efficacy of nuclear deterrence is predicated on the ability of these weapons to induce terror. It presupposes a rational calculus, as well as actors who, at the height of tension, will put logic before emotion. Recent events in South Asia have put all these into question. We therefore fear that perhaps a new chapter may someday have to written in textbooks dealing with the theory of nuclear deterrence.

Time is short. The role of the United States is key. It has begun to worry more about the spectre of nuclear armed islamic terrorism than the prospect of a South Asian nuclear war. But the Bush administration's unconstrained, unilateral, imperial vision has little space for restraint, treaties, and undermines the possibility of peace and disarmament for all.

There are a few steps that may begin to take us down the path to safety.

Crisis after Crisis

There is a fundamental link between crises and nuclear weapons in South Asia. Soon after the defeat of Pakistan by India in the 1971 war, Prime Minister Zulfiqar Ali Bhutto called a meeting of Pakistani nuclear scientists in the city of Multan to map out a nuclear weapons program. Pakistan was pushed further into the nuclear arena by the Indian test of May 1974, seen as a means to further consolidate Indian power in South Asia. Challenged again in May 1998 by a series of 5 Indian nuclear tests, Pakistan was initially reluctant to test its own weapons out of fear of international sanctions. Belligerent statements by Indian leaders after the tests succeeded in forcing it over the hill. But success brought change. Pakistan saw nuclear weapons as a talisman, able to ward off all dangers. Countering India's nuclear weapons became secondary. Instead, Pakistani nuclear weapons became the means for neutralizing India's far larger conventional land, air, and sea forces.

In the minds of Pakistani generals, nuclear weapons now became tools for achieving foreign policy objectives. The notion of a nuclear shield led them to breath-taking adventurism in Kashmir. Led by Chief of Army Staff General Pervez Musharraf, Pakistan sent troops out of uniform along with Islamist militant fighters across the Line of Control to seize strategic positions in the high mountains of the Kargil area. The subsequent Kargil war of 1999 may be recorded by historians as the first actually caused by nuclear weapons.

As India counter-attacked and Pakistan stood diplomatically isolated, a deeply worried Prime Minister Nawaz Sharif flew to Washington on 4 July 1999, where he was bluntly told to withdraw Pakistani forces or be prepared for full-scale war with India. Bruce Reidel, Special Assistant to President Clinton, writes that he was present in person when Clinton informed Nawaz Sharif that the Pakistan Army had mobilized its nuclear-tipped missile fleet. (If this is true, then the preparations for nuclear deployment and possible use could only have been ordered by General Pervez Musharraf at either his own initiative or in consultation with the army leadership.) Unnerved by this revelation and the closeness to disaster, Nawaz Sharif agreed to immediate withdrawal, shedding all earlier pretensions that Pakistan's army had no control over the attackers.

Despite the defeat in the Kargil War, Pakistan political and military leaders insisted that Pakistan had prevailed in the conflict and that its nuclear weapons had deterred India from crossing the Line of Control or the international border. This belief may be especially strong in the military, who would otherwise have to accept that their prized weapons were of no military utility.

Back to the Brink

On 13 December 2001, Islamic militants struck at the Indian parliament in Delhi sparking off a crisis that has yet to end. Indian Prime Minister Atal Bihari Vajpayee exhorted his troops in Kashmir to prepare for sacrifices and "decisive victory", setting off widespread alarm. It seemed plausible that India was preparing for a "limited war" to flush out Islamic militant camps in Pakistan administered Kashmir.

Sensing a global climate now deeply hostile to Islamic militancy, India's ruling BJP have sought to echo the U.S. "war on terror" slogan as a way to garner international support for their military campaign in Kashmir. Although an embattled Musharraf probably had little to do with the attack on the Indian Parliament, India cut off communications with Pakistan. The Indian ambassador in Islamabad was recalled to Delhi, road and rail links were broken off, and flights by Pakistani airlines over Indian territory were disallowed.

Such Indian reactions have played into the hands of jihadists in Kashmir who now operate as a third force almost autonomous of the Pakistani state (this operational autonomy is typical of such large scale covert operations, where there is a political need for the state patron to be able to plausibly deny responsibility for any particular action taken by such forces - the U.S. support for the Contras in Nicaragua and the Mujahideen in Afghanistan in the 1980s were classic examples of this relationship). There is a real possibility that jihadists will commit some huge atrocity - such as a mass murder of Indian civilians. Indeed, their goal is to provoke full-scale war between India and Pakistan, destabilize Musharraf, and settle scores with America.

Nuclear threats started flying in all directions. In May 2002, as fighter aircraft circled Islamabad, in a public debate with one of us (PH), General Mirza Aslam Beg, the former chief of Pakistan's army, declared: "We can make a first strike, and a second strike, or even a third." The lethality of nuclear war left him unmoved.

"You can die crossing the street," he observed, "or you could die in a nuclear war. You've got to die some day anyway." Pakistan's ambassador to the UN in Geneva, Munir Akram, reiterated Pakistan's refusal of a no-first-use policy.

Across the border, India's Defence Minister George Fernandes told the International Herald Tribune "India can survive a nuclear attack, but Pakistan cannot." Indian Defence Secretary Yogendra Narain took things a step further in an interview with Outlook Magazine: "A surgical strike is the answer," adding that if this failed to resolve things, "We must be prepared for total mutual destruction." Indian security analyst, Brahma Chellaney, claimed "India can hit any nook and corner of Pakistan and is fully prepared to call Pakistan's nuclear bluff."

Nuclear Denial

As India began to seriously consider cross-border strikes on militant camps on the Pakistani side of the Line of Control, it became convenient for those urging action to deny Pakistan's nuclear weapons by challenging its willingness and ability to use them. This is not the first time this notion has been exercised, but it has now gained astonishingly wide currency in Indian ruling circles and carries increasingly grave risks of a misjudgment that could lead to nuclear war. Two months before the May 1998 nuclear tests by India and Pakistan, a delegation from Pugwash met in Delhi with Prime Minister Inder Kumar Gujral. As a member of the delegation, one of us (PH) expressed worries about a nuclear catastrophe on the Subcontinent. Gujral repeatedly assured PH - both in public and in private - that Pakistan was not capable of making atomic bombs. The Prime Minister was not alone. Senior Indian defense analysts like P. R. Chari had also published articles before May 1998 arguing this point, as had the former head of the Indian Atomic Energy Agency, Dr. Raja Ramana.

Although Pakistan's nuclear tests had dispelled this scepticism, senior Indian military and political leaders continue to express doubts on the operational capability and usability of the Pakistani arsenal. Still more seriously, many Indians believe that, as a client state of the US, Pakistan's nuclear weapons are under the control of the US. The assumption is that, in case of extreme crisis, the US would either restrain their use by Pakistan or, if need be, destroy them. At a meeting in Dubai this year in January, senior Indian analysts said they were "bored" with Pakistan's nuclear threats and no longer believed them. K. Subrahmanyam, an influential Indian hawk who has advocated overt Indian nuclearization for more than a decade, believes that India can "sleep in peace."

To fearlessly challenge a nuclear Pakistan requires a denial of reality, which some Indians seem prepared to make. It is an enormous leap of faith to presume that the United States would have either the intention - or the capability - to destroy Pakistani nukes. Tracking and destroying even a handful of mobile nuclear-armed missiles would be no easy feat. During the Cuban missile crisis, the U.S. Air Force had aerial photos of the Soviet missile locations and its planes were only minutes away, yet it would not assure that a surprise attack would be more than 90 percent effective. More recently, in Iraq, U.S. efforts to destroy Iraqi Scuds had limited success. No country has ever tried to take out another's nuclear bombs. It would be fantastically dangerous because one needs 100 percent success. Nonetheless, there are signs that India is boosting its military capability to where it might feel able to overwhelm Pakistan.

Pushing The Arms Race

Since the 1998 nuclear tests, there have been very large increases in Indian military spending. The Indian defence budget for 2001-2002 was set at 630 billion rupees ($13 billion). This is nearly three times Pakistan's and follows an earlier increase of 28%, which was larger than Pakistan's entire military budget. A further increase of 4.8% is intended for purchases of fighter planes, submarines, advanced surveillance systems (including Phalcon airborne early warning systems from Israel), and a second aircraft carrier. In a paper entitled "Vision 2020", the Indian Air Force has laid out its requirements - it proposes increasing the number of squadrons from 39 to 60 by 2020 and replacing the aged MiG-21 planes with more modern fighters, such as the Russian Sukhoi-30s, or the Mirage-2000 or Rafael fighters from France. This Indian air force internal document is reported also to advocate the creation of a first-strike capability.

A missile regiment to handle the nuclear-capable Agni missile is being raised. Military officers are being trained to handle nuclear weapons and there have been statements by senior officials about Agni being mated with nuclear warheads. All of this is consistent with eventual deployment.

Pakistan's generals would like to keep up with India in this effort but the economy is faltering and cannot stand the strain. A recent World Bank report is worth quoting at length :

"The 1990s were a decade of lost opportunities for Pakistan. From independence to the late 1980s, Pakistan outperformed the rest of South Asia. Then in the 1990s progress ground to a halt. Poverty remained stuck at high levels, economic growth slowed, institutions functioned badly, and a serious macroeconomic crisis erupted."As and when the economy begins to revive, Pakistan's military leaders will no doubt resume the race.

Towards War

Pakistani generals know why they want nuclear weapons. They anticipate that in the event of hostilities, India is likely to take losses in a terrain unsuitable for heavy armour or strike aircraft. So it could shift the theatre of war - escalating horizontally but without attacking nuclear facilities. Thereafter India would have several options available to it:

- Push into lower Punjab or Upper Sindh to sever Pakistan's vital road and rail links.
- Destroy the infrastructure of the Pakistan military (communication networks, oil supplies, army bases, railway yards, air bases through the use of runway busting bombs).
- Blockade Karachi, and perhaps also Gwadur, Pakistan's other port, currently under construction.

Pakistan's generals have sought to make it impossible for India to achieve these goals. They have articulated a set of conditions under which they will use their nuclear weapons. Pakistani nuclear weapons will be used, according to General Kidwai of Pakistan's Strategic Planning Division, only "if the very existence of Pakistan as a state is at stake" and this, he specified, meant:

1. India attacks Pakistan and takes a large part of its territory
2. India destroys a large part of Pakistan armed forces
3. India imposes an economic blockade on Pakistan
4. India creates political destabilization or large scale internal subversion in Pakistan

India, in turn, has started to prepare its military to be attacked by nuclear weapons on the battlefield and to continue the war. The major Indian war game Poorna Vijay (Complete Victory) in May 2001, the bigggest in over a decade, was reported to center on training the army and airforce to fight in a nuclear conflict. Taken together, Indian military options and Pakistani planning would seem to ensure that that any major India-Pakistan conflict would lead inexorably to the use of nuclear weapons.

Fearless Nuclear Gambling

In early 2002, with a million troops mobilised and leaders in both India and Pakistan threatening nuclear war, world opinion responded fearfully, seeing a fierce and possibly suicidal struggle up ahead. Foreign nationals streamed out of both countries, and many are yet to return. But even at the peak of the crisis, few Indians or Pakistanis lost much sleep. Stock markets flickered, but there was no run on the banks or panic buying. Schools and colleges, which generally close at the first hint of crisis, functioned normally. What explains the astonishing indifference to nuclear annihilation?

In part, the answer has to do with the fact that India and Pakistan are still largely traditional, rural societies, albeit going through a great economic and social transformation at a furious pace. The fundamental belief structures of such societies (which may well be the last things to change), reflecting the realities of agriculture dependent on rains and good weather, encourage a surrender to larger forces. Conversations and discussions often end with the remark that "what will be, will be," after which people shrug their shoulders and move on to something else.

Because they feel they are at the mercy of unseen forces, the level of risk-taking is extraordinary. But other reasons may be more important.

In India and Pakistan, most people lack basic information about nuclear dangers. A 1996 poll of elite opinion showed that about 80% of those wanting to supporting Pakistan acquiring ready-to-use nuclear weapons found it "difficult" or "almost impossible" to get information, while about 25% of those opposed to nuclear weapons had the same concern. In India, a November 1999 post-election national opinion poll survey found just over half of the population had not even heard of the May 1998 nuclear tests. In the middle of the spring 2002 crisis, the BBC reported the level of awareness of the nuclear risk among the Pakistani public was "abysmally low". In India, it found "for many, the terror of a nuclear conflict is hard to imagine."

First hand evidence bears out these judgments. Even educated people seem unable to grasp basic nuclear realities. Some students at the university in Islamabad where one of us teaches (PH), when asked, believed that a nuclear war would be the end of the world. Others thought of nuclear weapons as just bigger bombs. Many said it was not their concern, but the army's.

Almost none knew about the possibility of a nuclear firestorm, about residual radioactivity, or damage to the gene pool. In Pakistan's public squares and at crossroads stand missiles and fiberglass replicas of the nuclear test site. For the masses, they are symbols of national glory and achievement, not of death and destruction.

Previous crises have also seen such lack of fear about the threat and use of nuclear weapons. With each crisis, there seems to be a lessening of political restraints and greater nuclear brinksmanship. A key factor is the absence of an informed and organized public opinion able to keep political and military leaders in check and restrain them from brandishing nuclear weapons. Close government control over national television, especially in Pakistan, has ensured that critical discussion of nuclear weapons and nuclear war is not aired. It is harder to understand the absence of such critical debate in India.

Because nuclear war is considered a distant abstraction, civil defense in both countries is non-existent. As India's Admiral Ramu Ramdas, now retired and a leading peace activist, caustically remarked, "There are no air raid shelters in this city of Delhi, because in this country people are considered expendable." Islamabad's civil defense budget is a laughable $40,000 and the current year's allocation has yet to be disbursed. No serious contingency plans have been devised—plans that might save millions of lives by providing timely information about escape routes, sources of non-radioactive food and drinking water. It is unimaginable to think of providing adequate protection against nuclear attack to the many millions in South Asia's mega-cities. We have not been able to provide homes, food, water and health care to so many even in peace time. There is, nonetheless, something to be said for having credible plans to save as many as possible from the folly of their leaders. The development of and debate over such plans, in itself, may serve to convince some people of the horrors of what may be in store and motivate them to protest to survive.

The US and South Asian Nuclear Weapons

During the Cold War, to all intents and purposes, the superpowers were able to ignore the rest of the world. The fears and entreaties of other countries counted for little in super power strategic planning and policy. In South Asia, the United States and to a lesser extent the international community loom large. This is an important difference and as the Kargil war and the 2001-2002 crisis showed, it can be crucial.

Following India's 1974 nuclear test, perceiving the threat of proliferation and the consequences of India-Pakistan nuclear rivalry, the United States tried unsuccessfully to block the development of a Pakistani nuclear weapons capability through the use of sanctions of various kinds. By the early 1990s, President Bill Clinton was fruitlessly engaged in a campaign to persuade both countries to cap, and then ultimately roll-back their programs. After the 1998 nuclear tests, the hope was that the two states could be made to sign the Comprehensive Test Ban Treaty. In early 2000, this was on the verge of being signed by Pakistan and India. However,

Clinton's efforts were undermined by the refusal of the Republican controlled Senate to ratify the Treaty. The treaty died, leaving open the possibility of a resumption of nuclear testing by the U.S. and inevitably by the other nuclear weapons states, including in South Asia. This possibility has grown because of the policies of the Bush Administration.

Under President George. W. Bush, the U.S. seems set to undo any and all arms control treaties, except those that clearly favor the US. The CTBT was the first victim. The Biological Weapons Convention followed.

The U.S. withdrawal from the Anti-Ballistic Missile Treaty is the first withdrawal from any arms control treaty by a state, creating a possibly terrible precedent. These steps have cleared the way for a more aggressive set of nuclear policies.

The Bush Administration's January 2002 Nuclear Posture Review (NPR) calls for development of operational strategies that would allow use of nuclear weapons by the US even against those states that do not possess nuclear, chemical, biological or other weapons of mass destruction; it proposes that U.S. military forces, including nuclear forces, will be used to "dissuade adversaries from undertaking military programs or operations that could threaten U.S. interests or those of allies and friends." [emphasis added]. New special-purpose nuclear weapons such as deep penetration weapons (bunker busters) are already being developed.

As the U.S. has focused on further developing its military capacity to achieve its goals it the post-Cold War world, it has worried less about what India and Pakistan may do to each other. With both India and Pakistan seeking to woo the United States over to their side, the U.S. has little to fear from either.

Although it seems to have taken out insurance. The Nuclear Posture Review recommends "requirements for nuclear strike capabilities" might include "a sudden regime change by which an existing nuclear arsenal comes into the hands of a new, hostile leadership group." Events since the terrorist attacks on the United States on September 11 suggest Pakistan may be a particular concern for the U.S. in this regard.

Pakistan's Loose Nukes

Immediately after the September 11 attack, although Pakistan's military government insisted that there was no danger of any of its 25-40 nuclear weapons being taking for a ride, it wasn't taking any chances. Several weapons were reportedly airlifted to various safer, isolated, locations within the country. This nervousness was not unjustified - two strongly Islamist generals of the Pakistan Army (the head of Pakistan's ISI intelligence agency, Lt. General Mehmood Ahmed, and Deputy Chief of Army Staff, General Muzaffar Hussain Usmani), close associates of General Musharraf, had just been removed.

Dissatisfaction within the army on Pakistan's betrayal of the Taliban was (and is) deep - almost overnight, under intense American pressure, the Pakistan government had disowned its progeny.

Fears about Pakistan's nukes were subsequently compounded by revelations that two highly placed members of the nuclear establishment, Syed Bashiruddin Mahmood and Chaudhry Majid, had journeyed several times into Afghanistan during the last year. Both scientists are well known to espouse radical Islamic views.

It is not impossible that the two Pakistanis could have provided significant nuclear information or materials potentially useful to Al-Qaeda's allies and subsidiaries in other parts of the world. If it turns so out, this will scarcely be the first instance of nuclear leakage. In 1966, sympathizers of Israel working in the U.S. Nuclear Materials and Equipment Corporation were instrumental in diverting more than 100 kilograms of highly enriched uranium for the Israeli nuclear weapons program, material which was reported by the CIA to most likely have "been used by the Israelis in fabricating weapons."

Pakistan's loose nuke problem underscores a global danger that may already be out of control. The fissile materials present in the thousands of ex-Soviet bombs marked for disassembly, the vast amounts of radioactive materials present in nuclear reactors and storage sites the world over, and the abundance of nuclear knowledge, make it only a matter of time before some catastrophic use is made of them.

5

Threats of Another Proxy War in Pakistan

The Pakistani Parliament, after deliberation in joint sittings, decided to maintain neutrality on civil war in Yemen. The consensus resolution called for maintaining neutrality, opposing sending troops to Yemen, but resolving to protect territorial integrity of the Kingdom of Saudi Arabia (KSA) (*Dawn*, 2015).

At the start of the joint sitting, Defence Minister Khawaja Muhammad Asif, sharing policy statement on Yemen crisis, revealed that the KSA had requested the government of Pakistan to send its fighter jets (to pound bombs on the rebels) and ships (to check the delivery of arms and wherewithal, allegedly being supplied by Iran). In the same debate, the defence minister, while laying out Pakistan's sacrifices in the war on terror, even questioned as to which country came to help Pakistan in its long war.

To be sure, even though parliamentarians vowed to help the KSA, should there be any threat to it, they largely conceded there was no imminent danger to the territorial integrity of the Kingdom or the two sacred sites.

Broadly, Pakistan Tehreek-e-Insaaf (PTI), Muttahida Quami Movement (MQM), and Awami National Party (ANP) openly and strongly opposed the idea of sending troops to Yemen. The Pakistan People's Party (PPP) stayed somewhat vague. The religious parties looked unsure on how to react. The Jamaat-e-Islami (JI) and Jamiat Ulema-e-Islam (JUI-F), two main religious-political parties subscribing to Sunni sect of Islam, also opposed dispatching troops to Yemen. The PTI rather took pride in having pushed the government to insert the word "neutrality" in the original resolution, said to be drafted by the Foreign Office (*Express Tribune*, 2015).

MPs feared that by jumping into Yemen quagmire, Pakistan would face another wave of sectarian violence. While a few of them rejected the perception that civil war in Yemen was not a Shiite-Sunni conflict, many believed the violence would have deep repercussions for Pakistan, in case it decided to take sides. Parliamentarians argued both Iran and the KSA were furthering their strategic interests in Yemen, from which Pakistan should stay away. By joining the KSA-led coalition against Houthi rebels, Pakistan might annoy neighbouring Iran, several lawmakers feared.

After the Parliament passed that unanimous resolution, the UAE's minister of state for foreign affairs, Dr Anwar Mohammad Gargash, warned Pakistan of paying a heavy price for its neutrality. Pakistan and Turkey, he said, must abandon the so-called mantra of neutrality and help Arab countries quell the rebellion in Yemen (*Khaleej Times*, 2015).

Many saw his reference to Yemen as an epicentre of crisis for the entire Muslim as exaggerating. Yet, many believed Prime Minister Nawaz Sharif tried to allay the concerns of Arab countries, by, for instance, terming Houthis as "rebels" and clarifying that Pakistan was against the illegal occupation by rebels of Yemen's territory.

To be sure, Pakistan is heavily dependent on Saudi economic assistance. Around two million Pakistanis work in the KSA and UAE, contributing over $15 billion annual in foreign remittances. Pakistan's economic cooperation with Iran is not yet ideal, even though the two share strategic interests. But, more than that, KSA and Iran fund the individuals and entities of their choices, in Pakistan.

PROXY WAR IN PAKISTAN

As political parties were debating the issue inside parliament, several religious outfits, blatantly divided on sectarian lines, started staging street protests. The outfits like Ahle Sunnat Wal Jamaat

(ASWJ) even vowed to send their*mujahedeen* to fight alongside Saudi forces, if Pakistan refused to send its troops. The outfits hailing from Shiite school of thought warned against accepting Saudi demands.

For long, Pakistan has been a favourite place of both Iran and the KSA to fight their proxy war on sectarian lines, to the disadvantage of the people of Pakistan.

Many seminaries in Pakistan have long been regarded as incubators of religious extremism and sectarianism. They provide manpower to violent extremist entities belonging to Shiite, Sunni, Deobandi and other sects. Several efforts were launched to reform the seminaries, but failed to yield the desired results owing to multiple reasons (Witter, 2007).

In early 2015, the interior affairs ministry informed Senate, in a written reply, that "financial assistance for religious or sectarian purposes was discouraged, because it was detrimental to law and order and sectarian harmony in the country" (Gishkori, 2015).

At the same time, Pakistani government admitted about over 70 seminaries receiving foreign funds amounting to 300 million rupees in 2013 and 2014 (Gishkori, 2015).

A sorry beginning

Islamization of Pakistan during the entire 1980s sowed the seeds of poison ivy, which has now developed into a full-grown tree. And, what all the successive governments did was to chop off the branches, instead of eradicating the roots. The influx of petro-dollars and hard cash from Washington during the Soviet war plagued the Pakistani society with elements, which continue to haunt the entire nation.

That Islamization, led by military ruler General Zia, was tilting towards Sunni Islam, thereby alienating Shiites, "who saw it as a majoritarian attempt to make the country more Sunni" (Rafiq, 2014). The campaign coincided with Iran's Islamic revolution, which revived Shia political activism across the Muslim world, including Pakistan.

This contrasted sharply with the religious and sectarian diversity of Pakistan. From the onset, differences were set aside in favour of peaceful living. But since 1980s, Pakistan experienced sectarian divide, aggravating further after 9/11, when militants turned against the state. Largely, Sunni/Deobandi militants have attacked Shia Muslims (Rafiq, 2014).

SAUDIS'S FEARS AND HOPES

To the Saudi monarchy, post-revolutionary Iran represents a direct adversary, both for ideological and strategic regions. The two have been eager to wrest power in the Muslim world.

Earlier, in 1980s, Pakistan became a fertile ground for the KSA to safeguard its strategic interest. During the Afghan War, Saudi Arabia wholeheartedly backed the Afghan and Arab *mujahedeen.* According to one estimate, the Saudi government split the cost of that with the U.S., bearing cost of more $20 billion (Atwan, 2006).Fundraising committees were formed under the chairmanship of Prince Salman bin Abdul Aziz, the governor of Riyadh district. Imams at mosques were encouraged to deliver fiery sermons exhorting young men to join the fight.

Moreover, the relations of Saudi royal family with Sharifs in Pakistan date back in history. When Pakistan detonated nuclear devices, in May 1998, the KSA doled out Pakistan, then ruled by Nawaz Sharif, oil worth of $2 billion. A year later, when he was ousted in a military coup, the Saudis got him and his family off the hook, providing them refuge in KSA. In 2007, Nawaz Sharif came back to Pakistan, his return asked by King Abdullah, to participate in elections in 2008. When five years later, Nawaz Sharif became Prime Minister for another term, the state of economy was in tatters. Once again, the KSA gifted $1.5 billion in Pakistan's kitty.

Although Iran and KSA have been waging proxy fight inside countries like Pakistan for long, the recent nuclear deal of Iran with the west raises a further point of concern for the Saudi Arabia. To the Kingdom, the deal will open more space to Iran.

As of now, not only the KSA demand fighter jets and ships from Pakistan, but a large contingent of its soldiers to participate in ground operation, whenever it is launched inside Yemen. As discussed, the Pakistani Parliament had already rejected the demand and urged the government to stay neutral. Demanding troops could have been understandable and normal, but what perturbed many people in power corridors was the KSA specific demand of Sunni soldiers for Yemen. Besides, the KSA also wanted that all army officers who would visit Saudi Arabia as part of training or assistance program should hail from Sunni sects (Muhammad, 2015). To some strategic analysts, this was a pathetic attempt to divide the Pakistan army on sectarian grounds.

To be sure, despite all that so-called goodwill gestures and positive attitude, the KSA never made an attempt to heavily invest in Pakistan. The entry of China with $46 billion of investment over next few years, Pakistani government is thinking differently. One of the main conditions of Chinese to keep their investment secure was that Pakistan should maintain good relations with its neighbours, especially Iran and Afghanistan. And by taking side with the KSA in Yemen civil war, Pakistani leadership does not want to annoy the Chinese.

Fallout: sectarian violence

What is pertinent to note is that sectarian difference between Shiites and Sunnis didn't turn violent until 1979. Two external events, the Islamic Revolution in Iran under Khomeini and the Soviet invasion of Afghanistan, rather set the path to violence in Pakistan.

According to South Asian Terrorism Portal, more than 5000 Pakistanis were killed in sectarian violence since 1989. Majority of the assassinated were Shiites.

After 9/11, hard-core Sunni sectarian groups landed under the umbrella of al-Qaeda and Tehreek-e-Taliban Pakistan (TTP). They unleashed an unchecked killing spree across Pakistan, much because there has been a strong nexus between sectarian groups, Taliban, and al-Qaeda (Rehman, 2012). Sectarian violence would be a long-term challenge.

The sectarian tension refused to die down permanently, though there are regular intervals in which it subsided only to blow after any triggering event. An example was witnessed in late 2013 in the city of Rawalpindi. When the main Muharram procession was passing outside a Deobandi mosque in the city, the mosque's cleric reportedly passed objectionable remarks against Shiites. Some mourners allegedly entered the mosque and set it on fire. Several people were killed. Later on, the stalwarts of Sunni/Deobandi religious and proscribed outfits resorted to violence and burnt a few *imambargahs* (Shia mosques) in the vicinity. The tension and peril gripped the city for weeks. In order to control the situation, the authorities had to impose curfew.

Catch-22 situation

Pakistan seemingly is a catch-22 situation on how to respond to the lingering Yemen crisis.

If it comes openly in support of KSA, the next-door Iran will complain, besides possibly imperilling the much-needed Chinese investment in the country. If Pakistan, on the other hand, rejects KSA's stance on Yemen, or even stay neutral for long, Saudi Arabia might be forced to revisit its historic ties with Pakistan.

In both cases, sectarian outfits of one or other school of thought, with or without backing from KSA or Iran, will raise voice against Pakistan's stance.

Still further, the persistence of Yemen crisis will be detrimental for the internal security and economic stability of Pakistan.

Conclusion

In the given situation, for Pakistan a steady progress on long-term measures is necessary, which include neutralizing sectarian outfits working under different nomenclatures, reforming seminary, modernizing curriculum, bringing sectarian mongers and criminals to justice, striking balance in relations with Iran and KSA, persuading both countries to find out an amicable solution to Yemen crisis, etc.

One thing Pakistani leadership can do is to build a national narrative, that whatever is happening in Yemen will never threaten territorial integrity of the KSA. This will subside the growing concerns among majority Sunni/Deobandi population of Pakistan, which now believes that the two holiest sites are under attack because of Iranian conspiracies against the KSA.

PAKISTAN: IDEOLOGICAL MOORINGS AND INDIVIDUALITY EMERGENCY

Since the beginning of the 1990s, one question that is haunting many Pakistani well wishers is, where is that country heading? Some observers and commentators have gone to the extent of calling it a "failed state." Others have even started expressing fears that the nation state of Pakistan may collapse if corrective measures are not taken immediately to sort out the contradictions within the body polity. Whatever may be merits and demerits of these assessments and predictions, there is near unanimity among Pakistanis and among its well wishers outside, that the nation is in a major crisis or as some would like to say, Pakistan, after fifty years of independence, is at the cross-roads.

An attempt has been made in this chapter to examine this peculiar situation in which Pakistan has placed itself in its 50th year of independence within the framework of the ideology and identity of Pakistan.

IDEOLOGICAL MOORINGS

Before analysing the ideological moorings of Pakistan as a nation state, three factors need to be noted. First, Pakistan is the first state to be carved out in the post-World War II with religion as an ideology. In fact, the only other state that took birth with similar orientation was Israel which came into existence eight months after the birth of Pakistan. However, the difference between the two is that while Israel became the homeland of Zionists of the entire world, Pakistan remained a home for only a section of the Muslims of the Indian subcontinent.

Second, a close scrutiny of the history of the Indian subcontinent from the 18th century onwards clearly shows that the Muslim aristocracy was not reconciled to the fact that they had lost their Empire to the British. And the ascendancy of the East India Company first and then by Her Majesty's Government from London, was interpreted as a failure of the Muslims to adhere to the basic tenets of Islam. In retrospect one could draw the conclusion that this rationalisation was made by the Muslim aristocracy just to cover up their failure in the governance of state. In the process, the Indianisation of Islam, in terms of absorbing the progressive ideas that started filtering from Europe, was rejected. Interestingly, this was the time when non-Muslim reformist movements, especially among Hindus, were born and infused some of the Western liberal ideas into the Indian polity. This enabled the Hindus to give up some of the dogmatic approach 'to religion and its rituals.

In other words, by the end of the 19th century, the elite among the followers of Islam, by and large, were not able to cope with the process of modernisation that was set in by the British rule. This failure of the elite among the Indian Muslims resulted in recourse to religion, more and more dogmatically. On the other hand, the virtues of the European civilisation, were quickly absorbed by the rest and incorporated into the body polity. This resulted in distict compartmentalisation of the Indian society into Muslims versus the rest. This percolated to the lower levels over a period of time, resulting in Muslims, especially in northern India, getting alienated from the rest of the people. This was cleverly exploited by the elite among the Muslims to argue that Muslims and Hindus cannot live together.

Lastly, this Muslim aristocracy's unwillingness to give up their expensive habits and change with the times resulted in their being relegated to the sidelines in the emerging socio-economic set-up in British India. By the beginning of the 20th century, the Muslim socio-economic status reached its lowest level; and they found it extremely difficult to compete with other communities. Once again, these frustrations remained largely a north-eastern India phenomenon.

These frustrations among the Muslims were projected by the elite as exploitation of the Muslims by the Hindus. It took a concrete shape, in poet-philosopher Allama Iqbal's speech at Allahabad in December 1930. Giving it a rationalisation, Mohammad Ali Jinnah wrote to Gandhi that "Hindus and Muslims belong to two different civilisations which are based mainly on conflicting ideas and conceptions."

The idea further crystallised in the form of the Lahore Resolution of 1940 of the Muslim League and Pakistan was born in August 1947. In other words, a group of people among Muslims of the Indian subcontinent achieved their objective in less than 17 years. And this was achieved as a part of the British departure from India. For the British leaving India, the main force was the Indian National Congress (INC). The Muslim League, while supporting the INC's cause, managed to have their share of the cake without much effort.

As has been mentioned earlier, some Pakistani commentators also argue that before the British came, Muslims were the rulers of the Indian subcontinent (they mean Delhi), and this made them look upon the British as usurpers of their power and authority. The Hindus, on the other hand, collaborated with the enemy's enemy, that is the British, to overcome the Muslims to recapture positions of power and authority. In the process, the Muslims felt insecure and demanded a separate homeland for themselves.

Whatever may have been the compulsions of the Muslim League for the creation of Pakistan, three things have happened which question the basic premise for the creation of Pakistan.

Foremost among them is that a majority of the Muslims decided to stay back in to India. In the process, they disproved the thesis that Muslims in India were being exploited by non-Muslims. One could even argue that this perception of non-Muslims persecuting Muslims was largely a phenomenon of the elite Muslims living in the northern parts of India only.

Second, the Indian republic declared itself as a secular state from the beginning and ensured equality of all religions before the state. This Indian experiment of unity in diversity became unique in contemporary world history. This proved to be against the very spirit of Pakistan; and from time to time, some of the Pakistani intelligensia tried to ridicule the Indian state's secularism and majority rule.

Lastly, even after fifty years of independence, Pakistan was not able to absorb the Muslims who migrated from India to Pakistan. They are still known as Mojahirs; and looked upon by a section of the Pakistani elite as aliens. In the process these Indian migrants were not able to develop the emotional linkages with Pakistan; and over the years they acquired a separate identity of themselves.

After five generations, some of these Mojahirs started talking in terms of a separate state for themselves.

The same cannot be said about people who migrated from Pakistan to India. They were rehabilitated quickly and made partners in nation building. With the result, they developed their emotional bondages quickly with the new nation.

In addition, the founders of Pakistan assumed that followers of the great religion Islam can become a homogeneous group. This assumption proved wrong first in December 1971 when Bengali speaking Muslims separated themselves from West Pakistan and became an independent state, Bangladesh. Again with the sectarian differences surfacing in the 1980s and 1990s, first the Ahmediayas were declared as non-Muslims.

The story has not ended there. The Shias and Sunnis started a fresh round of violence in the name of cleansing the polity. A new dimension was added to this controversy in terms of the Mojahirs—whether they are Pakistanis or not. In the process, the issue of who among the two—Shias or Sunnis—should hold the reins of power in Pakistan became a controversy questioning the very ideological foundations of the state. One could even say that more Muslims were killed in these sectarian clashes in Pakistan, than say, in its three wars with India.

Here the dilemma of Pakistani Constitutional makers was far more visible. The lawyers turned politicians of the Pakistan movement wanted that Ijma and Ijtihad (consensus of the community and the concept of continuing interpretation and judgement of Islamic Law) should form the basis for the democratic process. In contrast stood the traditional Ulema whose position was a legalistic one based on the unity of religion and politics in Islam. And the third group was led by Islamic fundamentalists who had some romantic ideas and tried to define Islamic identity.

In other words, from the beginning, the ideological moorings of the Pakistani state were fragile. The assumptions made by the founding fathers proved to be not close to the ground reality. Unfortunately, the elite of Pakistan, even after assuming power failed to acknowledge this fact and did nothing to strengthen the ideological foundations of the new state.

The first Constitutional Assembly of August 1947, in spite of outliving its mandated terms of five years, failed to produce a Constitution defining the core values of the new state. Its only achievement was the Objective Resolution of March 1949, which specified that the Constitution would be Islamic, democratic and federal. But there was no agreement on how these objectives would take form, no details and, no calming of fears of minorities. The second Constituent Assembly did manage to produce a Constitution in 1956, but it was abrogated by General Ayub Khan in October 1958 on the eve of general elections in March 1959.

In the process, the new nation state's elite set themselves an abstract goal—surpassing India in every sphere. This became more or less the basic theme of the state of Pakistan. This goal made the country enter into all types of alliances (e.g. South-East Asia Treaty Organisation—SEATO and Central Treaty Organisation—CENTO) without fully understanding the subtle conditionalities that went with them and the impact they would have on the ideological foundations of the country.

The Sandhurst trained General found everything wrong with the political process that was evolving in Pakistan. He felt that Pakistani politicians were a bunch of "rascals."8 His Western education and long years of military training made him look at Pakistan polity as secular. He also perceived, like the politicians, that surpassing India was the primary task and in the process rapid economic development became a watchword. In fact, Z.A. Suleri, a leading political commentator of Pakistan, writing about these developments observes that Ayub Khan assuming power "was a turning point in our history." Not only democracy was given the go-by "but what was the real tragedy, the ideology (of Pakistan) was consigned to a limbo" (emphasis added). He goes on to add that the administration might have run well for a number of years and industry might have flourished and the industrial magnates might have had a field day during the Ayub years, but "the spirit of the people was crushed and the destiny of the country was changed."

The developments in the subsequent years no way lessened the seeds of secularism. By declaring "idhar hum udhar tum" (we are here, you are there), Z.A. Bhutto tore apart the election results of 1970 and in the process buried permanently the concept of religion as a bond. And this automatically brought in race, language, and geography to the centre-stage of Pakistani polity. Bhutto went a step further by declaring that there are two majority parties as per the election results—one in West Pakistan and another in East Pakistan (now Bangladesh) and he reinforced this arguement by boycotting the newly elected Constituent Assembly session. What happened afterwards is well known to all students of the subcontinent's history.

Z.A. Bhutto went a step a further by quickly according recognition to the new nation state, Bangladesh and eliminating any prospects of reunion with Pakistan, even at a later stage.

The Pakistani armed forces' dismal performance in the December 1971 war with the India-Bangladesh forces, and the surrender of 90,000 Pakistani soldiers to the joint command had a devastating effect on the Pakistani national psyche. The very basis for the creation of Pakistan—Islamic oneness, and in the process, the much talked about two-nation theory—got invalidated. The national agenda of overtaking India in all spheres by the Pakistan elite, especially the armed forces, proved to be a myth; and Pakistan failed miserably in achieving its goal.

The folklore and myths built around the Pakistani armed forces (one of the popular slogans in the 1950s and 1960s used to be: one Pakistani is equal to ten Hindustanis) proved to be no longer valid; and suddenly the nation found that it could not defend itself against an adversary. This sent the nation into a spin.

Interestingly, a majority of the Pakistani commentators blame themselves for these unfortunate developments. To quote Suleri again, "The worst thing that has happened in our history is the installation of Bhutto in power after the break up of Pakistan...The empowerment of Bhutto empowered secularism and banished the concept of Muslim nationhood on which Pakistan is based. Let us face the fact that Bhutto counts far more in (today's) political arena than Quaid-e-Azam. How many parties are fighting in his name and how many are the flag bearers of the founders of Pakistan? As a result, we are confronted with the bitter reality that there is no sense of nationhood around. The man who mobilised Muslims into nationhood and led them to creation of Pakistan is dead and buried fathoms deep. His heritage has been lost" (emphasis added).

General Zia-ul-Haq did try to turn the tide against secularism and bring in Islam back to the national philosophy of Pakistan. But Zia's Islam and Muslim nationhood were totally at variance with what Quaid-e-Azam M.A. Jinnah pursued. In addition, Zia had three major disadvantages as compared to Quaid-e-Azam. Zia was not a leader. He usurped power through questionable means. This resulted in his lack of any legitamacy to rule. Therefore, in spite of his best intentions, to bring the Islam of his interpretation, the people of Pakistan always looked upon his actions as made to consolidate his position. Added to this, Zia was in no way a charismatic leader like Quaid-e-Azam M.A. Jinnah or Bhutto. He was known as an average soldier, who came to the top by an accident of history. Lastly, unlike Bhutto or Quaid-e-Azam M.A. Jinnah, he had no party to support his programmes and policies. Though did try to cultivate theocratic parties like the Jamaat-e-Ulema Islam who lacked any mass following.

In these circumstances, Gen Zia adopted coerceive tactics to bring back his interpretation of Islam as the core value of the nation state of Pakistan. This automatically resulted in a dilemma about whether Pakistan should move towards the secularism of Ayub-Bhutto or the Islamisation of the Gen Zia variety. In the process, the foundations of the Pakistani nation state got further weakened. If Gen Zia had continued in office, he would probably have made his ideology acceptable to the people of Pakistan. But that is a moot point to discuss. His sudden death in an aircrash and the return of the popular government in 1988 in no way altered the situation. The two terms of Benazir and one term of Nawaz Sharif have shown that the ruling elite of Pakistan still vacillate between secularism and Islam, making compromises wherever and whenever necessary.

IDEOLOGY DILEMMA IN THE ARMED FORCES

The ascendancy of the armed forces in the Pakistani polity resulted in a sort of politico-military fusion leading to the armed forces developing stakes in keeping their predominant position intact, if not better, in the evolutionary process of the nation state. Unfortunately, the Pakistani armed forces are not a cohesive unit, as they were projected to be, to take up such a role. This resulted in three significant developments.

Foremost, they proved to be professionally not as competent as they had projected themselves to be to the Pakistani people. In the three major wars they fought with India, from their own accounts, they lost the 1948 war and were defeated in the 1971 war. In fact, 90,000 troops surrendering to the Indo-Bangladesh joint command, in December 1971 lowered their image considerably. Every Pakistani felt, understandably, that their Generals, who were the rulers, had let them down. They failed to perform their basic duty.

This brought to the forefront a number of issues both at the popular level and within the armed forces. The most important is the strong criticism against the Punjab province's domination of the armed forces justified on the British created myth that Punjabis are a martial race. This resulted in subnationalist feelings emerging everywhere. And the ruling elite instead of quietly sorting it out, decided to ignore it.

At the same time, the Pakistani armed forces, to demonstrate that they mean business, behaved ruthlessly, first in East Pakistan (1970-71), then in Baluchistan (1972-73) against civilians during Z.A. Bhutto's regime and again in Sindh (1993-95). This resulted in further strengthening the people's perception that the Pakistani armed forces can at best deal with unarmed Pakistani civilians only.

Second, there is an ideological debate going on in the Pakistani armed forces. The central point of this debate is whether Pakistani armed forces are to be secular or whether they are soldiers of Islam. The oath taken by every Jawan and officer of the Pakistani armed forces reads as follows:

"I,....do solemnly swear that I will bear the true faith and allegiance to Pakistan and uphold the Constitution of the Islamic Republic of Pakistan, which embodies the will of the people, that I will not engage myself in any unlawful activities whatever, and that I will honestly and faithfully serve Pakistan in the Pakistani Army/Navy/Air Force as required by and under the law.

"May Allah Almighty help and guide me (Ameen)."

Secularists argue that the Constitution of Pakistan embodies the will of the people rather than the command of the Almighty Allah. The people of Pakistan are a composite entity. Besides, Muslims, there are Hindus, Christians, Parsis, Agha Khanis, etc. in Pakistan. The armed forces have, besides Muslims, a sprinkling of all these non-Muslims in their rank and file. According to Brig (Retd) A.R. Siddiqui, "As per the term Islamic Republic of Pakistan, used in the official oath, the state per se is a secular institution and functions on secular lines, regardless of the prefix 'Islam' attaching to the character."

The armed forces' sole official organ, Hilal, in its issue dated January 27-February 2, 1996, wrote of an "order" received "to secularise" the armed forces. The editorial is untriguingly entitled Afwaji Pakistan se Islam Ki Rukhsati (exit or explusion of Islam from Pakistani armed forces).14 The editorial which opens with the cryptic line Hukm aya hai (an order has been received) without mentioning the issuing authority, states:

(a) the armed forces of Pakistan need to be secularised;
(b) the armed forces of Pakistan should be patterned (or recognised) after the armed forces of certain countries of the Middle East and Africa;
(c) all officers possessed of Islamic thought and action should be scrupulously weeded out of the armed forces; and
(d) promotions of "bearded officers" stopped. No bearded officer or Jawan to be seen in the armed forces in the future.

While this secularisation of the Pakistani armed forces was going on, Hilal also carried articles and editorials calling Pakistani armed forces the soldiers of Islam. For instance, in its Pakistan Day issue (March 23, 1996, datelined Lahore where the Pakistani Resolution was adopted) Hilal spoke of the armed forces of Pakistan as "soldiers of Allah," the Navy as "the war cry of Khalid" and the Air Force as "the charge of Hamiza." According to one commentator, in this whole exercise of Hilal there was little to indicate anything more than the use of a motivational ploy as distinct from a shared strategic perception.

What is interesting is that similar sentiments were voiced by the Chief of Army Staff, General Jehangir Karamat at the Pakistan Military Academy parade on April 11, 1996. He told the gentleman cadets:

"These men are true soldiers of Islam and they value truth, justice, impartiality and courage—both moral and physical—and you can lead them well if your own conduct is based on the values of Islam."

Similar sentiments were echoed by the then Prime Minister, Benazir Bhutto, too. In the Pakistan Military Academy (PMA) graduation parade on October 12, 1995, Benazir Bhutto's Defence Minister, Aftab Shah Mirani, went a step further. According to him, the Pakistan military establishment "is motivated by Islamic values and imbued with true Islamic traditions."

This ideological debate in the premier institution of the Pakistan polity indicates that even the armed forces, due to the contradictions in the polity, lost their bearings. The leadership's effort to project itself as Islamic in character, clearly indicates that the rest of the communities of the country are no longer relevant. This is more or less the mistake Pakistan made up to 1971, resulting in the country getting divided into two. At that time, the Pakistani ruling elite failed to respect the Bengali sentiments and treat them as equal partners. One gets the feeling that the same is being repeated even now.

IDENTITY CRISIS

This resulted in the second problem for Pakistan—an identity crisis. For some inexplicable reasons, Pakistan does not want to own the rich history of 3,000 years of the Indian subcontinent. They know that they cannot claim to be the sole inheritors of the Indus Valley Civilisation and the subsequent history of the Indian subcontinent. This becomes quite clear from even a cursory glance at the Pakistani school level or college level history books. In fact, Pakistani historians are in a dilemma about whether to accept the dynamic rule of the Mauryas and the Golden Age of Guptas of ancient Indian history or not. Similarly, whether King Ashoka, who is a part of the Indian subcontinent folklore, belongs to them or to India. In fact, some of the Pakistani history books skip or make just a cursory mention of the some of the glorious periods of ancient Indian history. Apparently, Pakistani historians feel that projecting these Hindu and Buddhist Kings may place them in a tight spot.

Similarly, the Mughal Kings ruled from Delhi and not from Lahore or Rawalpindi. After Aurangazeb, the Mughal dynasty squandered their riches and proved to be incompetent rulers. This enabled the British to usurp power from the mid-18th century onwards. These are well recorded facts of history. But Pakistani historians refuse to accept these facts of history. Some Pakistanis even argue that the British managed to usurp power because Hindu Maharajas collaborated with the colonial masters. If one goes by the history books, nothing significant happened between the Indus Valley Civilisation and the advent of the Mughal period in the Indian subcontinental history!

Even in modern Indian history, Pakistani historians refuse to accept that Gandhi's non-violence and non-cooperation prompted the British to leave India and think in terms of independence, and Jinnah joined it only in the early 1930s.

At another level, Pakistan had the problem with their national language, Urdu. Whether the birthplace of Urdu is Lahore or Lucknow or Hydrabad in southern India, can be debated endlessly. Pakistanis claim Muslims brought Urdu to the Indian subcontinent and made it the official language of the Delhi durbar of the Mughal Kings. But many Indian Muslims feel that it became a rich language only in Lucknow (Uttar Pradesh) and Hyderabad (Andhra Pradesh). And interestingly enough, Urdu has been recognised as an official language by the Indian Constitution.

The Pakistani ruling elite tried to impose Urdu as a national language on its former eastern wing (now Bangladesh) resulting in large scale violence.

This unwillingness on the part of Pakistan to accept that Indian civilisation is a common heritage of both the countries brought in a lot of distortions in the Pakistani psyche. The information revolution from the 1970s onwards proved to many Pakistanis that what they have been told and studied is totally baseless and false. They realised that this quest for a separate identity from India brought in complete distortions about their roots. And after the 1971 India-Pakistan war, when Pakistan was divided into two, the myth of religious bondage was totally exposed.

As will be discussed later, Pakistan's quest to identify itself with the Islamic world and trace its roots to the Arab world created further complications. In fact, whether Pakistan belongs to South Asia or to the Islamic world of Persian Gulf/West Asia which in many ways is alien to them, except in the context of religion, created further problems for its people.

In the process, Pakistan got confused with its historical and cultural bearings. This get reflected in instances like in the late 1970s and 1980s when the film Mughal-e-Azam (history of Great Mughal King Akbar's son Saleem and his beloved Anarkali), was produced in India and telecast over the Indian Television, and everybody in the Indian subcontinent was able to watch it. Life in Pakistan used to come to a standstill on such an occasion, as everybody would be glued to the TV. An average Pakistani who watched it started asking how the "Hindu" India could show such a story on the government controlled television, that too about a Mughal Emperor. When some religious fanatics in Pakistan called it a cultural invasion, the average Pakistani got further confused. He was not clear how it could be a cultural invasion? All that was shown was a beautiful love story of a Muslim prince, and in all the right earnestness by an Indian film director. And when the film won laurels all over India, a discerning Pakistani realised that there is something wrong in what he reads and is told.

One could extend this to music, art, literature, etc. Indian music is copied in Pakistan and vice versa. Lata Mangeshkar and M.S. Subbalakshmi are as popular in Pakistan as they are in India.

In other words, when the electronic media broke the artificial barriers created by the ruling elite, an average Pakistani was able to sort out myth and reality about India and Pakistan. And in the process, he realised that his roots lie somewhere else and not in Pakistan. One could say this resulted in the lowering of stakes in the nation state he is living in. The contrast in governance of the nation state between the two countries became too obvious. While India was able to evolve a political system based on majority rule, Pakistan degenerated into a sort of authoritarianism and rule of the few. When India is maturing as a democracy, Pakistan is still experimenting with what form of government it should have. If recent reports in the Indian media are to be believed, the Council for Defence and National Security, created by a Presidential Ordinance in 1997 is going to evaluate the performance of the elected representatives.

This crisis of identity resulted in two important developments. First, nobody seems to have developed a stake in the Pakistani state. In fact, the ruling elite used the state of Pakistan to amass their personal wealth, rather than working towards nation building. The structure of governance changed according to the whims and fancies of the ruling elite at any given point of time. And the people who wield maximum firepower, the armed forces, became the sole arbitrators in deciding who should rule.

Second, as it happens in such situations, the credibility of the government got reduced to almost zero level. The absence of a credible government resulted in social development becoming the first casualty. Even after 50 years of independence, Pakistan cannot claim that it has any high quality educational institution in the country about which the country can boast. The ruling elite seems to be have lost its direction and nobody seems to be clear about what to do now. The best example is, when the nation is in its worst financial crisis, the armed forces decide to modernise their equipment and start negotiations for buying a French fighter aircraft!

In other words, as the years passed by, the ideological moorings of Pakistan started petering out resulting in an identity crisis. Only the elite of Pakistan refused to acknowledge it. In fact, Quaid-e-Azam Mohammad Ali Jinnah, visualised these problems in 1947 itself. In his famous speech to the Pakistan Constituent Assembly in August 1947, he said "...change your past and work together in the spirit that every one of you, no matter what community he belongs to, is first, second and last, a citizen of the state with equal rights." Apparently this was lost sight of in the first few months of the creation of Pakistan; and Quaid-e-Azam realised it. If Jinnah's last words, according to the doctor attending on him were that he committed a "blunder" by creating the state of Pakistan17 are true, then he must have foreseen that his successors were not going to uphold the values he strived for. Recalling these words in the 50th year of independence of Pakistan is a harsh judgement on men and matters of five generations. But that is the way the history of Pakistan is unfolding.

6

Proxy War in Kashmir: Jihad or State-Sponsored Terrorism

Since Pakistan-sponsored militancy first erupted in the Kashmir Valley in 1989-90 and cries of azadi (independence) rent the air, the pendulum of public opinion in Kashmir has swung away from thoughts of jehad to more mundane 'bread and butter' issues. While the security situation in Kashmir Valley has improved considerably, Pakistan is now endeavouring to spread the cult of militancy and terrorism to new areas south of the Pir Panjal range in the Jammu region, so as to create an ethnic and sectarian divide and trigger a communal backlash. Pakistan's increasing frustration and desperation can be gauged from the number of incidents of terrorism that its mercenary agents have been perpetrating since the situation in Kashmir Valley began to slip out of control in 1997-98. Pakistan's aim is clearly to de-stabilise India by all possible means. A protracted 'proxy war' and sustained political and diplomatic offensives, are part of a well-crafted strategy to keep India engaged in internal squabbles and impose a heavy burden on the Indian economy. Pakistan has achieved considerable success in projecting the Jammu and Kashmir (J&K) issue as an international 'flashpoint'.

Pakistan also aims to ensure that the Indian Army and Central Para-Military Forces (CPMFs) remain increasingly engaged in counter-insurgency/internal security operations in J&K and the north-eastern states, so as to degrade India's superiority in conventional combat through a process of strategic fatigue. While ensuring that violence in the ongoing low intensity conflict is maintained at a low level so that it does not lead to a conventional war (that is, it does not cross India's perceived threshold of tolerance), Pakistan can be expected to continue to develop its nuclear and missile capabilities to match Indian capabilities in these fields. Pakistan hopes that such capabilities would further deter India from resorting to conventional conflict to resolve the Kashmir issue.

The Indian Government, on the other hand, has exhibited remarkable restraint in the face of grave provocation. It is now engaged in taking stock of the emerging developments to evolve a co-ordinated civil and military 'action plan' to ensure that the initiative does not remain with Pakistan and that India is able to safeguard its national security and territorial integrity, as well as, eventually root out militancy from J&K and other parts of India. Though military operations against the Pakistan-sponsored militants and terrorists have been extremely successful, the nation has paid a heavy price in terms of civilian and military casualties. The economic costs have also been staggering and obviously cannot be sustained indefinitely. It is imperative that the impact of the various complexities and nuances of the J&K issue is carefully evaluated so that pragmatic decisions can be made to resolve it expeditiously.

THE HISTORY OF KASHMIRI JIHAD

More than half a century after Partition, the vexed Kashmir issue continues to fester, threatening to plunge India and Pakistan into the throes of nuclear war. Meanwhile, an estimated 80,000 Kashmiris have lost their lives in the on-going civil war in the area, leaving thousands more raped, orphaned and permanently maimed for life. Religion plays a central role in defining the very way in which the Kashmir issue is seen, by the Kashmiris themselves, and by both India and Pakistan. As a Muslim majority state, albeit with a significant Hindu minority, Pakistan insists that the very logic of the 'two-nation' theory on which it is founded demands that Kashmir should be a part of it. India, on the other hand, claims that the Kashmiris had thrown in their lot with it in 1947, thus forcefully challenging the legitimacy of the theory of Hindus and Muslims being two separate and antagonistic nations. For many Kashmiri themselves, religion per se is not at the root of the problem, which is seen as essentially political, a quest for self-determination of their own political future. A considerable section of the Kashmiris themselves would seem to support the idea of an independent Kashmir. Indeed, the Kashmiri nationalists who launched the militant struggle in the region in the late 1980s aimed at setting up a sovereign, democratic state, with equal rights for all its citizens, irrespective of religion. From the early 1990s, however, owing particularly to growing Pakistani involvement, Islam emerged as a central issue defining the way in which the Kashmiri struggle came to be framed. For a new breed of Islamist militants, their struggle against India was seen as an Islamic jihad, fired by an irrepressible zeal against the 'enemies' of the faith. This so-called jihad is now being sought to be taken further into India, with attacks by Islamist suicide squads on temples, government buildings and other sensitive locations in various parts of the country.

Muslim militancy in Kashmir and Hindu militancy in India feed on each other, with Hindu chauvinist outfits portraying the conflict in Kashmir as a defence of the indivisible 'Hindu' motherland from marauding Islamic hordes. The events in Kashmir have led to a complete breakdown of inter-faith relations in the state of Jammu and Kashmir, with most of the Hindus of the Kashmir valley having fled their homes, and scores of Hindus and Muslims having lost their lives in internecine violence. Elsewhere in India, the Kashmir imbroglio has contributed to a general heightening of Hindu-Muslim strife and conflict, as well as a rapid deterioration of relations between India and Pakistan, setting off fears of a nuclear catastrophe in the region.

This chapter looks at how the terms of discourse of the Kashmiri struggle have been transformed over time, and how the secular, nationalist Kashmiri movement has been overtaken by radical Islamists pursuing a very different political project, as represented by the Jama'at-i Islami of Jammu and Kashmir and the Lashkar-i Tayyeba. It focuses, in particular, with the issue of how Islam has been understood by Islamists to legitimize their involvement in the current struggle in the region as a jihad, looking at what this means for relations between Kashmiri Muslims and the Kashmiri Hindus and for the ways in which the former are expected to relate to the Indian state. It seeks to grapple with the crucial question of the shifting identities of the Kashmiri Muslims, faced with the might of the Indian state, increasingly defined by an aggressively militant Hindu agenda, on the one hand, and with the increasing salience of Islamist organizations, on the other.

Roots of Revolt

The early Kashmiri independence movement, whose roots go back to the uprising against the Hindu Dogra regime in the 1930s, saw itself principally as a nationalist struggle. From the 1930s till 1947, the Kashmiri movement, under the charismatic Shaikh Muhammad 'Abdullah, aimed at challenging the autocratic rule of the Dogras, demanding proper representation for the Kashmiri Muslims in the administration of the state. In 1947, most of Kashmir came under Indian rule, and from then onwards, a sizeable section of the Muslims of Kashmir carried on, largely through peaceful agitation, a movement for the establishment of an independent state. As 'Abdullah's charisma's gradually declined, with the failure of his National Conference to meet the aspirations of the people and to preserve the autonomy of Kashmir, a new breed of Kashmiri nationalists emerged, disillusioned with what they saw as 'Abdullah's complicity with the Indian state. The leadership of the movement was provided by young Kashmiri Muslims who had received a modern education in the colleges that began to be set up in the region after 1947. Their principal demand was that India should fulfil its commitments to the United Nations and allow a plebiscite to be held in the territory to enable the people to decide their own political future. Challenging the legitimacy of Indian rule, these Kashmiri nationalists advocated an independent, secular democratic Jammu and Kashmir. The ideology informing their nationalist project was that of Kashmiriyat or 'Kashmiri identity', which they saw as a unique amalgam of traditions drawing upon local Muslim, Hindu and other sources. The Kashmiri nationalist project was spearheaded by several organizations and parties, the foremost being the JKLF, established in 1964. The JKLF demanded that the state of Jammu and Kashmir as it existed prior to 1947 be united as 'one fully independent and truly democratic State'. It advocated 'equal political, economic, religious and social rights' for all citizens in the proposed state, 'irrespective of race, religion, region, culture and sex'.

Parallel to the rise of the Kashmiri nationalists, Kashmir in the late 1930s also witnessed the emergence of an Islamist movement. The roots of the Islamist emergence can be traced to the reformist efforts of the Ahl-i Hadith ('People of the Prophetic Tradition'), established in Kashmir in 1925. The Ahl-i Hadith saw themselves as inheritors of the legacy of the Prophet and his Companions, crusading against popular Sufism, the dominant form of Islamic expression in Kashmir, branding it as un-Islamic. Given the deep-rootedness of the Sufi tradition in Kashmir, the Ahl-i Hadith singularly failed to develop a mass following. Rather, it remained, as it does even today, a largely elitist phenomenon, with its core support base among a limited section of the urban middle classes. Ahl-i Hadith-style reformism did, however, provide fertile ground for the emergence of other Islamist trends from the 1930s onwards. Islamism in Kashmir found its most vocal champion in the Jama'at-i Islami, established in 1941 by Sayyed Abul 'Ala Maududi, and organised as an independent organisation and political party in Kashmir in 1952.

The Jama'at-i Islami of Jammu Kashmir (JIJK) remained, at least at the political level, a marginal force in Kashmir till the 1980s, but with the launching of the armed struggle in 1989 it came to play a central role in Kashmiri politics. It forcefully sought to present the armed struggle as a jihad between Islam and disbelief (kufr), thereby challenging the Kashmiri nationalists' definition of the struggle as one between the Kashmiri nation and the Indian state. The Jama'at sees the struggle as a war between Muslims and the 'enemies' of the faith, and is bitterly critical of the notion of a separate Kashmiri national identity. Rather, it insists that the Kashmiris are simply a part of the worldwide Muslim ummah, not a nation by themselves, for, according to it, Islam and nationalism are incompatible with each other. Hence, it argues, the mission of the Kashmiri struggle is not to set up an independent state, which is what the nationalists' project is all about, but, rather, to make Kashmir a part of Muslim Pakistan.

The JIJK's efforts at restructuring the framework of discourse within which the Kashmiri struggle sought to express itself has, from the early 1990s, been given further impetus by the growing intervention in Kashmir of Islamist groups based in Pakistan. These groups tend to see the Kashmiri struggle not simply as a jihad between the Muslims of Kashmir and the Indian state, but in far wider terms: as a 'holy war' between the Muslims of the world, on the one hand, and the Hindus as an entire community, in league with other 'disbelieving' 'enemies of Islam', on the other. In this grand battle, all national and geographical barriers are completely demolished—all Muslims, wherever they may be, are seen as being responsible for contributing in some way or the other in this jihad. On the other hand, Hindus are seen as complicit in the oppression of the Kashmiri Muslims, and hence, considered as enemies. Interestingly, the Hindus are regarded as being hand in glove with other 'enemies' of the Muslim ummah—the Jews and the Christian West—against whom, too, a jihad needs to be waged.

The JIJK and the Kashmiri Jihad

The JIJK was established as an independent organization in 1952, although from the late 1930s a growing number of Kashmiri Muslims had come under the influence of the founder of the Jama'at, Maulana Maududi, principally through his powerful writings. The JIJK presented itself as committed to establishing an Islamic state in Kashmir based on the shari'ah, but using democratic means of peaceful persuasion for attaining its goals. This was stressed in its Constitution, adopted in 1953. Article 2 [b] of its Constitution states that

The Jama'at shall not employ ways and means against ethics, truthfulness and honesty or which may contribute to strife on earth.

Article 2 [c] of its Constitution lays down that the Jama'at shall use democratic and constitutional methods, while working for the reform and righteous revolution. Till the late 1960s, the JIJK sought to cultivate a constituency for itself through publishing and distributing literature, establishing reading rooms and discussion groups, setting up a network of schools all over the state, and through public lectures. In 1969, for the first time, the JIJK decided to enter the electoral fray, by sponsoring a number of candidates for the local level (panchayati) elections which were held on a non-party basis. Apparently, it was felt that by remaining outside the sphere of electoral politics it was being rendered increasingly ineffective. It was thought, therefore, that elections were 'the best platform to popularize the message of the movement'. Later, the JIJK went on to participate in successive provincial as well as general elections as an independent political party. It failed, however, to win an impressive number of seats in any election, owing both to widespread rigging engineered by the Indian authorities as well as a definite lack of enthusiasm for the JIJK's agenda on the part of the electorate.

The last time that the JIJK participated in the electoral field was in the 1987 elections, as part of the eleven-party alliance, the Muslim Muttahida Mahaz (Muslim United Front or MUF), a group of several Kashmiri parties championing the right to political self-determination of the Kashmiri people. It was widely expected that the MUF would do well in the elections and might even be able to win a majority. However, these elections, like all the others previously held in Kashmir, were marked by massive rigging by the Indian authorities, as a result of which only four MUF candidates were officially declared elected. The election results met with an upsurge of rage and opposition, with mass demonstrations being held against the Indian state for subverting the democratic process. Then, in 1988, having tired of the democratic path of seeking to win the right to self-determination, an armed struggle for the liberation of Kashmir from Indian rule was launched. On 31 July 1989, two massive bomb blasts in the heart of Srinagar, the capital of the state, heralded the launching of the armed struggle. The JKLF claimed responsibility for the act.

The armed struggle launched by the JKLF for the independence of Kashmir found mass support among the Kashmiri Muslims, disillusioned as they were with Indian rule and with the subversion of democratic institutions in Kashmir. The MUF initially hesitated in joining the armed struggle, directing its four representatives within the state assembly, including Sayyed 'Ali Gilani, chief ideologue of the JIJK, to retain their seats so as to be able to air the grievances of the people. However, the rising tide of the JKLF-led struggle soon proved too much for the MUF high command to ignore, and in 1989, it instructed its members in the state assembly to resign and to join the struggle. The JIJK now decided to fully immerse itself in the militant movement, and in 1990 it set up its own militant wing, the Hizb ul-Mujahidin ('The Army of the Holy Warriors', HM).

Given the JKLF's immense popularity among the Kashmiri Muslims, and the mass support for its goal of an independent, democratic and secular Jammu and Kashmir, the JIJK and the HM had to struggle against great odds in putting forward their own agenda of making Kashmir part of Pakistan and establishing an Islamic state in the region. One of the major hurdles that the JIJK had to face in expanding its base beyond a narrow circle of middle class sympathizers was its perceived attitude towards popular Sufi traditions. The JIJK, rooted as it was in a fierce opposition to popular Sufism, was seen by many Kashmiris as opposed to the Sufi saints as such, whom they held in great respect, and despite its efforts to convince people that this was not the case, the JIJK was unable to dispel the notion. Since Sufism is still a dominant form of Islamic expression in Kashmir, this was seen by many as hostility towards Islam itself. Making the JIJK's project more difficult for itself was the fact that although most Kashmiri Muslims were certainly disillusioned with India, it is unlikely that a majority of them would have preferred to join Pakistan instead or to be ruled under a strict Islamist regime, as the JIJK and the HM advocated. To make matters even more difficult for the Islamists was the widespread abuses of human rights by the Indian armed forces, resulting in the killings of many Kashmiri Muslims, among whom were several known Islamist activists and sympathizers.

Despite the immense odds that the Islamists had to contend with, from both the Kashmiri nationalists as well as the Indian armed forces, they strove, through publications, mass meetings, public rallies and the work of their activists, to convince the Kashmiris that the solution to the crisis lay in the project that they were advocating, a counter to both Indian rule and demands for independent nationhood. In this manner, a shift was sought to be made in the terms within which the liberation struggle was being waged. Islam, not Kashmiriyat, and accession to Pakistan, not an independent Kashmir, were presented as the solutions to the Kashmir problem. Such arguments now began to exercise a broader appeal, especially with the rise of militant anti-Muslim Hindu groups in India, and the subsequent large-scale killings of Muslims in the wake of the destruction of the Babri mosque in 1992. Indeed, the growing popularity of the Islamists in Kashmir and the consequent marginalization of the Kashmiri nationalists has much to do with the rapid spread of the radical Hindu Right in India. The very real dangers that the rise of Hindutva posed to Muslim lives and identity in India, and to the Muslims of Kashmir as well, made the argument more convincing that the struggle being waged in Kashmir was one between kufr and Islam.

The Islamist reworking of the discursive framework in which the Kashmiri struggle has sought to express itself is well illustrated in the case of the writings of Sayyed 'Ali Shah Gilani. Gilani has held many top positions in the JIJK, and was for long the chief political spokesman of the party, besides holding the post of chairman of the All-Parties' Hurriyat Conference, an alliance of thirty-four Kashmiri Muslim parties and organizations fighting for Kashmir's freedom from Indian control. He is one of the most senior present-day Kashmiri political leaders and also has the distinction of being the most prolific writer among them all.

Gilani's major writings all date to the 1990s, a period when the JIJK had already immersed itself in the armed struggle, in which Gilani himself played a key role, and for which he was forced to spend several years in various jails. Not surprisingly, Gilani's writings focus almost solely on the issue of Kashmir's freedom from Indian control. He devotes little attention in his writings to Islamic law, theology and doctrines, for being an ideologue of the JIJK, he takes Maududi's voluminous writings on these subjects as authoritative. Gilani's concern is to place the

Kashmiri struggle within the Islamist discursive framework. Thus, the struggle is depicted as a jihad, the goal of which is the merger of Kashmir with Pakistan and the establishing of an Islamic state in the region. As we shall see, however, Gilani's understanding of the struggle differs at some crucial points with the views of the Pakistan-based jihadist outfits, being considerably less radical and uncompromising, at least in some crucial aspects.

Three features are of particular importance in Gilani's description of what he calls the Kashmiri jihad. Firstly, the jihad is seen as directed against the Indian state and its agents, and not against Hindus or Indians as such. Secondly, the jihad has the limited goal of freeing Kashmir from Indian control. Thirdly, the mujihadin have no intention of intervening in Indian internal affairs after the liberation of Kashmir. Once the Kashmir issue is solved by freeing the territory from Indian control and merging it with Pakistan, India and Pakistan, Gilani writes, will be able to establish peaceful and cordial relations with each other, for the root cause of the tensions between the two countries is the dispute over the issue of Kashmir.

Gilani sees the armed struggle being waged in Kashmir not as a war of national liberation, but as a jihad between Islam, on the one hand, and the forces of kufr or disbelief, on the other. He argues that a combination of various developments—India's denial to the Kashmiris of their right to self-determination, its brutal suppression of the Kashmiri struggle which has resulted in the deaths of many thousand Kashmiris, and the rapid rise in India of anti-Muslim Hindu chauvinism—have necessitated the launching of a jihad against India. He writes that the Indian state has, by its actions, 'proved its extreme hostility towards the religious and moral sensibilities [of the Muslims] and the tenets of Islam'. 'Wherever and whenever the laws of Islam are held out for insult and the religious rights [of the Muslims] are trampled upon', he declares, 'jihad becomes a binding obligation (farz) for all Muslims'. Such a situation, he says, prevails in Kashmir, and hence the need for a jihad to be waged there. This jihad, he stresses, calls for the participation of all Muslims, not just Kashmiris alone. In a telephonic interview in 1992 with a Lahore-based journalist soon after his release from a long spell in prison, Gilani declared: It has now become incumbent, in the light of the teachings of the Holy Qur'an, upon all the people of Pakistan to participate in the [Kashmir] jihad. They should now stand up determinedly and assist their Kashmiri brethren in the practical jihad. This jihad is a religious duty binding not only on the people of Pakistan, but, in fact, on the entire Muslim ummah [...] The extreme oppression that the Kashmiri Muslims are having to face is an open challenge for the entire Muslim ummah. All Muslims must now move ahead, help the oppressed Muslims [of Kashmir] and stop the hands of the oppressors.

While declaring the armed struggle a jihad, Gilani makes it clear, however, that the armed struggle is directed against the Indian state and not against Hindus or Indian citizens per se. He makes a clear distinction between the Indian state, on the one hand, and ordinary Indians and Hindus, on the other. Thus, in an appeal to the Kashmiri militants in April 1992 Gilani asserted that, 'The mujahidin have just two enemies: the Indian state and its agents. To waste the power of our youth on targets other than these two is like pouring salt on the wounds of our oppressed people'. Gilani has, on numerous occasions, appealed for communal harmony between Hindus and Muslims in Kashmir. He stresses that Hindu-Muslim relations in the state have traditionally always been cordial, and that in the past the Valley has never known the wild bloodletting between Hindus and Muslims that has erupted periodically, and now on a menacingly increasing scale, in India. Defending the armed struggle from charges of being anti-Hindu, he asserts that the mass exodus of the Kashmiri Pandits in the early 1990s was actually instigated by the Indian authorities in order to project the Kashmiri struggle as an 'Islamic terrorist' movement, so as to discredit it in the eyes of the West. Gilani has issued several appeals to the Kashmiri Pandits who have fled from their homes to return and join their Muslim brethren in the struggle. He has also warned the mujahidin that they should desist from any actions 'which will give their opponents a chance to brand them as terrorists'.

Gilani's opposition to the Indian state is limited insofar as his prime objective is to liberate Kashmir from Indian control. The jihad against India, in other words, is circumscribed by the limited objective of freeing Kashmir from Indian rule. Thus, he asserts that after Kashmir is freed from Indian occupation, the JIJK would 'like to see India as free, prosperous and peaceful'. Criticizing certain un-named Kashmiri militant groups for spreading anti-India hatred, he says:

Emotional slogans such as 'Crush India!' are neither realistic nor do they reflect the spirit of Islam. At root, Islam is based on invitation to prosperity, witness to the truth, salvation in the Hereafter, protection of the truth, the ending of every form of oppression and creating understanding between all children of Adam. This, indeed, is the message of the life of the Prophet Muhammad (may peace be upon him). Even when the people of Ta'if unleashed a wave of unlimited oppression on the Prophet of Islam (may peace be upon him), he did not pray to God that they should be destroyed but, rather, that He should guide them [to the right path]. This is why I believe our struggle should be geared only to gaining our rights [...] The slogan of Islam is not one of destruction but of invitation [to the Truth], prosperity, peace and truth.

The legitimacy of the category of the 'Kashmiri nation' that forms the subject of Kashmiri nationalist discourse is vehemently denied by Gilani, this being a logical outcome of his own Islamist position that sees Islam and nationalism as being in complete contradiction to each other. Here, of course, Gilani seeks to question the very basis of the political agenda of the major rivals of the JIJK, the various Kashmiri nationalist groups such as the JKLF. Gilani argues that nationalism is a 'poisonous philosophy' which the 'enemies of Islam', foremost being 'various Western philosophies', have deliberately sought to infect Muslims with so as to divide and weaken them so that they can be kept under their control. He insists that the Muslim world-wide ummah is one, monolithic ideological community, cemented together on the basis of 'common belief and faith', which sees no differences of colour, race, language, caste, tribe or family. He asserts that 'whenever Muslims have ignored the principles of Islam, which sees no boundaries of region, they have lost their power and have become like any other community'. Territorial nationalism, he writes, has proved to be the bane of the Muslims, for it has divided them into different states and, thereby, has deflected them from the task of 'changing the conditions of the entire human race'.

Islam, says Gilani, makes a clear distinction between 'love for their country' (watan dosti), which it allows, and territorial nationalism or 'nation worship' (watan parasti), which it clearly forbids. 'Nation worship', based on the principle of 'my nation, right or wrong', Gilani writes, leads to group prejudice, a quality of the period of the pre-Islamic period of jahiliya, an age of utter darkness. He lays much of the blame for strife, war and bloodshed that characterizes the world today on territorial nationalism. 'Nationalism is the slogan of the jahiliya', he argues, because the nation has usurped from Islam the 'right to decide the criterion for what is right and what is wrong'. Because of this, large states, such as India, prey on smaller, weaker states, causing endless suffering and misery, 'with millions of people being sacrificed at the altar of nationalism'—in the Kashmiri case, 'at the hands of the priests of Mother India'. However, he asserts, by denying the narrow boundaries that 'nation worship' has inscribed, Islam has 'destroyed into smithereens the idol of nationalism until the Day of Resurrection'.

All Muslims being considered as one nation, Muslims and Hindus in India, and Kashmir as well, are considered to be members of two different nations despite living in the same territory. This, Gilani says, is 'an undeniable truth' (na qabil-i tardid haqiqat). He writes, conveniently glossing over the remarkable degree to which Muslims in India and Kashmir share a common culture with the Hindus, that not just in matters of faith, beliefs and customs do the two differ, but that they are also distinct and sharply set apart from each other in such matters as food, clothing and lifestyles. For Muslims to stay among Hindus or in an environment which is very different from their own is said to be as difficult as it is 'for a fish to stay alive in a desert'. Muslims, he says, cannot live harmoniously with a Hindu majority without their own religion and traditions coming under a grave threat, one major factor being Hinduism's capacity to absorb other religions and communities into its fold. Hence, for Islam to be preserved and promoted in Kashmir, he insists, it is necessary for Kashmir to be separated from India. Curiously enough, he is silent on the fate of the over 150 million Muslims living in the rest of India.

If all Muslims form one nation and nationalism is antithetical to Islam, then, Gilani implicitly argues, the Kashmiri nationalist project of groups such as the JKLF is itself 'un-Islamic'. From this it follows that the 'Islamic' solution to the Kashmir question is not the establishment of an independent Kashmiri nation-state but, rather, the incorporation of Kashmir into an already-existing existing Muslim state, Pakistan. This is seen as the first step towards the eventual unity of all Muslims. In a pamphlet titled Masla Ka Hal ('The Solution to the Problem'), issued in 1992, Gilani expressed this view thus:

To advocate that one Muslim group (qaum) be kept apart from the rest would be against the very definition of a people (millat), whose communal identity is based only on one pure creed (kalima tayyiba), especially so when that group shares common ideological, cultural and communal relations with a neighbouring [Muslim] group as well as a common border [...] For such a group to maintain a separate political identity of its own is against the broader interests of the entire Muslim millat.

The JIJK has, in fact, been among the most vocal champions of the merger of Jammu and Kashmir with Pakistan. In a letter to Nawaz Sharif, the then Prime Minister of Pakistan, in June 1993, Gilani commented that in Kashmir the JIJK and the HM 'were the most reliable groups supporting the ideology of Pakistan', and declared that the final goal of the JIJK was Kashmir's accession to that country. In the Kashmir jihad, therefore, the Pakistanis state is seen as having a central role to play, in addition, of course, to the Pakistani people, who are asked to assist the jihad. Thus, in his letter Gilani appealed to the Pakistani Prime Minister for further assistance, but bitterly criticized Pakistan's alleged policy of 'taking everyone together', by which he meant Pakistani support for Kashmiri nationalist groups, in addition to the Islamists. Gilani complained that such a policy was not only 'un-Islamic'; it also is against the very interests of Pakistan itself. He labeled the nationalists as 'enemies of the jihad', and foes of Pakistan, and cautioned that assistance to such groups as advocate secular nationalism posed a grave threat 'to Pakistan's stability and existence'.

PAKISTANI JIHADISTS AND THE KASHMIR JIHAD

The Islamic Revolution in Iran in 1979, followed by the jihad in Afghanistan (1979-89) against the Soviet occupation soon turned Pakistan into what one commentator termed as 'the original staging ground of Jihad as an international movement'. Large sums of money and huge quantities of arms now began pouring into Pakistan from various sources, particularly from the USA and Saudi Arabia, apprehensive as both of them were of Soviet expansionism and the Iranian-style anti-monarchical and anti-Western Islamic radicalism in the region. From the early 1980s, Pakistan emerged as the major launching pad for numerous militant Islamist groups fighting in Afghanistan, with large numbers of activists flocking there not only from Afghanistan, but also from the Arab world and from Muslim communities in the West, fired by an irrepressible zeal for the cause of the jihad against the godless Soviets. Several Pakistani Islamic parties, particularly the Jama'at-i Islami, the Jami'at-i 'Ulama-i-Islam and the Jami'at-i 'Ulama-i-Pakistan were also drawn into the jihad, and set up or sponsored their own militant wings. Numerous Islamic seminaries (madrasas) sprang up all over the country, lavishly patronized by the Pakistani military dictator Zia ul-Haq and the Saudis, almost all based on sectarian affiliation, to train their students for the jihad. The consequent spread of what has been called the 'gun-culture' in Pakistan was a major consequence of all these factors. Thus, with arms and funds easily available, Pakistan was rapidly faced with widespread internal conflict, which took several forms—ethnic, between Mohajirs and Pathans in Karachi; and sectarian, between Sunnis and minority Shi'as and, among Sunnis themselves, between Deobandis and Barelwis.

Besides the Soviet presence at Pakistan's very doorstep, several internal factors were responsible for Zia's patronage of radical jihadist outfits. Having captured power through a military coup in 1977, and lacking legitimacy for his rule, he sought to win support for his regime through appeals to Islam, introducing cosmetic changes in the law, such as Islamic punishments, in the name of Islamization, for which he won the warm support of Islamist groups such as the Jama'at-i Islami. Linked to the Islamization project that Zia and Pakistani rulers after him sought to pursue at home was Pakistan's Kashmir policy. To begin with, Pakistan is believed to have extended armed support to the JKLF, arranging for training some of its fighters in the wake of the beginning of the armed uprising in Kashmir in 1989. Soon, however, it was clear to the Pakistani establishment that the JKLF, with its agenda of a free, democratic Kashmir, would not only not toe its line but also pose a threat to its own strategic interests. Hence, from the early 1990s began a policy of deliberate marginalization of the Kashmiri nationalists by the Pakistani establishment, alongside with the cultivation of Pakistani Islamists, who had emerged in the years of the Afghan war, to enter the Kashmir jihad, coupled with lavish patronage extended to Kashmiri Islamist groups such as the JIJK and the HM.

As a result of this change in Pakistan's Kashmir policy from the early 1990s onwards, particularly since the mujahidin victory in Afghanistan in 1992, numerous jihadist outfits in Pakistan began turning their attention towards Kashmir. By the late 1990s, these Pakistani jihadists were playing a key role in the fighting in Kashmir, eclipsing even local Kashmiri groups. Thus, a report brought out by the Indian army in 2000 highlighted the fact that almost all the militant groups active in Kashmir were pro-Pakistan or Pakistan-based, and that the JKLF, the only non-Islamist group included in its list, was 'presently on a low profile'. It estimated that there were some 2750 pro-Pakistan Islamist militants active in Kashmir, while it put the number of JKLF militants at only 60. The groups to whom these Islamists belonged groups were actively assisted by the Pakistani establishment, in particular by its ISI.

With increasing Western criticism of the Pakistani state's role in sponsoring what some have termed as 'Islamic terrorism', an increasing 'privitization of jihad' has occurred. Thus, Pakistan-based organizations that claim to be autonomous of the Pakistani establishment, but are, of course, still dependent on it for patronage, have taken up the task of spearheading the jihad. What is particularly striking about most of these groups is the relatively small Kashmiri presence in both the leadership as well as cadre levels, with almost all their leaders being Pakistani and most of their fighters being Pakistani nationals as well as some Afghans, Arabs and others. Apparently, it is felt that Pakistani strategic interests can be secured only if the leadership and even the rank-and-file of the jihadists remain in Pakistani hands. It has also been argued that the failure or the unwillingness of Kashmiri militant groups to engineer large-scale killings of non-Muslims in Jammu and Kashmir so as to reduce the Hindu population has been an important factor in the promotion of Pakistani-based groups, who have little such compunctions, to take over the armed struggle.

Jihadist Discourse: The Markaz Da'wat ul-Irshad and the Lashkar-i Tayyeba

If the JIJK seeks to seriously question the legitimacy of the discursive framework of the Kashmiri nationalists by seeking to present the Kashmiri armed struggle as a jihad between Islam and disbelief, a further radicalization of the jihadist discourse is clearly evident in the writings and statements of the several Pakistan-based Islamist organizations actively involved in fighting in Kashmir. The most prominent of these groups are the Harkat ul-Ansar, also known as the Harkat-ul Jihad-i Islami, al-Badr, Jami'at ul-Mujahidin, al-Jihad and, probably the most influential of them all, the Lashkar-i Tayyeba ('The Army of the Pure'). All these groups share a common Islamist ideology and advocate the merger of Kashmir with Pakistan.

The Pakistan-based Islamist groups actively involved in the Kashmir conflict are thus today central players in the Kashmiri armed struggle. One of the consequences of their emergence and growing influence has been the further radicalization of the terms of discourse within which the JIJK has sought to portray the Kashmiri armed struggle, arguing against the claims of the Kashmiri nationalists and further developing certain themes that are only vaguely touched upon in Gilani's writings. The jihad is no longer limited to liberating Kashmir from India, but goes far beyond, as we shall see. This is strikingly illustrated in the publications and statements of the Lashkar-i Tayyeba, the 'new masters of Kashmir', and said to be 'the largest jihadi organization in Pakistan'.

The Lashkar is the military wing of an organization called the Markaz Da'wat ul- Irshad ('The Centre for Preaching and Guidance'), set up in 1986 by two Pakistani university professors, Hafiz Muhammad Sa'eed and Zafar Iqbal. Its headquarters are located in a sprawling 160-acre campus at Muridke, a small town in the Gujranwala district of Pakistani Punjab, some thirty kilometres from Lahore. The Markaz is affiliated to the Ahl-i Hadith school, known for its fierce opposition to Sufism and to the established schools of Islamic jurisprudence, insisting that Muslims must go back to the original sources of inspiration—the Qur'an and the Hadith. It seeks to refashion the worldwide Muslim community in the mould of the Companions of the Prophet. It sees itself as the inheritor of the legacy of the first major jihadist movement in modern times in India, the movement launched by Sayyed Ahmad Barelwi and his band of followers, who, in the early nineteenth century, attempted to set up an Islamic state in the Pathan borderlands and launched an abortive jihad against the Sikhs. The Markaz is believed to be closely linked to the Pakistani establishment as well as to the Jama'at-i Islami of Pakistan.

The Markaz, like many other Pakistani Islamist outfits, was originally designed to serve as a training base for Pakistani militants involved in the Afghan jihad against the Soviets. In 1987, a year after its founding, it set up a training centre inside Afghanistan itself, at Jaji in the Patkia province, and then, shortly after, another in the Kunnar province. It claims that the warriors produced at these centres 'performed outstanding operations' against the Russians. In Afghanistan it carried out its jihad in league with an Afghan outfit, the Jama'at al-Da'wat il al-Qur'an. As the Markaz's activities rapidly grew, it was decided to divide its work into two separate but related sections: the educational and the jihadist. Thus, in 1993, the Markaz established its separate 'jihadic and warfare' wing, the Lashkar. The Lashkar later established four training centres in Pakistan and Afghanistan, where, 'thousands of mujahidin from all over the world are being trained'. Markaz authorities claim that militants produced at these centres have played a leading role in the armed struggles in Afghanistan, Bosnia, Chechenya, Kosovo, the southern Philippines, Kashmir and 'in other areas where Muslims are fighting for freedom'. According to one report, in recent years the spread of the Markaz in Pakistan has 'been phenomenal', and today it has some five hundred offices all over the country, most of them in Punjab, which operate as recruitment centres for would-be mujahidin.

At its Muridke headquarters, the Markaz runs an Islamic school and university, most of whose students are local Pakistanis, with some from Pakistan-administered Kashmir, a few Kashmiris from the Indian-ruled part of the state, and several Afghans and Arabs. Besides, the Markaz has established a network of over seventy schools, mainly in Punjab, where Islamic and modern education are imparted. Young boys of the age of eight are taken in and are given a twelve-year training. A strict military atmosphere is enforced, students must wear military uniforms, abide by military discipline and 'properly assimilate the commandments of their theologians and military instructors that their future profession—as mujahidin—will be in great demand in the Muslim world on the threshold of the new millennium'. At its four training centres, would-be mujahidin are given rigorous military training. This is of two kinds. Firstly, a short twenty-one day course, the daura-i 'ama ('general course'). Secondly, a three month intensive course, the daura-i khasa ('special course'), geared to guerrilla warfare, in which trainees learn how to handle small arms as well as survival and ambush techniques. These courses, it is claimed, 'change the course of life' of the trainees completely', and a sign of this is said to be that they 'no longer shave' and 'wear their shalwars above their ankles, as enjoined by the Prophet Muhammad'.

As in the case of the other Pakistan-based militant groups active in Kashmir today, the Markaz's direct participation in the Kashmir conflict dates to the end of the Afghan war in 1992, in which an estimated 1600 of its militants are said to have participated. After the Soviet withdrawal from Afghanistan, it shifted its attention to Kashmir to 'help the oppressed and innocent

Kashmiris who were undergoing Indian aggression for the past fifty years'. In this, they were assisted by the Jama'at-i Islami of Pakistan and the Pakistani intelligence agency, the ISI, key players in the Afghan jihad. The Lashkar is said to have first entered Kashmir in 1990, and then to have 'upgraded' its jihad there in 1993, when its militants attacked an Indian army base in Poonch. In 1994 it began sending large numbers of its fighters into Kashmir, most of them non-Kashmiris. From 1995 it claims that its fighters have been 'engaged properly and striving hard' against the Indian forces. 1996 witnessed a major shift in the Lashkar's Kashmir strategy, with greater attention being paid to the border districts of Jammu, particularly Rajouri and Poonch, as well as Doda. Reports suggest that some of the mass killings of Hindu villagers in these areas have been the work of the Lashkar, with the aim of causing an exodus of the Hindu population of these areas so as to make their task easier. By 1998, it was estimated that the Lashkar had some 350 mujahidin present in Indian-controlled Kashmir. Its fighters are considered by the Indian armed forces to be the best trained among all the militant groups in the region.

In mid-1999 India and Pakistan almost came to war after Pakistan-based militants, believed to be backed by the Pakistani army, occupied certain strategic heights in the Kargil sector in the Ladakh province in the remote northern part of Indian-controlled Kashmir. The four principal militant groups taking part in this operation, all Islamist and manned almost entirely by non-Kashmiris, were the Harkat ul-Mujahidin, the Tahrik-i Jihad, al-Badr and the Lashkar. These groups together formed a joint military command to co-ordinate their military operations against the Indian army. The Lashkar contingent consisted, among others, of several students from its college at Muridke, led by one 'Abdur Rahman 'Abid, a graduate of Medina University. They were joined by some two hundred militants from the Nuristan province of Afghanistan, the first time that such a large number of Afghan fighters had entered Kashmir in recent years.

The Pakistani attempt to enter Kashmir through Kargil failed, however, and under pressure from the West, the country's then Prime Minister, Nawaz Sharif, appealed to the militants to withdraw from the heights that they had captured. The militants, on their part, were reluctant to obey, and they saw Sharif's capitulation to the USA as a betrayal of their jihad. Instead of toeing Sharif's line, they announced what they called 'the second stage' of the Kashmir jihad—taking the battle against the Indian army right inside the Kashmir valley itself, in order, as Zaki ur-Rahman Lakhvi, the amir of the Lashkar, put it, 'to avenge' the atrocities of the Indian army. According to the amir of the Markaz, Hafiz Muhammad Sa'eed, in this second phase 'the jihad would spread all across Kashmir. It would spread to every peak, every forest and every path'. As part of this new strategy, the Lashkar came up with a new means of attack—suicide bombers, which it named as Ibn Taimiya Fida'i Missions, in memory of the medieval Arab Islamic scholar who crusaded against what he saw as un-Islamic practices, and to whom the Ahl-i Hadith as well as the Lashkar owe much of their inspiration. So far, the Lashkar has conducted scores of fida'i missions in Kashmir and beyond. In all, the Lashkar claimed that by early 2000, it had killed some 2100 Indian army personnel, including senior officers, and to have lost some 500 of its own men in its Kashmir operations.

In the wake of a Lashkar attack on the Indian army headquarters in Srinagar, the capital of Kashmir, in 1999, the head of the Markaz, Hafiz Muhammad Sa'eed declared before an audience of an estimated three hundred thousand people that his fighters could now 'strike anywhere in India', threatening to target even the Indian prime minister's office if India did not stop its aggression on the Kashmiri Muslims and vacate Kashmir.

The jihad, declared Hafiz, was not limited simply to freeing Kashmir from Indian control. Rather, he stressed, it was aimed at 'liberating' India itself. He revealed that the Lashkar was now planning to extend its activities beyond the borders of Kashmir, deep inside India. 'To set up a mujahidin network across India is our target', said Zaki ur-Rahman Lakhvi, chief of the Lashkar, addressing the same congregation. He claimed that his organization was 'preparing the Muslims of India against India' and that once they were ready, 'it would be the start of the disintegration of India'. Some 50,000 Pakistani youth are said to have responded to this appeal to join the grand anti-India crusade.

GENESIS OF MILITANCY IN KASHMIR

Ever since Pakistani raiders and razakars invaded J&K in October 1947 and the state acceded to India, Pakistan has been unable to accept what it perceives as a wrongful oss. The state remains a bone of contention between the two countries even after over 50 years of independence. The Pakistan Government calls it the 'core' issue and says that the eventual merger of J&K with Pakistan is the only acceptable solution to the problem and that it is the 'unfinished agenda of partition'. Having failed to annex J&K by force in the several wars initiated by it against India over the last 50 years, and emboldened by its acquisition of nuclear weapons in 1987, Pakistan hatched a new conspiracy for the annexation of J&K by waging a covert 'proxy war' against India through a strategy of 'bleeding India by a thousand cuts'.

Operation 'Topac', under which Pakistan launched its proxy war against India, was brilliantly conceived and skilfully executed. Pakistan's President, General Zia ul Haq's concept was to exploit the religious sentiments of the Kashmiri people, whip up passions on communal and sectarian lines, fan the flames of religious fundamentalism and, in the process, gradually create conditions for waging a jehad. Before launching its proxy war in Kashmir, Pakistan also initiated measures to exploit the disgruntled elements among the youth of Punjab to fight for the creation of an independent Sikh state of Khalistan. The intention was to destabilise India by creating conditions of insecurity in two contiguous front-line Indian states and to tie down the Indian security forces, particularly the Indian Army, in internal security duties. It was expected that prolonged employment in internal security duties would weaken the Indian Army and degrade its conventional superiority over the Pakistan Army. All this was to be achieved through a low-cost option, without getting directly involved.

The Inter-Services Intelligence (ISI) Directorate of Pakistan was entrusted with the responsibility of executing the plan. The ISI had gained immense experience in organising guerrilla warfare in Afghanistan, with sabotage and terrorism as the weapons of choice, while working together with the US Central Intelligence Agency (CIA). The ISI had also surreptitiously siphoned off nearly

60 per cent of the small arms, light weapons, ammunition and explosives supplied to it by the CIA for onward despatch to the Afghan mujahideen. It has been reported that arms and ammunition worth US $5 billion had been pumped into Afghanistan by the US and its allies. In addition, the erstwhile Soviet Union had supplied arms and ammunition worth US $5.7 billion. Large numbers of these weapons became available to the ISI for equipping Kashmiri militants when the Soviet forces withdrew from Afghanistan in 1989. Profits from the clandestine sale of freely available narcotics from Afghanistan, "donations from Muslim zealots in other countries" and profits from large-scale smuggling activities across the Indian border, provided adequate funds to finance an uprising in J&K. Massive rigging of elections to the J&K Assembly in March 1987 and the Kashmiri people's disillusionment with Mr. Farooq Abdullah's allegedly corrupt and inefficient administration, led to spontaneous protest and a call for azadi (independence). Thus the situation was ripe for exploitation and the ISI, which was ready and waiting, stepped in to fan the flames.

The strategic design of Operation Topac was to launch a proxy war against India in a phased manner. The salient aspects of Pakistan's plan were as under :

* Initiate a low-level insurgency to interdict communications networks and subvert the police and financial institutions.
* Subsequently, exert direct pressure along the Line of Control (LoC) by large-scale sabotage and infiltrate mercenaries and Special Forces to attack vital targets in rear areas.
* At an appropriate stage, using religion as a motivating and binding factor, give a nudge to the jehad to peak and, if necessary, be prepared to exercise the military option to liberate J&K.

While J&K was to remain the focus of all ISI activities, Operation Topac also envisaged the provision of support and encouragement to insurgent and militant groups in the north-eastern states of India and thespread of terrorism progressively to other parts of India, in keeping with the strategy of bleeding the country through a thousand cuts. It is axiomatic that for the Pakistanis, a continuing crisis in Kashmir and tensions along the LoC with India provide an excellent diversion from frustrations at home. These are time-tested methods for mobilising the masses, for gaining the support of fundamentalist Islamic parties and the mullahs within Pakistan and in other Islamic states. It also enables the civilian rulers and the bureaucracy to keep the Pakistani Army gainfully employed in directing and supporting the slickly packaged 'just cause' of the Muslim brethren of Kashmir and, as a corollary, away from harbouring thoughts of another military coup. Another major aim is to internationalise the Kashmir issue, contrary to the spirit of the 1972 Shimla Agreement, by raising the bogey of the denial of the Kashmiri people's right of self-determination. It is conveniently ignored that Pakistan itself had impeded the process of the holding of a plebiscite in J&K by not vacating its illegal occupation of Pakistan Occupied Kashmir (POK), which is called Azad Kashmir in Pakistan. The playing up and highlighting of trumped up human rights violations in the international media is also part of a well-orchestrated campaign.

Pakistan's proxy war campaign is carefully calibrated to ensure that India's perceived 'threshold of tolerance' is not transgressed. Though Pakistan would prefer to avoid escalation of the present low intensity conflict (LIC) situation to conventional war, it has apparently vectored in the risks involved in pursuing its proxy war strategy into its operational plans. Yossef Bodansky writes that, "Pakistan knows that the active pursuit of the current Kashmir strategy may lead to an escalation of the face off with India. Islamabad is ready to deal with this eventuality while increasing its all out support for the Kashmiris."

In mid-February 1995, a Foreign Ministry spokesman warned that 'if India carries out another aggression and war breaks out between Pakistan and India, it would not be a war of a thousand years or even a thousand hours, but only a few minutes and India should not be oblivious to the potential destruction.' Pakistani officials add that "Pakistan is really in a position to strike a heavy blow against India through its nuclear capability." Pakistan also believes that its nuclear weapons and missiles provide the cheapest option for peace. Gen Mirza Aslam Beg writes: "The nuclear and missile deterrence have helped maintain peace in the sub-continent for over two decades."

However, it is self-evident that a foreign power can sow the seeds of insurgency only when discontentment and dissent are already widespread among the people and the situation is ripe for exploitation. Due to decades of poor governance13 and neglect, compounded by rampant corruption, cynical nepotism, alienation from the national mainstream and political mismanagement, the situation in J&K was as bad as it could possibly have been in 1988-89. It is only belatedly that true realisation has dawned regarding the various sins of omission and commission with which the post-independence history of J&K is replete. J&K Governor, Mr. Girish Chandra Saxena, recently told Prakash Nanda in an interview that, "We are considering the situation on the political, administrative and democratic fronts. We realise that maladministration, corruption and unemployment have also been responsible for the growth of militancy in the past."

ISI'S CURRENT MODUS OPERANDI: STATE-SPONSORED TERRORISM

In the early 1990s, when local recruits were not hard to motivate, the ISI relied on Pakistan trained militants (PTMs) for organising ambushes of security forces convoys and patrols (using AK-47s and machine guns). PTMs were also employed for executing hit-and-run raids on the Central Police Organisations (CPOs) bunkers and pickets inside urban areas (for which hand grenades and rocket propelled grenades were used). For low-risk tasks such as the planting of anti-personnel land mines and improvised explosive devices (IEDs) and to act as couriers of arms, ammunition and messages, locally trained militants (LTMs) wre generally employed. The ISI had declared 1994 as the year of 'barood' (explosives). Though a fairly large measure of autonomy was given to the area and district commanders of militant outfits such as Hizbul Mujahideen (HM), the Jammu and Kashmir Liberation Front (JKLF) and Harkat ul Ansar (HUM—banned as a terrorist organisation by the US State Department) to conduct operations, overall control was retained by the ISI as it held the purse strings and was the single largest source of supplies of arms and ammunition. Orders to the various outfits used to be relayed over a clandestine radio station located in POK. However, the Kalashnikov culture that swept Kashmir Valley soon extracted a predictable toll. The power of the gun gradually corrupted the PTMs and they soon began to indulge in extortion, loot, rape and murder for petty jealousies.

The criminal activities of the militants soon alienated the Kashmiris. "Even political leaders aligned with militant groups have acknowledged that the abuses undermined the militants' support in Kashmir." At the same time, counter-insurgency operations by the security forces also gained momentum and a large number of militants were killed in action or apprehended. Kashmiri families soon became wary of sending their sons for what they realised was a futile jehad. The result was that, beginning around 1994-95, the ISI's recruitment base in Kashmir Valley gradually dried up, though recruitment by force continued for some more time. The ISI then placed its reliance for further operations in Kashmir predominantly on foreign mercenaries. The ISI's USP (unique selling point) was that Islam was in danger in India, in general, and in Kashmir, in particular. Mercenaries from POK, Pakistan, Afghanistan, several Gulf and West Asian countries including Saudi Arabia and Iraq and many African countries including Egypt, Libya and Algeria, were hired, trained and inducted into the Kashmir Valley. In addition, criminals undergoing long imprisonment sentences in Pakistani jails were also enticed into participating in the so-called jehad. They were told that their sentences would be reprieved if they successfully completed a tenure of ISI ordained duty in J&K. Gradually, the presence of foreign mercenaries among the militants went up from 15 per cent in 1994 to 40 per cent in end-1998.

The modus operandi was to give the mercenaries some rudimentary military training and knowledge about using explosives, arm them with an AK-47 with four magazines of ammunition and give them a few thousand Rupees in Indian currency. At an opportune moment, they were infiltrated through the porous LoC with the support of the Pakistani Army. The Army provided a safe passage through its own defences, guidance by hired gujjars and bakkarwals (Kashmiri shepherds) and covering fire from small arms, machine guns and even artillery, to draw away the attention of Indian troops on the LoC. The command and control set up was loose and flexible. The mercenaries were usually assigned to operate in specified areas and co-ordinated their operations with each other and the remnants of Kashmiri militants. The mercenaries soon found that the people in Kashmir Valley enjoyed an unfettered right to practice their religion. Namaz was performed by the devout five times a day and the mosques were functioning without any kind of interference. In fact, the mullahs were quite used to and rather fond of spewing venom and inciting the people to rise in revolt. Though the local population tolerated them as 'guest militants' the mercenaries did not get the promised support from the Kashmiri people, contrary to what they had been briefed by their masters in Pakistan. Food and shelter were hard to come by and the constant flight from the security forces was tiresome and most inconvenient. Also, they found that the security forces, particularly the Indian Army, were a tough force to reckon with and discovered that a militant's life span in Kashmir was a maximum of four to six months before he was hounded out and killed or apprehended. In 1998, as many as 320 foreign mercenaries were killed.

All this disillusioned the mercenaries very quickly. The story of extortion, loot, rape and murder was soon played out aain. Some of them even began to run their own harems. While the people of Kashmir had initially actively participated in a struggle for azadi (independence) and had even encouraged their sons to join the movement, they were not willing to put up with the errant and domineering ways of the foreign mercenaries with whom they did not identify in any manner whatsoever. They soon began to give real-time intelligence— euphemistically called 'actionable' intelligence—about the whereabouts of the mercenaries to the security forces. From then onwards, the days of the foreign mercenary in Kashmir Valley were numbered. The tide finally turned around the summer months of 1996 when the ISI found that it was no longer profitable or even cost effective to persist with the induction of additional mercenaries in the Valley sector. At this stage, the ISI, in conjunction with the Pakistani Army, appears to have decided to shift the focus of its activities to the areas south of the Pir Panjal range. It was also apparently decided at this time to rely more on terror tactics to discredit the Indian administration, incite a communal and sectarian divide among the people and, by simultaneously raising the ante in Siachen glacier and along the LoC, project Kashmir as an international 'flashpoint'.

The ISI also enlarged the sphere of its diabolical activities to other areas in India. South India soon became a new front in the covert war against India, as evidenced by the incidents of terrorism in 1997-98. In December 1997, there were three bomb explosions in trains in Tamil Nadu. On February 14, 1998, simultaneous bomb blasts in Coimbatore, at the venue of the Bhartiya Janata Party President's election meeting, the bus stand, the railway station, near a hospital and in a bazaar, mimicked the Mumbai bomb blasts of March 1993. The obvious objectives were India's democratic and secular values, political stability and economic growth. The sea route was followed to smuggle explosives to India's west coast for the serial explosions in Mumbai. A new dimension was added to the ISI's relentless effort to spread terrorism in India when, "On December 17, 1995....... an AN-26 aircraft flew into India from Karachi, refuelled at Varanasi in broad daylight, airdropped about 400 AK-47s and thousands of rounds of ammunition over Purulia in West Bengal, and the flew on to Thailand.......The aircraft was intercepted five days later on December 22, just as it was about to leave Indian airspace near Gujarat." Only two months later, an Iranian and a Swiss national drove a truck full of weapons through the Wagah border check post between Lahore and Amritsar to New Delhi and were caught purely fortuitously. On February 11, 1998, a gang of international gun runners was intercepted in the Andaman islands with a consignment of 145 rifles and machine guns and 40,000 rounds of ammunition meant for insurgent groups in the country's north-eastern states. "Thus today we have a situation where land borders, sea coasts and now island territories have become porous and vulnerable to infiltration of weapons and terrorists alike (sic)."

In J&K, the ISI provides comprehensive support to five major militant groups. These include Hizbul Mujahideen (approximate strength 1,000 militants), Harkat ul Ansar (350), Lashkar-e-Toiba (300), Al Barq (200) and Al Jehad (150). In all, about 2,500 militants, mostly foreign mercenaries, belonging to these and other smaller militant groups are operating in J&K at present. The ISI spends about Rs. 60 to 80 crores every year for prosecuting Pakistan's proxy war against India in J&K alone, that is Rs. 5 to 6.5 crores per month. It is quite obvious that Pakistan's doddering economy can ill afford such expenditure. As the ISI's links with the narcotics trade in Afghanistan and the agency's active participation in the illegal arms trade flourishing in Pakistan's North West Frontier Province are well known, it can only be assumed that funding for its nefarious activities in India is being generated by the ISI itself, with the active connivance of the Pakistan government and the Army.

Just before the Secretary-level talks between India and Pakistan, held at New Delhi in November 1998, Indiaome Minister, Mr. L K Advani called Pakistan a 'terrorist state'. During the talks, the Indian team submitted the following four proposals to the Pakistanis:-

* Give up state sponsorship of terrorism in India and dismantle the terrorist camps in Pakistan for arming and indoctrinating militants.
* Close down more than 30 training camps functioning in the so-called Azad Kashmir.
* Deny use of Pakistani territory and facilities to fundamentalists and militant organisations to fuel religious violence.
* Hand over to India 32 terrorist and underworld operators of Indian origin currently in Pakistan.

WHITE PAPER ON ISI OPERATIONS

The ISI wishes to float and sustain an 'overground conglomerate' to project itself as the 'third party' to the dispute representing the 'wishes and aspirations' of the Kashmiri people. To sustain the Kashmir movement at minimal cost, the ISI plans to cause disaffection and alienation, play the Islam-in-danger card, highlight the non-performance of the elected government and atrocities allegedly committed by the security forces. Pakistan wants to pursue the 'Qurban Ali Doctrine' or the inevitable balkanisation of India by sending intensively trained and motivated Pakistani agents to carry out acts of sabotage and subversion.

The objectives of Pakistan's covert action plan against India are to:-

* Sustain the Kashmir movement at minimal cost.
* Force a settlement of the Kashmir problem on terms acceptable to Pakistan.
* Weaken India's potential strength and national will by hitting at its perceived 'fault lines'.
* Prevent India from emerging as a strategically dominant power in the region.
* Make Indian borders porous and India's border states vulnerable to exploitation.

Pakistan wishes to embarrass India by internationalising the Kashmir issue, projecting India as a violator of UN resolutions and accusing it of human rights violations. In pursuance of its objectives, the ISI is engaged in spreading the tentacles of terrorism not only in J&K but also in Punjab, Assam and Nagaland by carrying out subversive propaganda on fundamentalist and communal lines. The ISI has established operational links with drug syndicates and fundamentalist Islamic groups in Pakistan, Afghanistan and India.

In response to demands made by members of the Parliamentary Consultative Committee attached with the Ministry of Home Affairs, the Government of India has proposed to bring out a White Paper on ISI activities in the budget session of Parliament. Details of some of the issues which are likely to be included in the proposed White Paper have appeared in some sections of the Indian press. The growing ISI presence along the Indo-Nepal border is another cause for concern. India has taken up the issue of ISI's anti-India activities, which include the infiltration of militants and agents and the smuggling of arms, explosives and narcotics through Nepal into India, with the Nepalese Government at the highest level. The increasing influx of Bangladesh nationals in the strategically sensitive Siliguri Corridor in north Bengal has changed the demographic pattern in the area. The population of Muslims has increased from 15 per cent in 1971 to 70 per cent at present. The ISI is using the Siliguri Corridor for smuggling arms and narcotics from Bangladesh into the north-eastern states of India. Along the Rajasthan border also, the ISI is actively involved in setting up madrassas (Islamic schools) inside Indian territory and in smuggling arms, explosives and narcotics. These developments are pointers to the larger Pakistani gameplan to further extend the areas in India in which internal security is not fully under the control of the civil government and, consequently, to dissipate efforts to fight the menace of militancy and terrorism.

PRESENT STATE OF MILITANCY IN J&K

1999 is the tenth year of militancy in Jammu and Kashmir (J&K). Despite vociferous denials to the contrary, Pakistan continues to finance, train, equip and support Kashmiri militants and actively abet their ttempts at infiltration across the Line of Control (LoC). As the initial recruitment base in the Kashmir Valley has very nearly completely dried up, Pakistan is increasingly resorting to sponsoring Islamic mercenaries to let loose a reign of terror in J&K. A suo motto statement made by the Defence Minister in the Lok Sabha on August 5, 1998, explained Pakistan's frustrations and its desperation to raise the ante in Kashmir. Extracts from the statement are reproduced below. "Pakistan has always resorted to firing along the LoC to facilitate infiltration by Pakistani and foreign militants who are organised, trained equipped, financed, armed and finally infiltrated with active covering fire and support from Pakistani Army deployed along the LoC. In recent months, especially since May 1998, our security forces have been able to intercept and reduce the level of infiltration, thereby frustrating Pakistan's designs. As if to give vent to its frustration, Pakistan has started targeting not only our Army posts but also civilian inhabited areas, with Batalik, Kargil, Kanzalwan, Tangdhar, Karen and Uri becoming the main targets.

"These actions by Pakistan are in consonance with its calculated design to obstruct and stall peaceful bilateral dialogue and to create a sense of alarm by orchestrating incidents on the border which will project Jammu and Kashmir as a 'flashpoint'. Pakistan's desperation is becoming acute in view of the fast declining Kashmiri support in the Valley to militancy, control of which has passed into the hands of Pakistani militant organisations, patronised by Pakistani political figures; and foreign mercenaries directed by Pakistan's Inter Services Intelligence."

With the Indian security forces in almost complete control of the security situation in the Kashmir Valley, the centre of gravity of Pakistan's Inter Services Intelligence (ISI)-controlled and directed mercenary activities is gradually shifting to new areas south of the Pir Panjal Range which separates the Jammu region from the Kashmir Valley. These include Doda (Kishtwar and Bhadarwah), Punch and Rajouri. Sporadic acts of wanton terrorism were also perpetrated in and around Jammu City and Udhampur during 1997-98. Serious attempts are also being made to widen the arc of militancy to areas in the states bordering J&K such as in the Dalhousie-Chamba area of Himachal Pradesh.

As most areas south of the Pir Panjal Range in Jammu region are predominantly Hindu majority areas, unlike the Kashmir Valley, which is a Muslim majority area, the aim is clearly to create a communal and sectarian divide. Acts of terrorism targeted primarily against Hindus are designed to engender mass migrations by whipping up a fear psychosis on the pattern of the exodus of Hindus from the Kashmir Valley in 1990-93, with a view to gradually changing the demographic pattern in the Jammu region and adjacent areas. Tables 1 and 2 show the brutal and savage acts of terrorism perpetrated in the Kashmir Valley and the areas south of the Pir Panjal Range in 1996-98, masterminded by the ISI and executed with ruthless precision by foreign mercenaries.

In addition to the massacres enumerated in the accompanying tables, the killing of 20 Hindus on February 20, 1999, in three separate incidents, two in Rajouri district and one in Udhampur district, coincided with Indian Prime Minister Vajpayee's historic bus ride to Lahore in Pakistan to achievea breakthrough in Indo-Pakistan relations.

In Doda, "the entire operational command has been handed over to foreign mercenaries belonging to Pakistan, Afghanistan,

Sudan and Turkey, sidelining Kashmiri militants." Doda district comprises rugged mountainous terrain which affords ample opportunity to the militants to operate from well-concealed hideouts. The countryside is ideal for the mercenaries to establish their headquarters and radio communications centres and to stockpile arms, ammunition and explosives. Due to the lack of adequate surface communications, it is difficult for the security forces to respond in a timely manner to prevent incidents of terrorism, or to chase and eliminate militants after they strike. It is even more difficult to establish a viable intelligence network. In particular, the gaining of 'actionable' intelligence for launching surgical strikes against the militants is extremely problematic. As such, the ISI has succeeded in achieving major successes in killing members of the minority community in order to create a communal divide and force migrations from the area. It has also achieved success in blowing up bridges and culverts to further slow down the security forces and in targeting schools, government buildings and property. Even places of worship have not been spared.

In a perceptive piece after the Prankot massacre in April 1998, Ved Marwah, former Police Commissioner of Delhi and former adviser to the Governor of J&K, Jagmohan, expressed the following views:-

"The shift to Jammu is deliberate and is likely to continue. The number of foreign mercenaries is likely to increase in the coming months in the region, with more trained and experienced Afghan mujahideen being available for infiltration into the state. Harkat-ul-Ansar and Lashkar-e-Toiba have been operating there since 1993 and many more such groups have entered the Jammu region since then...... What is called for is concrete action—an immediate strengthening of the security arrangements in the region with the active support of the state police and the civil administration."

Since the setting up of the Unified Command in J&K in December 1996 (after elections to the State Assembly in September 1996), with the Chief Minister of the State as the Chairman and the General Officers Commanding 15 and 16 Corps as Security Advisers, there has been much greater co-ordination between the State Government, the Army and the CPOs in the fight against militancy. The re-vamped Jammu and Kashmir Police (JKP) and the better trained, equipped and motivated Jammu and Kashmir Armed Police (JKAP) have begun to operate in close co-ordination with the central security forces and greater synergy has been achieved in counter-insurgency operations. The intelligence network has also been strengthened. The Joint Intelligence Committee (JIC) has become more effective in co-ordinating intelligence acquisition, collation, analysis, synthesis and dissemination.

The Army has enhanced its vigil over the LoC to further reduce infiltration through a three-tier, static-cum-mobile deployment plan combined with vigorous patrolling in the rear areas, particularly during the hours of darkness and poor visibility. Equipment and technology deficiencies of the past are now being redressed to improve and further enhance the quality of surveillance. Sophisticated electro-optronic observation and surveillance equipment, including hand-held battlefield surveillance radars (BFSRs), is gradually being inducted to further enhance the quality of surveillance over the LoC. The long-standing requirement of passive night vision devices (PNVDs—based on the principle of thermal imaging), for the troops deployed on the LoC, is also being addressed. Unattended ground sensors (UGS), which can detect the movement of human beings through the generation of acoustic, magnetic or electrical signatures, are also likely to be acquired and emplaced in difficult terrain through which infiltration can take place.

However, no amount of hi-tech gadgetry such as BFSRs, PNVDs and UGS, can completely eliminate infiltration. The rugged mountainous terrain, covered by dense forests in the Punch and Rajouri areas, comprises innumerabe deep ravines, nullahs and re-entrants and is tailor-made for infiltration as the initiative for deciding on a route for infiltration, from among the numerous choices available in a given area, lies with the militants. Even if the number of infantry battalions deployed on the LoC could be doubled, it would not be possible to stop infiltration altogether. Hence, the present emphasis is on making the villagers capable of fending for themselves through the establishment of village defence committees (VDCs). The members of the VDCs are being provided elementary training, light weapons and limited communications equipment. In Doda district alone, 800 VDCs have been established.

Simultaneously, the number of police posts is being increased to enhance the presence of the civil administration in the affected areas in Punch, Rajouri, Udhampur and Doda districts. The aim is to instil confidence among the people, deter terrorist strikes by denying the militants the capability of unfettered movement in the area, gain intelligence, identify harbourers and sympathisers who provide shelter to the militants, exercise command and control over the VDCs and for quick reaction against the terrorists when they mange to launch strikes. This JKP scheme is called 'Police Security Grid' and involves the setting up of 90 border posts (on the likely routes of infiltration behind Army posts in Punch and Rajouri districts), 385 defence posts (inside selected villages) and 118 operational posts (to launch active counter-insurgency operations against the militants) in the four districts. When finally implemented, these measures will help to prevent forced migrations of members of the minority community and enable the JKP and the people of the affected areas to play a more effective part in eliminating militancy in J&K. In Punjab, the tide had turned only when the local people stood up to the militants and the Punjab Police, under the able guidance of the State's outstanding Director General, Mr. K P S Gill, took the lead in rooting out the scourge of militancy and terrorism from the State with the active support of the people.

India's Military Response: Paying a High Price

If the situation in Kashmir Valley has been brought under control despite the viciousness and ruthlessness of the ISI-sponsored campaign to wrest Kashmir from India, the credit must go to the Indian Army and the other central security forces such as the BSF and the CRPF. The Army's relentless effort in conducting counter-insurgency operations under the most trying circumstances, while resolutely adhering to the application of the principle of 'minimum force', is indeed commendable and possibly unparalleled. "In contrast to similar situations elsewhere in the world, where tanks, aircraft, artillery and mortars have been freely used with attendant non-combatant casualties, the Indian Army has conducted no more than a police operation in Kashmir. In keeping with its training and style, it has carried this out in a methodical fashion, ferreting out and arresting individuals rather than punishing a community, seeking combat with the militants, rather than waiting to be attacked in places where civilians could be hit."

Weapons such as RPGs (rocket propelled grenade launchers), infantry mortars and anti-aircraft missiles, have been recovered in smaller numbers. In addition, 1,403 radio sets, most of them extremely sophisticated, have also been recovered. The above mentioned figures are in respect of militants neutralised and recoveries made during Army operations. The success achieved by the CPOs and JKP/JKAP would make the tally much higher.

In reply to Dr. Jayanta Rongpi's Unstarred Question No. 205, answered in the Lok Sabha (Lower House of the Indian Parliament) on May 28, 1998, the Defence Minister, Mr. George Fernandes stated the following:

"At present, 72,000 defence personnel are directly deployed in counter-insurgency/internal security in J&K, while about 47,000 are deployed in north-eastern states. In addition, there are also personnel of supervisory and other formations who are involved in supervisory roles whose number is not included in the above figures.

"Prolonged employment of Army for such duties, besides adversely affecting the Army's preparation for its main task also imposes an extra burden on the defence budget which, in turn, affects Army's modernisation programmes. In addition, casualties suffered by the Army in peacetime affect the morale of the Army personnel.

"The maintenance of law and order is basically the responsibility of the State Governments and the defence forces are deployed for counter-insurgency/internal security duties only against a specific requisition by the State administration and/or when they are statutorily required to render such duties under the provisions of the relevant laws such as Armed Forces (Special

Powers) Act, 1958, etc. "The consistent policy of the Government in this regard has been that the defence forces should be deployed for internal security duties very sparingly and only if the State Government is not in a position to handle the situation and the deployment of defence forces becomes absolutely necessary. The Rashtriya Rifles was sanctioned by the Government to relieve the Army, to the extent possible, form counter-insurgency duties. This has, however, helped only to a limited extent in view of the increased commitment of the Army in counter-insurgency operations."

It emerges from the Defence Minister's statement that a total of 119,000 Army personnel were deployed for counter-insurgency and internal security duties in J&K and the north-eastern states of India in May 1998. Since the number of supervisory and supporting personnel is over and above this figure, it could be concluded that approximately 132 infantry battalions were committed for such duties. (The approximate strength of an infantry battalion may be taken as 900 personnel.) Of these units, 36 battalions are of the Rashtriya Rifles. Hence, about 96 infantry battalions were employed for such duties. As the situation has not changed substantially since 1993-94 (except that while militancy has come militarily under control in the Kashmir Valley, the security situation in the areas south of the Pir Panjal range has deteriorated), it could be assumed that about 90 to 95 battalions are being employed continuously for counter-insurgency/internal security duties.

In addition, for the last five years, five to eight infantry battalions of the Territorial Army and about 25 battalions of the Assam Rifles, a para-military force funded by the Ministry of Home Affairs but officered by and under the operational control of the Army, have also been employed for active operations within the country. Hence, overall 162 to 165 regular Army and Army-led para-military battalions are actively engaged in counter-insurgency/internal security operations and duties. To this list, details of the units of Central Police Organisations (CPOs) which are being employed for similar tasks, need to be added to get an overview of the enormity of the effort involved in combating militancy which is mainly Pakistan-sponsored, aided and abetted. As per the details reported to be contained in the White Paper proposed to be released by the Government in the budget session of Parliament, Pakistan-sponsored terrorism in India has claimed the lives of 29,151 civilians and 5,101 security forces personnel. 2,78,601 persons have been rendered homeless. The loss to public and private property is estimated at Rs. 2,000 crores. The cost of compensation paid to victims, for border fencing and the amount expended on the raising of local anti-terrorist force, works out to Rs. 18,500 crores. The expenditure on the Army and para-military forces is approximately Rs. 46,000 crores.

Besides the casualties being suffered almost on a daily basis and their adverse impact on morale, the Army's prolonged involvement in counter-insurgency operations has several other major disadvantages. The financial costs of sustaining a successful counter-insurgency campaign are staggering. It has been estimated that the Army spends approximately Rs. 2,500 crores (US $600 million) out of its annual budget on counter-insurgency operations. This is about 13 per cent of the Army's 1997-98 budget of Rs. 19,000 crores approximately (Revised Estimates). The outcome is that the Army spends almost 57 per cent of its budget on pay and allowances, about 40 percent on the maintenance of equipment and the replenishment of ammunition and other essential stores being consumed for counter-insurgency operations, and is left with only three per cent for modernisation, including capital acquisitions. Even the expenditure on the Rashtriya Rifles, amounting to approximately Rs 500 crores annually, is incurred from the Army's budget. It is obvious that the Army can ill afford an expenditure of 13 per cent on counter-insurgency operations from its budget without its operational efficiency for its primary task being significantly impaired. As the Defence Minister informed Parliament (see text of the Minister's statement above), the Army's modernisation programme has been adversely affected by its prolonged and continued involvement in counter-insurgency duties. This situation needs to be redressed as early as possible.

As most of the additional battalions required for counter-insurgency operations have been inducted from peace stations, the peace time tenures of infantry battalions have consequently had to be reduced correspondingly. This affects the Army's preparation for conventional war since intensive training at individual, section, platoon, company, battalion, brigade and divisional levels requires a systematic and methodical approach and stability of tenure is an important pre-requisite. Also, the requirement of serving tenures for counter-insurgency/internal security is over and above the existing requirement of serving in field/high altitude areas along the LoC and the Actual Ground Position Line (AGPL, on Siachen Glacier) with Pakistan and the Line of Actual Control (LAC) with China. This results in peace station tenures not only being shorter but also more spaced out. Once again, training and preparedness for conventional war are bound to be affected.

The wear and tear caused to first line weapons (small arms and light crew-served weapons), equipment, vehicles, extreme cold clothing (ECC) and camp items such as tentage due to excessive usage in counter-insurgency/internal security operations, results in a reduction in their life cycles. As it is not always possible to procure replacements duc to the inadequacy of funds, replacements have to be provided from the available war reserves which results in their depletion. Some units are inducted for operations temporarily during the summer months only or to fill emergent operational voids till new units can be brought in. The weapons and equipment that temporarily inducted units leave behind in cantonments, deteriorates due to inadequate maintenance.

Regarding the effect on the morale of the Army, given the fact that approximately 119,000 personnel are involved in exacting and sometimes exasperating and psychologically unsettling counter-insurgency/internal security duties, it can be stated that the Army has borne the rigours of prolonged employment in these operations stoically and resolutely. The nature of LIC is such that it exacts a heavy mental toll due to the absence of a clearly defined uni-directional threat and the assumed omnipresence of armed militants who may suddenly open fire form the least expected direction. The abundance of anti-personnel mines and remotely controlled IEDs and, the lurking fear of a hand grenade being hurled without warning from around a corner on a passing vehicle, also add to the pressures on a soldier's mind. Odd hours of duty and long marches through inhospitable terrain, while braving the vagaries of the weather (which in J&K comprises rain, snow, sleet, fog and blistering winds capable of chilling even a well-clad soldier to the bone marrow), exact a heavy physical toll as well. By all accounts, personnel of the CPOs have also withstood the challenges of internal security operations commendably well. However, the long-term implications of prolonged employment are not yet clear. Maj Gen Arjun Ray writes : "Troops who operate for protracted periods under stressful conditions are bound to suffer from psychological problems as well as disorders." Recently there have been reports that a number of CRPF personnel deployed in J&K have been afflicted by mental disease. These need to be taken note of as the reported incidents may be advance indicators of a larger malaise.

During an interview with the Times of India on the occasion of the 50th anniversary of Army Day, General V P Malik, PVSM, AVSM, ADC, the Chief of the Army Staff (COAS) stated that, "With increasing involvement in counter-insurgency and internal security operations, the operational preparedness was getting diluted.......Prolonged and large-scale deployment is neither good for the Army nor the country." The COAS was only reiterating what he and his predecessors have said on a number of occasions in the past. In the ultimate analysis, it is clear that the prolonged and continued employment of a large number of Army units in counter-insurgency/internal security operations, is likely to result in the reduction of the Army's combat potential and, consequently, in the degradation of India's conventional deterrence, particularly against Pakistan.

The Rashtriya Rifles force was raised to act as the Army's counter-insurgency strike force so that regular infantry battalions would remain available to train and prepare for their primary task even during periods when the Army's employment for counter insurgency/internal security operations is unavoidable. However, under the present circumstances, 36 Rashtriya Rifles battalions have proved to be grossly inadequate for the purpose as the requirement appears to have stabilised at approximately 130 to 135 battalions, including the Rashtriya Rifles battalions. It is imperative that the employment of regular infantry battalions of the Army for counter-insurgency operations be reduced to not more than 30 to 40 at a time so as to overcome the drawbacks of prolonged employment, if it cannot be stopped altogether.

Various options could be considered to find a solution to this problem. Firstly, the number of Rashtriya Rifles attalions could be increased to about 60 and the force given permanency as the counter-insurgency component of the Army, to be funded preferably by the Ministry of Home Affairs to avoid a heavy strain on the Army's budget or through an additionality to be given to the Army budget. Simultaneously, the strength of Assam Rifles could be increased to about 60 battalions (from the present 31). Secondly, a new national level counter-insurgency strike force could be raised with Army leadership and ethos, based on the existing Rashtriya Rifles as a nucleus.

Such a force, to be financed by the Ministry of Home Affairs, could comprise about 100 battalions, to be raised gradually in a phased manner over the 9th, the 10th and the 11th plans. Thirdly, the CRPF could be designated as the national counter-insurgency strike force. (The BSF must go back to its border guarding role which is not being performed with optimal efficiency at present as the force is heavily committed in counter-insurgency/internal security operations. Effective border management is a mandatory pre-requisite if the induction of weapons, ammunition and explosives, as well as foreign mercenaries and foreign trained Indian militants is to be checked and reduced.) The CRPF will need to be re-vamped for this new role and its leadership and training standards will need to be immensely enhanced. The lateral induction of volunteer Army officers with experience of counter-insurgency operations and trained Army instructors in the rank and file will go a long way in re-vamping the CRPF. Each of the options discussed above has several merits as well as many disadvantages. These need to be analysed in detail by a specially constituted joint Army and CPOs study group whose findings should be evaluated by the National Security Advisory Board

(NSAB) of the National Security Council (NSC). Recommendations made by the NSAB should be examined by the NSC and approved for early implementation.

A Solution Remains Elusive

Clearly, India's patience has been stretched almost to the limit and the strain is now showing. Demands for a more pro-active Kashmir policy are becoming vociferous. "The country has exercised restraint against Pakistan's proxy war and shown enough tolerance. We must make the costs unbearable for Pakistan. Why is the nation shying away from exercising the military option? Is there not provocation enough? In a sharply critical article in September 1998, Mr. K Subrahmanyam wrote: "It would appear that the Government of India has no policy about a possible solution to the Kashmir issue but hopes that so long as the issue is kept out of international attention and the insurgency and terrorism are contained through attrition, the problem will go away."

Mr. Farooq Abdullah, the Chief Minister of J&K, a long-standing advocate for recognising the LoC as the international border between India and Pakistan, is now of the view that the Kashmir issue should be frozen for 25 years and that the two countries should build bridges on other aspects like trade, tourism and cultural exchanges. Mr. K.P.S Gill, former Director General of Punjab Police, is critical of the country's reliance on 'the niceties of diplomacy' to resolve the Kashmir problem and says that, "No nation in the world would have displayed the restraint and the patience that we have in the face of the scale and intensity of violence that has been unleashed upon us. It is time, now, to cry halt." However, he acknowledges that "the overwhelming reality is that the people of the sub-continent do not want conflict."

It is axiomatic that there can be no military solution to an insurgency. The security forces can only restore functional normalcy so that the law and order situation is under control and the writ of the civil administration runs in the state. The level of violence can be curtailed to a large extent and the number of incidents can be considerably reduced by co-ordinated operations. However, the security forces cannot eliminate the insurgency. To do that, the root causes of the insurgency have to be identified and tackled and the people's perceived grievances redressed. That is a task which only the civil administration and elected political leaderscan undertake. The security forces can assist by carrying out 'civic action' on behalf of the civil administration, 'show the flag' by virtue of their presence in the area, particularly the villages in the interior, and provide security cover to civil officials to enable them to perform their duties without fear. Exemplary state and national level leadership and a resolute and unwavering political will are necessary to root out insurgency.

A lasting solution to the Kashmir issue can only be found if both the external and the internal dimensions of the problem are successfully addressed, as both are inextricably interlinked. Unless Pakistan 'turns off the tap' of infiltration, no amount of effort, both military and civilian, will succeed in eliminating militancy from J&K. By now it should be clear to Pakistan that its proxy war will not succeed under any circumstances and that it would be in its own interest to renounce this path and seek mutually beneficial co-operation with India. However, George Santayana's classic definition of a fanatic is that he is a person who re-doubles his effort on losing sight of his goal. The fanatics in the Pakistani Army and the ISI can only be expected to re-double their efforts.

It is difficult to believe that the Pakistani Government does not understand that its sponsorship of insurgencies and its support to virulently fundamentalist organisations such as the Taliban militia, will eventually boomerang on Pakistan itself. It does not require great prescience to predict that the Taliban backlash is eventually bound to create unmanageable problems for Pakistan. Perhaps, having created a Frankenstein monster, the Pakistanis now find it difficult to regain control; or, they have deluded themselves into believing that they can get away with it lightly. Either way, Pakistan is apparently set on a course of self destruction.

In case the present proxy war leads to conventional or, even the unthinkable, nuclear war, it should be obvious to the Pakistanis that they will suffer much more than India. During an address to the National Defence College, New Delhi, General V P Malik, the COAS, warned that, "Pakistan's proxy war is dangerous not only for India but for the entire region. If militancy grows too big, both the initiator and the affected nation are tempted to use conventional means of war." Perhaps, the civilian rulers of Pakistan have already gone too far with the latitude given to the ISI and the Pakistani Army to wage a proxy war against India and are now unable to control the Frankenstein monster. The February 1999 massacre in Rajouri and Udhampur districts, masterminded by the ISI to coincide with Indian Prime Minister Vajpayee's bus ride to Lahore, could not possibly have been timed to send a message to the Indian Government as such incidents often have been in the past. This time, clearly, the message was from the Pakistan Army-ISI-Jamaat e Islami combine to Pakistan Prime Minister Nawaz Sharif, and its essence was: "Shake hands, play cricket and hockey, open up trade and encourage people-to-people contacts if you wish; however, lay off Kashmir—that is our agenda and it is non-negotiable."

Nevertheless, India should continue to strive to achieve normalcy in its relations with Pakistan and must keep all channels of communications open. Mr. K Subrahmanyam recommends that: "India should put forward a whole series of confidence building measures (CBMs) to reduce tension and restore peace in Jammu and Kashmir to enable meaningful negotiations between India and Pakistan. This should include an open skies plan along the border, international observers to check on Pakistani camps of terrorist organisations and agreed mining and fencing of borders." However, as long as Pakistan remains intransigent and believes that holding bilateral talks with India is futile, as advocated by the former Foreign Minister, Mr. Gohar Ayub Khan, prior to the Colombo summit meeting between the two Prime Ministers in July 1998, India should remain aware that not much is likely to be achieved by India's continued pursuance of the diplomatic option. Pakistan's efforts to secure third party mediation are irreconcilable with India's approach hat the problems between the two countries be resolved bilaterally in the spirit of the Shimla agreement.

India must project the Kashmir issue as one of international fundamentalist Islamic terrorism with widespread adverse ramifications, including for the western nations. Osama Bin Laden's terrorist training bases in Afghanistan which were hit by US cruise missiles in August 1998, were also training terrorists for operations in J&K. Mr. Naresh Chandra, India's Ambassador to the US, recently highlighted the convergence of Indian and US interests on terrorism : "Both India and the United States have been victims of terrorism perpetrated by individuals trained and equipped in the same schools of crime near India's borders." It would be in India's interest to further highlight through diplomatic channels and by launching a concerted public information/awareness campaign that Pakistan is the 'mother nation' of Islamic fundamentalist terrorism. The US State Department has so far been reluctant to list Pakistan as a sponsor of international terrorism "because of warnings by Pakistani Prime Ministers that such action would unravel the country's fledgling democracy and drive it into the hands of the virulently anti-American extremists." The US needs to be convinced that turning a blind eye to Pakistan's sponsorship of terrorism neither augurs well for peace and stability in the Southern Asian region, nor is it in the US' own long-term interest.

Regarding the internal dimension of the Kashmir problem, there is a lot more that can still be done. The first and foremost is the issue of the general consensus within the country to initiate talks with the militants. Mr. Prem Shankar Jha, a noted columnist, is of the opinion that the Muslims in Kashmir are not prepared to go back to the way things were before 1990. He writes: "Needless to say, India cannot offer independence to J&K, but if the Government wants a peaceful settlement in Kashmir, it must drop its insistence that it will hold talks with the militants only under the Constitution. This position......... is a non-starter.........The Government should have the courage to drop its insistence and agree to hold talks with the militants without pre-conditions." Mr. Muchkund Dubey, a former Foreign Secretary, recommends "opening a broad-based dialogue embracing all sections of society and evolving an acceptable package containing, among others, a cast iron guarantee that the experience of the recent past will never be repeated."

While consenting to hold talks with the militant groups is undoubtedly desirable, the issue raises several questions with major practical implications for ongoing counter-insurgency operations. Firstly, who represents the militants? The All Party Hurriyat Conference (APHC) is a fractured coalition of disparate political parties with discredited leaders. Surely, the Indian Government cannot be expected to hold talks with leaders of Pakistan-sponsored and controlled militant outfits like the Hizbul Mujahideen and Harkat ul Ansar. Secondly, is a cease-fire to be declared, as in Nagaland? If so, what is the guarantee that it will be observed faithfully by the militants? Who will ensure that Pakistani-sponsored militant outfits also adhere to the cease-fire agreement, or are they to be left out of the talks process? Will it then make sense to pursue negotiations at all? Thirdly, can the Government of India agree to hold talks with the Kashmiri militants without pre-conditions till the unanimous resolution of Parliament on the Kashmir issue is rescinded? Is it not necessary to first build a national consensus on the issue, given the presence of ultra right wing elements in some political parties who have been vociferously demanding that Article 370 of the Constitution (which confers a special status on the State of J&K), be scrapped? Finally, how is it to be ensured that whatever agreement is reached with the militant groups will be acceptable to the Government of Pakistan?

Obviously, it is difficult to see any light at the end of the tunnel as there are no easy answers to this intractable problem. The most pragmatic way ahead appears to be to further synergise counter-insurgency operation in J&K so as to bring about functional normalcy all over the state as early as possible, while simultaneously stepping up the industrial development of the State and the socio-economic upliftment of the people. The creation of employment opportunities for the youth, including schemes for self-employment, should be a high priority point for action. The Sufi tradition of tolerance and liberalism, for which Kashmir is well known, should be encouraged to bloom unhindered by the diktats of radical Islam.

A sustained political campaign must be immediately launched to win the 'hearts and minds' of the Kashmiri people, assuage their feelings of hurt and neglect and restore their bruised and battered dignity. The people of J&K need to be convinced that their future lies with India. However, J&K will need to be given a large measure of autonomy; indeed, this demand is entirely in keeping with the federal structure of the Indian Constitution and has been recommended strongly for all the states by the Sarkaria Commission. The hands of Mr. Farooq Abdullah's administration should be strengthened so that the Kashmir Government can further enhance the quality of its battle against militancy on all fronts. And, the Government must launch a sustained media campaign, both within the country and abroad, to highlight Pakistan's deep-rooted involvement in fostering terrorism and insurgency in J&K and other parts of India. International pressure must be brought to bear on Pakistan to desist from its nefarious interference in India's internal affairs and to stop sponsoring Islamic fundamentalist terrorism in the Southern Asian region and other parts of the world.

Above all, public opinion must be mobilised to express the nation's solidarity with the Kashmiri people in their long drawn out and courageous struggle against Pakistan-sponsored proxy war.

7

Pakistan Supporting Taliban: Proxy War in Afghanistan

Strange as it may seem to the outside observer, the last two decades in the history of Pakistan and Afghanistan have led to a situation wherein the two countries are invariably taken together as one. The evolution of the term "Pakistan-Afghanistan" region in any discussion on narcotics, terrorism, money laundering or gun running underlines the extent to which a once proudly independent country has been subsumed and nearly incorporated into the ambitious state next door. That such an event has occurred during the supposedly civilised times that we now live in—when virtual annexations are considered unthinkable—is difficult to accept. Yet for all practical purposes, the sinews of the state of Afghanistan lie in Pakistan. The currency used is Pakistani rupees, its border now no longer exists even on paper, and much of its "armed forces" are either Pakistani or linked to that country in diverse ways.

Yet it is to the constant worry of Pakistani policy-makers, that the process is not yet complete. One slice of Afghan territory continues to be held by the recognised government of Afghanistan, that of President Rabbani, while the rest is under the dubious control of a group that remains beholden to Pakistan for everything but its name.

Having said as much, it must be noted that the costs to Pakistan of this "virtual annexation" have been inordinately heavy. There is much to show that these costs also include the sacking of a democratic government by a military that has its own agenda in Afghanistan. Socially, the costs have been the most obvious, as Pakistan threatens to spin out of control in a paroxysm of violence that pits different radical religious sects against each other, in what observers call the "Talibanisation" of Pakistan. Diplomatically, Pakistan stands accused by both friends and others of being the main supporter of terrorism that emanates from Afghanistan. Economically, the constant violence and mayhem in financial centres like Karachi has meant a flight of capital and loss of foreign investment. Politically, the country has been the loser, with democracy once again hijacked, and the new regime justifying its move on the slogan that the greatest threat to Pakistan was internal and not external (that this statement was made at the same time that the army was planning its Kargil War is another matter).

Two sets of variables, therefore, influence the future Pakistani policy towards its western neighbour. First, Pakistan has to get its own internal situation under control and remove armed gangs and around five million weapons from its streets. In short, the state of Pakistan has to control the streets and to be seen as doing so. Development and investor confidence are directly linked to this event. Second, and linked to this is the fact that investor confidence can hardly invent itself as long as Pakistan stands suspect of providing sustenance and support to an array of terrorist groups, and, thus, remains virtually under the shadow of being declared a terrorist state. Pakistan has to either tame the tiger that it has created, or give up all its objectives in Afghanistan. On the ground this means that Pakistan has to win—and quickly—so that the Taliban can lay claim to the UN seat, and the stability that is assumed to go along with it. If it does not do so, then it must consider the alternatives.

This chapter traces Pakistan-Afghanistan relations in the period after Kargil, when the focus of international attention on the region was sharpened in the wake of the hijacking of an Indian Airlines aircraft, the sacking of a prime minister, and the ambitions of a military that appears to realise that this could very well be its last chance at ruling the country. This period is also evocative of the pulls and pressures within Pakistan, and indeed—as mentioned at the beginning of this chapter—provides a brief on Pakistan itself during an important phase of its history.

For the sake of cogent analysis, the paper begins with a summary of what Pakistan's objectives were to begin with in launching the Taliban. This is followed by a brief review of Pakistan-Taliban relations in the first phase (November 1994-June 1999), with the objective of getting an answer to two crucial and interrelated questions: Has Pakistan been able to achieve its objectives in Afghanistan? What are the constraints that apply to a full realisation of these objectives with regard to the new regime? In the final analysis, does Pakistan "control" Afghanistan? It must be noted that "control" here is taken to mean that the primary actor can influence the behaviour and actions of the secondary actor so as to lead to an outcome that is perceived as being satisfactory to the former and reasonably so to the latter.

Constants or Add Ons?: Pakistan's Objectives in Afghanistan

As is now well known, Islamabad began its campaign of covert war in Afghanistan as early as 1973, when it began to arm and train batches of 30-40 disaffected elements, an operation that was carried out with help from the CIA (Central Intelligence Agency), according to the then governor of the Frontier Provinces, General Fazle Haq. The former governor of the Frontier Provinces Maj General Nasirullah Babbar also confirms that Pakistan began training and arming of disaffected Afghans in 1973. Between 1973-77, Pakistan trained an estimated 5,000 dissidents and channelled aid to the Hazaras located in central Afghanistan. This programme, started by Prime Minister Zulfiqar Ali Bhutto, was essentially a move against the regime of Sardar Daud who was a strong proponent of "Pashtunistan"—which was essentially diplo-speak for Afghan ambitions on what was undoubtedly Pashtun territory in Pakistan. The operation nearly achieved its aims, since Kabul is said to have come calling to discuss the possibility of recognition of the Durand Line.

However, as the Soviets moved in, matters changed completely. The region was sucked into the vortex of Cold War competition, as American "aid"—which started at about $30 million in 1980 and exceeded $ one billion a year by 19895—began to flow into the region. The operation, which was controlled by the Inter-Services Intelligence (ISI) of Pakistan, tied in with the original objectives, as well as appeared to fit in with new ones. The Pashtun problem was subsumed under the banner of jehad, thus, propagating a pan-Islamic identity rather than an ethno-nationalist one. At one stroke, this negated what had till then been Kabul's trump card, and allowed Islamabad to hunt with the "devil" and run with the hounds. US aid was, thus, legitimised in the greater Islamic cause, even as Pakistan was projected as the courageous adversary against the Reds (the indifference of the government during the mob attack on the US embassy in November 1979 apparently having been forgotten).

Other objectives in this second phase were important "add ons". The nuclear programme initiated under Bhutto was clearly not one that the Americans would be at all comfortable with. The astute General Zia, therefore, managed to tie in Pakistan's new found status to the US turning a blind eye to its activities in this field. Moreover, a considerable amount of military equipment began to arrive for the courageous ally, all of which was supposed to protect it from the might of the Soviets. Aircraft, guns and tanks flowed into the armouries of Pakistan, even as the ISI was presented with the greatest gift of all—an unprecedented supply of light weapons, finance (in the form of drugs money) and no accountability. In the evocative words of a Pakistani intelligence officer. "We could have conducted operations on Mars..."

The third phase began in 1992 with the withdrawal of the superpowers, and the unexpected resilience of the Najibullah regime. The equally unexpected disappearance of the Soviet Union led to an expansion of Pakistan's aims. If the nominally Islamic regimes of Central Asia could be brought under the Pakistani fold (especially since it offered the nearest outlet to the sea that was not actively opposed by the US) this would mean an end to Pakistan's "South Asia—minimal power" status, and the emergence of Pakistan as "a pillar of the Muslim world."

However, by 1994, even existing trade between the Central Asian Republics (CARs) and Pakistan had stopped due to the chaos of infighting in Afghanistan. The truckers mafia controlled by the Pashtuns (who had enriched themselves considerably during the massive covert operation) began to pressure their own "man" in upper circles—the interior minister and former trouble shooter for Afghanistan, General (retd.) Nasirullah Babbar. Within Pakistan itself, Benazir Bhutto was trying to wrest the control of state policy, including foreign policy, from the ISI.

Thus, it was that the Taliban—groups of religious students who had indeed been operating even during the time of the jehad—were brought under the wing of the Interior Ministry, a fact that is now openly admitted by the general himself. And, thus, was born the force that was in a completely different operation than had been done before. This was so open as to mock the tag of "covert" assistance, so large as to make it a near "bottom up" exercise, and so extensive that it was difficult to think of one area where that force could manage on its own.

As observers note, everything from the tin plates for the rucksacks to the communications lines were Pakistani delivered. Thus, the objective now was the sustenance and creation of an army that was well equipped, and that was to be simply an extension of the Pakistan Army in all but name. (That the US had a fair—but unknown—share in the equipping of this army meant that some of the benefits would have to be shared with the US.)

Thus, it was that following an extensive review of army doctrine which led to the propagation of the doctrine of "offensive defence" (and the use of the Mujahideen during the exercise which preceded it), General Aslam Beg was heard to say that "Afghanistan and Pakistan were two countries but one people…and any future war will be our war, which gives the Pakistan army added capability". This perception was outlined in an article in a prominent defence journal which noted that the inclusion of the 500,000 battle-trained Mujahideen to the 500,000-strong Pakistan Army would forever change the balance of power on the Indo-Pakistani subcontinent. This emerged as the last point (so far) of the evolution of Pakistani policy and objectives towards Afghanistan. Thus, what started as a "border conflict", escalated into an objective of controlling an entire country as well as using it to further irredentist claims elsewhere.

The Taliban Today

However, all of this assumed that the "Taliban" would remain a fairly disciplined body that would prove amenable to Pakistani prodding, and grateful for assistance. Indeed, there was every reason to suppose that this prodding would succeed, given that Pakistani "assistance" was complete in certain crucial areas:

- Weapons and ammunition.
- Tactical direction.
- Training.
- Recruitment.

Additionally, it was the Pakistani knowledge (and leverage) with different commanders that "persuaded" them (either with money or the promise of a quick demise) to join up with the Taliban—which did much to propagate the false idea that this was a "social" movement rather than a propped up Kandahari clique.

Pakistani assistance at crucial points—like during the fall of Kandahar—emerged as a critical factor. When this was not present, the Taliban forays tended to be rather unsuccessful, revealing a poor knowledge of conventional battle (which is usually anathema to the average Pashtun). At a later date, Pakistani assistance to an extent was also able to hold together the Taliban "forces" which displayed a tendency to drift away once their own areas had been cleaned up. The input of continuous recruitment from the Pakistani side was, therefore, crucial. In addition to this were the following areas of assistance which tied Afghanistan with an umbilical cord of considerable strength to the Pakistani economy and politics:

- Fuel.
- Communications (telephone lines were linked to Peshawar).
- Road building.
- Technicians for airports, aircraft.
- Medical assistance.
- Cheap wheat imports (which prevented the growth of wheat in Afghanistan to replace the poppy crop).
- Funding (through drug caravans and the Afghan Trade and Transit Agreement—ATTA).

- Most importantly, as a diplomatic conduit

But this kind of intense Pakistani linkage was bound to affect the evolution of the Taliban itself. What started out as a genuinely local and highly ideologically orientated group has today become something of a mixed bunch. While the top echelons around Mullah Omar to an extent continue along the same lines, the motivations of the rest are naturally affected by the opportunities offered by their linkages across the border, and their own persuasions.

Some points need to be noted here regarding the creation of the Taliban. While the Taliban came out of the files of the Interior Ministry (with over 65,000 troops commanded by a serving army officer) it still had to have the approval of the army brass—especially the Pashtun sections.

The bottom most rung (which is the largest) has within it the few who have survived the initial battles of the Taliban (which were simply disorganised massed attacks) and who are still perhaps fired by ideology. Another segment of this same rung is made up of foreigners of various persuasions, some of whom (like the Pakistan Occupied Kashmir (POK) Pakistanis and some Kashmiris) are there to be "trained", including the AI Queda of Osama Bin Laden. At this level are those who have joined from Pakistani madrassas (the youngest age group) and the ones most prone to sliding into a life of crime or perpetual war.

The Pakistani segment is also the most useful in maintaining the facade of a jehad against the evil forces of the "West supported" Northern Alliance, and being relatively better educated, are most useful in handling communications and logistics. At the obverse end it also means that it gives Pakistan a vast and permanent intelligence gathering unit into almost every aspect of Taliban activity. This then is the Taliban which is accused of subverting Pakistan itself, and spreading terrorism into the neighbouring areas.

PAKISTAN AND THE TALIBAN—POST-KARGIL

By mid-1999, extensive reports of the Pakistani involvement in the Kargil conflict, as well as the Pakistani nexus with terrorism in Afghanistan at almost every level made prominent stories. News analysis underlined the Harkat-ul-Ansar's nodal role in allotting trainees to their different sectors and their importance in running the training camps. Reports noted that more than 8,000 Pakistanis were in the Taliban ranks with a diplomat quoted as saying, "The state is privatising war to advance its own goals". Photographs of Pakistani prisoners of war only added to this impression. In July 1999, the UN envoy for Afghanistan, Lakhdar Brahmi, was noting the involvement of Pakistani youth in what was essentially a local war. He noted, "They call it jehad. Nobody else does".

The US ambassador to Pakistan had taken the somewhat unprecedented step in May 1999 to publicly caution Pakistan that it risked antagonising the US if it continued to pursue its pro-Taliban policy. Policy circles in Pakistan saw this as additional pressure on Pakistan to use its influence on the Taliban. Indeed, the ambassador said as much, claiming that Pakistan was assisting the Taliban in "different fields". In August, exactly a year after the east African bombing of US embassies, rumours were rife that the US was moving in special forces to capture Bin Laden. This set the cat among the pigeons.

The rumour was given credence by Qatari TV which announced that two US military aircraft had landed at airports in Pakistan and commandos had taken up positions around the field. This led to a clarion call from Mullah Omar for "all Muslim states to stand by Afghanistan" and an outpouring of venom from extremist parties within Pakistan. The relatively moderate Jamaat-e-Islami—perhaps in a venture to appear even more revolutionary than the rest—joined issue with the Jamiat-e-Ulema-e-Islam (JUI) (Fazlur) which had already been threatening Washington with a hit "within 8 hours" of any act against Osama Bin Laden while the JUI (Samiul Haque) was equally graphic in its threats. Miranshah, Waziristan and other Pashtun tribal areas appeared to be up in arms against possible US action. This was followed by a massive exodus of Afghan youths (mostly under 17) from the madrassas of Pakistan. Reports from Pakistan noted that "thousands" of youths were enrolling in the Taliban ranks. Indeed, large madrassas like the

Darul Uloom Haqqania (Akora Khattak) remained shut for 10 days in response to the message from the Taliban leader. This was confirmed by the Taliban spokesman who noted that the students included both Pakistanis and Afghans sent to study in the seminaries. Clearly matters appeared to be coming to a head.

Meanwhile "consultations" were on, with Pakistan sponsoring talks at Dushanbe, with a contingent led interestingly by Interior Ministry officials. This was apparently aimed at power sharing arrangements with the Opposition but ended with the latter refusing to discuss a settlement till Pakistan stopped supporting the Taliban. Commander Masood was heard to note that over 1,000 Pakistani officers were present in Kabul to advise and assist the Taliban. The Taliban in its turn accused the Opposition forces of liaising with the Israelis, an accusation that seems to have been aimed at ending Iranian support for the group.

In Parliament, enraged senators—stung after the defeat at Kargil and using it as a bludgeon against the ruling party—were ironically warning that this constituted a "naked intervention" in the affairs of a neighbouring country. Across Pakistan, there was a rash of sectarian terrorist attacks (13 sectarian incidents in 10 days) adding fuel to the perceived threat from the "Talibanisation" and the spread of weapons from the war next door.

Within the government, tensions were high enough to be palpable. The post-Kargil rift between the inner decision-makers and the army was again apparent. In September 1999, a rather unusual number of persons were hurrying to Washington. One was Punjab Chief Minister Shahbaz Sharif, and the other was the Director General (DG) of the ISI, Lt General Ziauddin. Prominent papers speculated on these sudden visits, especially since the army chief had yet to make a visit (General Musharraf—unlike most of his fellow officers—has had no training/courses in the US at all). Sharif is said to have met Deputy Secretary of State Strobe Talbott, and Assistant Secretary of State for South Asia Karl Inderfurth among others. An in-camera meeting of the Cabinet (minus the military secretary) furthered rumours. Meanwhile, the visit of the ISI chief was declared as "routine consultations" though other reports noted that the DG was asked for a briefing in response to a fear of a "Talibanisation of a nuclear armed Pakistan".

Reliable reports from Pakistan noted that the US had warned the Pakistanis about a possible "international reaction" to Pakistan's failure to prevent patronage of terrorism. The threat of placing Pakistan under the State Department's list of terrorist states was reportedly held out. Side by side, it was known that the US was piloting a proposal at the UN Security Council for sanctions against the Taliban.

Many of these stories were confirmed when the DG-ISI visited Kabul with the "request" that the Taliban shut down terrorist training camps in Afghanistan. This reportedly led to an impasse with the army which had always controlled Afghan operations—though this was done through the front of the ISI. The Army Chief General Musharraf—who had taken the precaution of appointing his loyalists like General Mahmud Aziz as deputy chief of the ISI and packed other posts with his own men—ordered that all matters concerning Afghanistan would be shifted to the chief of General Staff's office. This was an absolute challenge to the political brass, who were not slow in responding.

In October 1999, the prime minister himself made the startling announcement that he had asked the supreme leader of the Taliban to shut down the terrorist camps. This charge was, according to him, made on "solid" evidence that had been put together for him by the intelligence agencies. As a daily observed, "Who on earth can believe that it was only last week that Islamabad came to know about Pakistanis given military training?" The overwhelming opinion was that this was a signal to official agencies to delink themselves from all militant groups—at least those under US scrutiny. But curiously, it was also noted that this "paradigm shift" had not even been discussed in the Defence Committee of the Cabinet (DCC) nor was the army given a perspective over the warnings from the US.

The prime minister's blunt message was hastily reworked by the Foreign Ministry which noted that the Taliban was helping Pakistan to deal with the problem, and that while Afghanistan was indeed a base, the Taliban was hardly involved. Sartaj Aziz noted that the Taliban's "help" was solicited, and this was hardly an unprecedented step. He claimed that the Taliban was not in control of the whole of Afghanistan, and indeed Pakistan "was not concerned whether or not people get training in Afghanistan. But when it comes to Pakistan, it becomes a key issue." To buttress this, the administration launched an anti-sectarian sweep in which over 100 men of the extremist Sipah-e-Sahaba were arrested.

The Taliban leadership reacted to this volte face, by noting that a clear distinction be made between terrorists and freedom fighters (a point of view that was to have a significant impact on the following government). One observer noted presciently"...the government is currently trapped between a rock and a hard place. In any case it will lose..."

The backlash from the Islamists was that the Nawaz "discovery" of Pakistanis being trained in Afghanistan was simply paving the way for US action, while news analysts were also wondering at this paradigm shift in Pakistan-Afghanistan relations, and the possible motivations for such a swift change. In Afghanistan, the threat had some curious effects. Mullah Omar announced that Afghanistan was ready to talk on terrorism to anyone in the world. Alongside this, however, he ordered a massive reshuffle in the Taliban administration. Some of the changes made are worthy of note here. Mullah Wakil Ahmed Muttawakil was elevated from the post of spokesman to that of foreign minister. An old guard Taliban like Mullah Khairkhawa was shifted out from the post of interior minister to governor of Herat, as well as the Helmand areas. Mullah Akunzada (once a powerful force in Helmand in the pre-Taliban days, and linked closely with the Pakistani elite) was made corps commander, Kabul. Mullah "Rocketi", known to have been responsible for the kidnapping of Chinese engineers, and an arms dealer for the Taliban, was moved from the sensitive Jalalabad area to the western frontier. Essentially this saw a shift of power to the core Taliban, while those with close connections to the Pakistani institutions or other circles were moved out of the areas near the Pakistani border.

This appeared to be in reaction to reports that Pakistani contingents, with CIA assistance, were moving to attack Afghan camps. On October 10, 1999, reports appeared of these groups, put at around 30-50 each, moving out from Torkham and Chaman.

This was apparently "confirmed" by bureaucrats, but there was no independent assessment nor indeed any further news of these commando raids. Whether they existed at all is open to some doubt. But the Afghan side obviously felt it was serious enough to quickly upgrade security at sensitive camps. Clearly, there was a rift between Islamabad and Kabul—real or simply created for the moment—with the former fearing air strikes, and the latter doing everything it could to fuel the stories in the Press of a "turnaround" in Pakistani policy.

On October 12, another incident highlighted the flux within the relationship. Mullah Omar was targetted in a truck bombing which narrowly missed killing him though it did hit several senior commanders. Oddly enough, the chief made haste to note that the USA was "not involved"—a statement that led to renewed suspicions that at least some sections of the US Administration still had "connections" with the Taliban. On October 12, 1999, the army took over power.

THE TALIBAN AND THE NEW REGIME

Ironically, the man who had planned Kargil and headed an institution that incorporated the use of jehadi irregulars as part and parcel of its strategy was initially seen as a "moderate" element who would prove to be more harsh on the Taliban extremist policies. Few cared to remember that the general had once been closely working with Bin Laden himself during the Afghan operations, and had used the group to quell a Shia uprising in Gilgit. However, to his credit, the general, while unorthdox in his methods, was apparently motivated by realpolitik rather than religion. In January 1999, he was heard to warn of internal dangers to Pakistan being at the forefront while he pointed to the "zero" possibility of war with India even as preparations for just such a war had been set afoot. Realpolitik, therefore, demanded that Pakistan do a little shifting and changing in its policy towards Kabul—even as the objectives were kept intact. Thus, General Musharraf appeared to have soothed the fears of the US ambassador when he called for a representative government in Kabul and indeed showed all initial signs of sweeping with a new broom in the country's foreign policy.

Meanwhile, the UNSC (United Nations Security Council) passed the resolution to impose limited sanctions on the Taliban (October 15) but which was due to go into effect as of November 14, 1999. Acting under Chapter VII of the Charter of the UN, the Security Council determined that the Taliban's failure to respond to demands to stop terrorism constituted a threat to international peace and security. The crucial clauses were that the Taliban give up shelter to, and training of, international terrorists, and use of the territory "under its control" for terrorist installations and camps, or for the preparation or organisation of terrorist acts against other states or their citizens. Another clause specifically demanded the handing over of Osama bin Laden to "appropriate authorities" who would bring him to justice. The next move of the new government appeared to contradict its stated posture.

It ordered the release of goods imported under the ATTA—a huge source of smuggling for the Taliban and the Pakistani transborder mafia—and additionally was reported to have waived Rs 8 billion worth of excise duty on these goods. Considering that Pakistan has been extremely shrill on the ramifications of the ATTA trade and the huge losses in revenue to the staggering economy, this was a surprising development. A few days later, the new administration was faced with yet another crisis. Just two days before the UN sanctions were to take effect, a series of seven rockets were fired at the US embassy, UN building, American cultural centre and downtown government buildings, wounding at least six people. All seven attacks appeared to have occurred within a two-minute time span, and were fired from cars parked in the vicinity. Representative Frank Pallone blamed Pakistan and its unstinting support for the Taliban, but the attackers themselves remained unidentified. Former chief of the ISI Javed Nasir, accused the Masood faction of perpetrating the blasts, while others pointed a finger at the Taliban, since it was they who had been "warning" against the imposition of sanctions. Mullah Omar himself condemned the blasts as "unIslamic"—which was at one with his earlier hair-splitting on what constituted terrorism and what constituted violence permitted by jehad.

With the sanctions coming into effect, Iran moved to open borders with the Taliban (at Islam Quilla), indicating its contempt for what was seen as US-sponsored sanctions, as well as its decision to keep the doors open to talks with the Taliban. Moves were also made to reopen the consulate—a move that was viewed with concern in Pakistani intelligence circles. Iran followed this up with two simultaneous conferences in Rome and Iran, which propagated the return of Zahir Shah and the calling of a loya jirga.

The sanctions themselves were, however, rather a sham. They required Pakistan—and other neighbours—to cut off diplomatic relations with Afghanistan, as well as all funds by "their nationals, or by any persons within their territory, to or for the benefit of the Taliban or any undertaking, owned or controlled, directly or indirectly, by the Taliban." As a former president of the Quetta Chamber of Commerce noted, the Taliban—or those who lived within those territories—hardly had any need for banking facilities, since all transactions were made in cash. Besides, all large deals were made in Pakistani rupees. The sanctions apparently helped boost the profits of the smugglers, and encourage the existing cross-border illegal trade to a considerable degree. This was apparent as an acute flour crisis deepened in the Frontier regions, and observers pointed out that this was due to the complicity of border officials with smugglers. The importance of the illicit trade in post-Taliban Afghanistan is underlined by Ahmed Rashid who notes that this rose from a mere $128 million in 1992-93 to a staggering $2.5 billion in 1997, which is more than half of Afghanistan's estimated gross domestic product (GDP). When the income from narcotics smuggling is added, this, according to Rashid, should amount to $5 billion. Thus, it was hardly surprising that the UN sought a report from Pakistan on the steps taken by it to impose sanctions.

Meanwhile, the Taliban responded by opening yet another border post (Nawa Pass) to apparently facilitate the crossing of relatives and others. However, Foreign Minister Abdul Sattar announced that all Taliban accounts had been frozen and that Pakistan would respect the sanctions. How this would affect the reported $2.5 billion illegal trade with Afghanistan, and the supply of all essential commodities and services (including electricity and communications) remained unclear.

Meanwhile, the administration sent home some 120,000 Afghan refugees, even as it sought "world neutrality" on Afghanistan. Speaking at the UN, Pakistan's ambassador noted that it was unproductive to demonise one side, and backed the six-plus-two initiatives as the only way out of the conflict. This statement appeared to be in reaction to a report by UN Secretary General Kofi Annan that castigated the Taliban's dismal human rights record, the increasing terrorising of the population, as well as the growing presence of thousands of young volunteers—some children under the age of 14—from religious schools in Pakistan.

The hijacking of the Indian Airlines flight from Nepal to Kandahar appeared to underline the role of the Pakistani connection. Indian decision-makers noted that radio intercepts between the hijackers and their contacts in Pakistan, and the later disappearance of the hijackers into Pakistan underlined the thesis. The Taliban's attitude was, however, more mixed. On the one hand, they offered cooperation on the issue, but, on the other, they effectively prevented any commando action by the Indians. Analysts noted that both the Indian negotiators and the hijackers had been pressurised by the Taliban, indicating a savvy and confident negotiating stance from the Taliban. This was further apparent as Taliban fighters simply lounged around the aircraft and drank tea, and to all appearances seemed content to sense no threat to anyone. The only jolt to this was the unexpected demand for a ransom of $200 million by the hijackers. This was one demand that was not only negotiable but might have been accepted by the Indians, especially since it clearly exposed the motivations of the "freedom fighters". Islamist groups as well as Taliban spokesmen noted that they were "stunned" by the demand, since this would make the hijackers lose whatever sympathy they might have gained. As it happened, this demand was denounced as "unIslamic" (condoning apparently the seizure of innocents as Islamic) before New Delhi could react, raising suspicions that the "cooperation" hid ulterior motives. Other sources like the Washington Post also noted, "Afghanistan and Pakistan are trying to have it both ways on terrorism. They play host to terrorist groups yet wax indignant when terrorists hijack an aircraft or...blow up US embassies."

International Reactions: The Pace Hots Up

A surprising event thereafter underlined the slowly building consensus among neighbours that Pakistan needed to rein in terrorism. China, long-time friend and nuclear ally, for the first time lodged a protest with Pakistan, noting the training that was being given to terrorists on its soil. This evidence had been unearthed after the arrest of 16 Shia Muslims in China. For the first time, China also noted the existence of 1,600 active members of the "Party of Allah" which was said to use heroin for funding terrorism. Noticeably, after pleading the porosity of Pakistan's border in regard to the entry of the hijackers, Pakistan was able to do a thorough search and "credibly" inform China that there was no evidence of any such movement or camps in any part of the tribal areas.

On January 16, 2000, the Taliban announced the formal recognition of Chechnya—a statement that led to a Russian outcry not only against the Taliban but also against Pakistan for its failure to prevent such an outcome. Russia's ire increased as former President of Chechnya Zelim Khan was accorded a huge welcome in Pakistan from the Islamists, even as he appears to have met all the leading policy-makers. Following the imposition of sanctions, Russia also noted that over 100 trucks had crossed over from Pakistan with ammunition and weapons for the Taliban units for the spring offensive.

A curious report at the tail end of the hijacking noted that Saudi Arabia had expressed annoyance that "scores of Arab militants" had been flown out of Peshawar around December 29, 1999, and were sent to Saudi Arabia, according to an Interior Ministry source. These men apparently had fake Afghan passports and had dispersed for unknown reasons. Yet another source noted that Egyptian terrorists were carrying fake Pakistani passports. Most telling of an apparent "isolation" of Pakistan was the refusal of the Turkish prime minister to visit Pakistan, lambasting the supporters of the Taliban, even as he made a trip to India.

Prior to the visit of the US president, there was a spate of reports from the US which specifically charged Osama Bin Laden and the Harkat-ul-Ansar with supporting the terrorist groups in Kashmir. However, M.R. Sheehan, the chief coordinator on anti-terrorism also noted that the Taliban fondly remembered US assistance in their freedom struggle, "I also believe that they do not want individuals or organisations to plan and conduct terrorist operations from their soil." This obviously meant that other powers or individuals were using Afghan territory for their own ends.

Back in Pakistan, Masood Azhar, the militant freed by New Delhi in the hijack incident—after a few days in "protective custody"—was received with fanfare at Banuri Masjid in Karachi. This is one of the many large seminaries that are often overlooked, and it remains one of the largest seminaries of "revolutionary" Deobandi activity, and the main sponsor of Harkat activity, according to Pakistani sources. The announcement of the formation of a new party, the "Jaish Mohammad" was made under the aegis of this seminary, led by Mufti Shamzai. The mufti is understood to be closely linked to Mullah Omar, and is respected by the various tiers of Taliban leadership. The subsequent declaration of a jehad against the US and India only served to confirm India's contention that the "religious scholar" was far from being simply an ideologue.

Plea of Talibanisation

Meanwhile, continuing evidence of Pakistanis being trained in Afghanistan (Isphol camp), with the Harkat ul-Ansar evidently involved at all stages, came to light even as reports of a group leaving for Chechnya surfaced in the Press. Other reports noted that Pakistan had the largest private army of Islamists, while yet others noted the "Afghan connection" to Islamic extremism—in particular the activities of the Harkat-ul-Ansar with its training camps in Afghanistan—with the Rishkor camp reportedly "supervised" by the dreaded Pakistani terrorist Riaz Basra (an ex-Mujahideen) and those in Pakistan itself on the Muzzafarabad road, and other areas of POK. The trend of these various articles was unmistakable—that the powerful Islamist lobby was slowly trying to seize political power, assisted by a well-armed and trained army. This was the essence of the warning of "Talibanisation" of Pakistan, where the onus was on Kabul for unleashing violent sectarianism on Pakistan. This tied in with the projection of the new regime as one that was against such activities and which condemned "terrorism" even while it supported self-determination. Such ideas were furthered when Qazi Hussain obligingly noted in London that were it not for the army, the Islamists would have been able to seize power. That this was completely negated by the admission of prominent jehadis—who should certainly be in the know—was not generally observed. The leader of the Lashkar-e-Taiba and others were heard to say that Nawaz Sharif's last days had proved to be tough, and that the army's return was, quite literally, an answer to their prayers. In fact, he noted that the coming of the army had led to the release of several jailed jehadis who had been imprisoned during the latter period of the Sharif government.

This kind of twin-track policy was apparent in the period prior to the Clinton visit. On the one hand, efforts were made to convince the media and the international community that Pakistan was indeed for taking action against terrorists for the sake of its own security, even as the same jehadi policy that encouraged terrorists in the first place was hardly touched. In fact, the focus of attention was kept continuously on Afghanistan, and the issue of "terrorism" that emanated from there.

Following a further protest by China, General Musharraf announced a surprise visit to Kabul and his decision to talk turkey to Mullah Omar. But this proactive policy has remained on paper as of the time of writing, and the general remained in Pakistan. At another level, a whirl of activity was apparent, with various Arabs being arrested with much fanfare on charges of being suspected Bin Laden aides—and more often than not released later. For instance, the announcement of the arrest of an Egyptian "aide" with over $35,000 and forged passports in his possession was subsequently found to be false.

Similarly, while Musharraf was reported to have asked a Rabbani-led team in February 2000 to resolve the Osama issue and form a broad based government, on the other hand, arms were pouring into Afghanistan from all sides in preparation for an offensive which began with a bloody opening by the Taliban. However, it appeared that strong ISI contingents were not present this time around, nor was there adequate intelligence at the tactical level—an asset that has been invaluable to the Taliban. The ISI, however, appeared to be busy in Pakistan itself, where a series of murders of moderate leaders ensured that no others emerged to challenge the Taliban.

In the same vein, Foreign Minister Sattar came out strongly against terrorism that emanated from Afghanistan, even as diplomatic moves went on at a frenetic pace to gain acceptability for the Taliban. After consistently refusing to attend (unless recognition was forthcoming), the Taliban was persuaded to take part in Organisation of Islamic Countries (OIC) sponsored talks in Saudi Arabia. This volte face was obviously aimed at breaking out of the isolation that was beginning to take a toll on Pakistan itself. Sattar also, however, differentiated between terrorism and militancy, noting that militancy was not a crime unless "a person commits an act of terrorism or uses force against an innocent person." Right on cue, the targetting policy in Kashmir shifted—with the now heavily foreign dominated jehadi parties targetting the Indian armed forces rather than the beleaguered people. This marked a significant shift in the history of terrorism in the subcontinent.

The Clinton visit itself was seen in diverse ways by different groups with one insisting that Pakistan had received "a slap in the face", while others crowed that it was a loss of face for Indian diplomacy. While the US president—or rather his entourage—made it obvious that the visit was hardly an "endorsement" of the Musharraf regime and the hijacking of democracy, and that the US was unhappy with Islamabad's record of supporting terrorism, there was also a clear decision not to push Pakistan too far on either issue. General Musharraf, in turn, reiterated his concerns on Kashmir, and publicly announced that there were "differences" over the handling of the Taliban issue. A prominent commentator, however, noted that Pakistan "has to deliver, and terrorism holds the key".

This appeared to be sage advice. Subsequently, the interior minister was quoted by Businessweek as saying that he would tell the Taliban that harbouring Osama was not "worth the price it is paying" in diplomatic and economic isolation. The magazine also quoted Pakistani officials as saying that the bulk of US-Pakistani discussions during the Clinton visit had focussed on counter-terrorism. The fact that the minister, during his visit to Washington, was accompanied by the new ISI chief and Musharraf loyalist General Mahmud was seen as heralding a new agenda. Back in Islamabad, Interior Minister Moinuddin Haider asked Afghanistan to close down all terrorist camps, and extradite sectarian extremists. A clear threat from the minister that the sectarian parties would have to stop or else "we will get them by the neck" appeared to be real enough, as the government continued this by passing strict arms control laws, and weapons collection measures.

The response to this was rather baffling. The Taliban was said to have asked Pakistani groups to close down a string of small camps near Jalalabad, Paktia, Khost and other parts—but reportedly allowed them to relocate to a bigger facility—all this without any outcry from Pakistan. The main camps at Rishkor continued to function, while those within Pakistan were not disturbed at all. The media found these moves equally puzzling. As the courageous Newsline noted, on the one hand, Pakistan was apparently concerned about terrorism, while on the other, it did nothing at all to prevent the grand conferences of Maulana Azhar which received considerable publicity—this at a time when the US was specifically asking Pakistan to close down terrorist camps. The argument from the interior minister and the Harkat chief was as before—that terrorism could not be equated with militancy and a freedom struggle. Given this interpretation, the Afghan foreign minister was not far off the mark when he said that there were no terrorist camps in his country.

Conclusion

In evaluating Pakistani policy towards Afghanistan, the first question that naturally arises is whether Pakistan has been able to achieve its objectives in Afghanistan and if so at what cost? This would be a barometer of the options before Chief Executive Officer

(CEO) General Musharraf and also the possible future options open to Islamabad. Here it is worth reiterating the main objectives of Pakistan:

- Ensure a friendly (pliant) regime in Afghanistan.
- Arising from this, ensure that the Pashtun issue is dealt with once and for all.
- Ensure a smooth trade route into the CARs.
- Propel Pakistan onto the world stage as a leader of the Islamic world, and a moderating influence in the area.
- Ensure that the irregular/jehadi forces of Afghanistan are readily available to Pakistan in the event of a war/limited war/conflict.

Regarding the first objective, it is difficult to envisage a friendlier regime to Pakistan than the Taliban. Ideologically, politically and functionally, it remains almost a part of Pakistan itself. As long as the Taliban continues in its present form, this will carry on with some variations, depending on personal and institutional equations.

The second objective is much more difficult. At present, it is vital that the Taliban controls the whole of Afghanistan. This is not just to consolidate the hold of the group, but also to prevent the reemergence of Pashtun nationalism that could so easily become the country's worst nightmare. The virtual disappearance of the Durand Line, the "tying" of Taliban infrastructure into Pakistan's border areas, especially Peshawar and its environs, and most of all the so-called "Talibanisation" of these bordering areas all point to danger signals of a Taliban that may settle down to an exclusively Pashtun identity. General Musharraf's call for a broad based government—which would naturally see a heavy presence of the Taliban rather than any real power sharing—should be seen in this light.

The third objective remains as yet elusive, though is likely to emerge in the near future. Trade with Central Asia already exists, but this cannot be exploited to the full till peace returns. Moreover, the crux of the trade comprises the offering of an exit route for Central Asian oil and gas, and there is as yet no movement in this direction.

The image of a moderate state that engages with the Taliban and against "fundamentalism" was one that Benazir Bhutto had tried hard to project. As noted above, this image has taken a beating, and recent visits of the CEO to Egypt and Indonesia show that this state of affairs continues.

The last objective has to an extent been successfully achieved. The presence of thousands of jehadis gives the Pakistan Army a deniable and extremely cheap source of power projection. As scholars have noted, the use of irregulars in the Pakistan Army has been consistent, and at present is unlikely to be given up—unless Pakistan decides to completely overturn its long-time strategy in both Afghanistan and Kashmir. In fact, so important is this policy to the Pakistani elite, that it was in part responsible for the imprisonment of a prime minister who was alleged to have tried to distance Pakistan from the Taliban, and from the jehad into Kashmir as well.

The Costs: Talibanisation

This is directly related to the perceived threat of Talibanisation that is seen to be the one of the main costs that Pakistan has had to bear. Here it is worth viewing "Talibanisation" in its proper perspective. The Taliban movement is essentially a national one, though its professed ideology—what there is of it—aims at sheltering and providing sustenance to Muslims everywhere. In reality, the Taliban is pretty much engaged in stabilising its own land rather than fighting elsewhere. Thus, Taliban leaders have indignantly denied that any of their cadres were present in Kargil—a fact which cannot be completely refuted. Neither are there any "Taliban" in Central Asia or anywhere else, though the ideology is undeniably one that is being used by a wide variety of actors, including drugs traffickers who support "fundamentalist" groups for their own ends. This ideology is also being used by the Pakistan Army to attain its objective against India, and justify its "moral" intervention in Kashmir. Therefore, much of the "Talibanisation" is by the Pakistanis themselves due to policies followed by successive governments in both appeasing the radicals, and pursuing a foreign policy that is based solely on the waging of jehad (which is Paki-speak for covert war). This explains why

Pakistan is the worst hit in seeing this phenomenon of the energising of the religious right. Thus, "Talibanisation" is a Pakistani creation, just as the Taliban itself was a Pakistani creation. In short, Pakistan has to first put its own house in order, and change the way it wants to deal with its neighbours. The Taliban has little to do with it.

Yet US decision-makers—who should know better—decided to adopt the "danger of Talibanisation" line. In January 2000, Deputy Secretary Strobe Talbott and Under Secretary Karl Inderfurth were warning of "Talibanisation", noting that "with the emergence of the Taliban, there is growing reason to fear that militant extremism, obscurantism, and sectarian will affect surrounding countries".

Interestingly, however, other sources also noted—in line with later US pronouncements—that there were "wheels within wheels…which continued to have truck with Osama, besides rendering valuable material support to the Taliban." Other sources were quoted as saying, "There is a vast network in your (Pakistani) intelligence community which does not listen to any government and which operates on its own. It is definitely happening in the case of the Taliban and Osama as well..." Later, after the massacre of Sikhs in Kashmir, President Clinton echoed the same perceptions when he noted that "elements" in the Pakistani government were backing the violence in Kashmir.

The Costs: Runaway "Elements"?

While at one point there was a period when the ISI was almost a free-wheeling body that dominated all other like institutions, today it appears to be under the firm control of the CEO or his loyalists. However, it is true that many within the army and its intelligence arm have grown to like the vast power that covert war brings. The huge apparatus that sends war material to the front, the internal power that arises from the influencing of the Islamists and their private armies, the financial power that comes with drugs trafficking, the institutional power that arises from the coming together of all these factors—all these are not easily given up. The greater danger to Pakistan, and indeed to the region, is the privatisation of the covert war by the most powerful institution in the country—the Pakistan Army. This at one stroke provides the greatest resistance to peace initiatives from any side, and the single element that provides the impetus to continuing instability.

THE FUTURE: DEALING WITH THE TALIBAN

As noted above, the CEO is under pressure—both from factors within and without—to rein in and close once and for all the Taliban adventure. The need to bring the war to an end on Pakistan's terms has already been discussed. However, pending that, the question of "influencing" the Taliban, and stemming the rot within his own country remains.

This raises the question of what influence can be brought to bear. This chapter referred to the roots of the Taliban, and its present structure which is divided into many layers, each with its own motivations. Within this, as noted, there are groups that are closely allied to Pakistani groups, as well as institutions. Thus, these groups/institutions can play a considerable part in influencing the direction of Taliban policy. Nearly all of these groups/ institutions—the transport mafia, the drugs mafia, and the Islamists—once functioned under the patronage of the military during the long years of Soviet occupation. Today, each has a measure of independence, yet all have to play the game under the rules drawn up by the military or its institutions.

At a more prosaic and easily understood level, it may be argued that the intelligence has only to cut off weapons aid to bring the Taliban offensive to a grinding halt. So the fact remains that there are many strings Islamabad can pull to ensure that the Taliban continue to heed its "advice".

But here Pakistani policy is somewhat in a bind. Pakistani policy presumes that if Islamabad cuts off aid, other neighbours like Iran would be only too happy to oblige. At one level, while it is true that the Taliban—due to its ties, bonding and the past—follows the dictates of Pakistani agencies, it is bound to become adept at avoiding a degree of vulnerability by turning ostentatiously—as it did in early 2000—to other sources of sustenance. At another level, Iranian or other assistance would in the end mean the virtual "disinventing" of the Taliban in its present form, which means twenty years of Pakistani effort going down the drain. This is the Pakistan fear. But there is an important caveat: while outside sources may offer some help, few—and certainly not Central Asia or Iran—can afford to prop up virtually an entire country and feed a dangerously indisciplined "armed force" for even a few years. Neither can Pakistan—which means that Islamabad and the Taliban are still getting their "aid" from diverse sources. The French believe that the US still has a hand here, while the Saudis continue to play the "front office".

There is an other important caveat here. Note that the US evinces no particular enmity towards the Taliban and never has. It was one of the first countries to move towards an implicit endorsement of the regime, and at present continues to have channels of communication with it. What it objects to are the sheltering of Osama and the terrorist camps that function under some "outside" control.

Dealing with Terrorist Camps

The question that is of interest, then, is—just who controls the Afghan terrorist camps? For this, it is necessary to note that many of these camps date back to the Mujahideen days, when they were used as bases to launch attacks. In the initial years especially, the main training camps were in Pakistan, not in Afghanistan. By the mid-1990s, however, as US policy veered towards serious counter-terrorism, and the emergence of various terrorists—like Ramzi Youseff of the World Trade Centre bombing and Aimal Kansi who killed the CIA officers at Langley—from Pakistani territory persuaded Pakistan to move many of these camps to just across the border. Control remained in the hands of the ISI as well as sections within the Frontier Corps.

After 1993-94, therefore, the running of these groups like the Harkat-ul-Ansar, Lashkar-e-Taiba and others, was handed over to the large seminaries—which being inside Pakistan were within the control of the state. These large outfits owe their land, patronage and power—and, more importantly, their weapons—either directly to the state or to state indulgence. Recall that the land at Muridke was donated by General Zia, that the JUI (Fazlur) received considerable land and money from Benazir Bhutto, and that the annual conventions of the Markaz Da'wat ul Ershad were regularly attended by the prime minister and his entourage. Recall also that the last Markaz meet was immediately after Kargil—and no impediment of any kind was put on this meeting by the new army regime. Note also the relief of the jehadis at the removal of Nawaz Sharif.

Today, the terrorist camps in Afghanistan do produce jehadis for the front. Where these are Afghans, they usually stay within their own country, or perish in the war, or return home. A few do move out in search of profit—but these are the individuals who are affiliated to the Pakistani-controlled Harkat and others. The largest numbers of terrorists are Pakistanis, followed by the Arab contingent. They are the jehadis but at other times they are also the terrorists who feed on Pakistani society itself. These former fighters stay on to be used as mercenaries by agencies for their own ends. Undoubtedly, the camps near Kabul as well as the "offices" of Uzbek or Tajik resistance are allowed by the Taliban—which are reflections of its own interests in dealing with the hostility of these neighbours (a ploy that has worked by pushing these regimes into opening "talks" with the Taliban). But the Taliban is not on a "jehadi spree". As noted earlier, firstly, it has enough on its plate to keep it occupied, and secondly, its brand of Pashtun, tribal, and extremist ideology cannot easily be transplanted to other societies—however "fundamentalist". The camps are not vital to Taliban policy—they are, however, completely central to Pakistani policy.

The bottom line, therefore, appears to be that the thrust of Pakistani policy in Afghanistan is tied surely to the objectives and nature of not only the Pakistan government itself, but also the ties within it. Pakistanis have to learn to change the way they deal with their neighbours, for as long as covert war continues, the CEO may not be able to control either his own backyard or the fallout from these adventures. Stability for the new regime can only flow from its own ability to control institutions like the intelligence or non-state bodies like the Harkat. The intelligence draws its power from covert war, as do the Islamist parties and their creatures who benefit from it. To control Pakistan, General Musharraf has to do one simple thing—he has to turn off the tap that funds and backs the jehad policy. Anything else can only be a sop to history. At present that is all that is visible.

TALIBAN ATTACKS ON SUPPLY LINES THROUGH PAKISTAN

In November and December 2008, there were multiple incidents of major theft, robbery, and arson attacks against NATO supply convoys in Pakistan. Transport companies south of Kabul have also been reported to pay protection money to the Taliban. In an attack on 11 November 2008, Taliban fighters in Peshawar hijacked a convoy carrying NATO supplies from Karachi to Afghanistan. The militants took two military Humvees and paraded them in front of the media as trophies.

The area east of the Khyber pass in Pakistan has seen very frequent attacks. Cargo trucks and Humvees have been set ablaze by Taliban militants. A half-dozen raids on depots with NATO supplies near Peshawar destroyed 300 cargo trucks and Humvees in December 2008. The Taliban destroyed an iron bridge on the highway between Peshawar and the Khyber pass in February 2009.

Coalition issues with Pakistan

An unnamed senior Pentagon official told the BBC that at some point between 12 July and 12 September 2008, President George W. Bush issued a classified order to authorize U.S. raids against militants in Pakistan. Pakistan however said it would not allow foreign forces onto its territory and that it would vigorously protect its sovereignty. In September, the Pakistan military stated that it had issued orders to "open fire" on American soldiers who crossed the Pakistan border in pursuit of militant forces.

On 25 September 2008, Pakistani troops shot towards ISAF helicopters, which belonged to American troops. This caused confusion and anger in the Pentagon, which asked for a full explanation into the incident, and they denied that American choppers were in Pakistani airspace. Pakistani President Asif Ali Zardari was quick to deny that shots were fired but instead insisted that the Pakistani troops shot flares to warn the Americans that they were in Pakistani airspace. A further split occurred when American troops apparently landed on Pakistani soil to carry out an operation against militants in the Khyber Pakhtunkhwa Province but 'Pakistan reacted angrily to the action, saying 20 innocent villagers had been killed by US troops'. However, despite tensions between Pakistan and the U.S., the United States has continued to increase the use of remotely piloted drone aircraft in Pakistan's border regions, in particular the Federally Administered Tribal Regions (FATA) and Balochistan; as of early 2009, drone attacks were up 183% since 2006. By the end of 2008, the Taliban apparently had severed remaining ties with al-Qaeda. According to senior U.S. military intelligence officials, there are perhaps fewer than 100 members of al-Qaeda remaining in Afghanistan.

In a meeting with General McChrystal, Pakistani military officials urged international forces to keep their fight on the Afghan side of the border to prevent militants from fleeing into Pakistan. Pakistan noted that it has 140,000 Pakistani soldiers on its side of the border with Afghanistan to monitor and address militant activities, while the Coalition only has 100,000 soldiers to police the Afghanistan side of the border.

2009: Southern Afghanistan

In response to the increased risk of sending supplies through Pakistan, work began on the establishment of a Northern Distribution Network (NDN) through Russia and several Central Asian republics. Initial permission for the U.S. military to move troop supplies through the region was given on 20 January 2009, after a visit to the region by General Petraeus. The first shipment along the NDN route left on 20 February from Riga, Latvia, then traveled 3,212 miles (5,169 km) to the Uzbek town of Termez on the Afghanistan border. In addition to Riga, other European ports include Poti, Georgia and Vladivostok, Russia. U.S. commanders have stated their hope that 100 containers a day will be shipped along the NDN. By comparison, currently 140 containers a day are shipped through the Khyber Pass. By 2011, the NDN handled about 40% of Afghanistan-bound traffic, compared to 30% through Pakistan.

On 11 May 2009, Uzbekistan president Islam Karimov announced that the airport in Navoi, Uzbekistan was being used to transport non-lethal cargo into Afghanistan. Due to the still unsettled relationship between Uzbekistan and the United States following the 2005 Andijon massacre and subsequent expulsion of U.S. forces from Karshi-Khanabad airbase, U.S. forces were not involved in the shipment of supplies. Instead, South Korea's Korean Air, which is currently involved in overhauling Navoi's airport, officially handles logistics at the site. Originally only non-lethal resources were allowed on the NDN. In July 2009, however, shortly before a visit by President Obama to Moscow, Russian authorities announced that U.S. troops and weapons could use the country's airspace to reach Afghanistan.

Additionally, human rights advocates are concerned that the U.S. is again working with the government of Uzbekistan, which is often accused of violating human rights. Nevertheless, U.S. officials have promised increased cooperation with Uzbekistan, including further assistance to turn the Navoi airport into a major regional distribution center for both military and civilian ventures.

Azerbaijan, which has sent its peacekeeping forces to be a part of ISAF, also provided its airspace and airports for transportation of vital supplies for the U.S. Army in Afghanistan. Apart from usage of Azerbaijani airspace by U.S. Air Force, over one-third of all of the nonlethal equipment including fuel, clothing, and food used by the U.S. military in Afghanistan travels through Baku.

Increase in U.S. troops

In January, about 3,000 U.S. soldiers from the 3rd Brigade Combat Team of the 10th Mountain Division moved into the provinces of Logar and Wardak. Afghan Federal Guards also fought along with U.S. Troops. The troops were the first wave of an expected surge of reinforcements originally ordered by George W. Bush and increased by Barack Obama.

In mid-February, it was announced that 17,000 additional troops would be deployed to the country in two brigades and additional support troops; the2nd Marine Expeditionary Brigade of about 3,500 from the 7,000 Marines, and the 5th Brigade, 2nd Infantry

Division, a Stryker Brigade with about 4,000 of the 7,000 U.S. Army soldiers. The U.S. commander in Afghanistan, General David McKiernan, had called for as many as 30,000 additional troops, effectively doubling the number of troops currently in the country.

On 23 September, NBC News reported that a classified assessment of the war in Afghanistan by General McChrystal included his conclusion that a successful counterinsurgency strategy would require 500,000 troops and five years of fighting.

In November, the U.S. ambassador in Kabul sent two classified cables to Washington expressing deep concerns about sending more U.S. troops to Afghanistan until President Hamid Karzai's government demonstrates that it is willing to tackle the corruption and mismanagement that has fueled the Taliban's rise. Ambassador Karl W. Eikenberry, a retired three-star general who in 2006–2007 commanded U.S. troops in Afghanistan, also expressed frustration with the relative paucity of funds set aside for spending on development and reconstruction in Afghanistan.

In subsequent cables, Ambassador Eikenberry repeatedly cautioned that deploying sizable American reinforcements would result in "astronomical costs" – tens of billions of dollars – and would only deepen the dependence of the Afghan government on the United States.

On 26 November 2009, Afghan President Hamid Karzai made a public plea to the United States to engage in direct negotiations with the Taliban leadership. In an interview with CNN's Christiane Amanpour, Karzai said there is an "urgent need" for negotiations with the Taliban, and made it clear that the Obama administration had opposed such talks. There was no formal American response.

On 1 December 2009, President Barack Obama announced at The United States Military Academy in West Point that the U.S. will be sending 30,000 more troops to Afghanistan. Antiwar organizations in the United States responded quickly, and cities throughout the U.S. saw protests on 2 December in response. Many protesters compared the decision to deploy more troops in Afghanistan to the expansion of the Vietnam War under the Johnson administration.

Kunduz Province campaign

In April, German forces stepped up their efforts to retake some rebellious areas of Kunduz province, considered to be the most dangerous part of Northern Afghanistan by ISAF commander McChrystal. The fighting centres upon the areas to the west and south of the city of Kunduz with a main focus on an area between the town of Chahar Dara in the West and the Kunduz river in the east. Up to now this campaign consisted of several large offensives linked by countless skirmishes and gunfights. Operations of German, Afghan, U.S., and Belgian troops were still ongoing as of December 2009. Insurgent militias suffered more than 650 casualties in this period. At least 86 coalition troops were wounded or killed. On 4 September, a devastating NATO air raid was conducted 7 kilometres to the southwest of Kunduz where Taliban fighters had hijacked civilian supply trucks, killing Up to 179 people including over 100 Afghan civilians.

Operation Khanjar and Operation Panther's Claw

We're doing this very differently. We're going to be with the people. We're not going to drive to work. We're going to walk to work. — Brig. Gen. Lawrence D. Nicholson, commander of the 2nd Marine Expeditionary Brigade, July 2, 2009.

On 25 June 2009, American officials announced the launch of Operation Khanjar ("strike of the sword").About 4000 U.S. Marines from the 2nd Marine Expeditionary Brigade and 650 Afghan soldiers are currently involved in Operation Khanjar, which will be staged on the Helmand River. Khanjar follows a British-led operation named Operation Panther's Claw in the same region. Officials call it the Marines' largest operation since the 2004 invasion of Fallujah, Iraq. Operation Panther's Claw was aimed to secure various canal and river crossings to establish a permanent International Security Assistance Force(ISAF) presence in the area.

Initially, Afghan and American soldiers have been moving into towns and villages along the Helmand River to secure the civilian population from the Taliban. The main objective of the operation is to push troops into insurgent strongholds along the river. A secondary aim was to bring security to the Helmand

Valley in time for presidential elections, set to take place on 20 August. The first aggressive phase will last 36 hours, where the secondary aim will be achieved first.

Taliban's gains

According to a 22 December 2009, briefing by Major General Michael T. Flynn, the top U.S. intelligence officer in Afghanistan, "The Taliban retains required partnerships to sustain support, fuel legitimacy and bolster capacity." The 23-page briefing states that "Security incidents projected to be higher in 2010." Those incidents are already up by 300 percent since 2007 and by 60 percent since 2008, according to the briefing. NATO intelligence at the time also indicated that the Taliban had as many as 25,000 dedicated soldiers, almost as many as before 9/11 and more than in 2005. On 10 August 2009, Stanley McChrystal, the newly appointed U.S. commander in Afghanistan, said that the Taliban had gained the upper hand. In a continuation of the Taliban's usual strategy of summer offensives, the militants have aggressively spread their influence into the north and west Afghanistan, and stepped up their attack in an attempt to disrupt 20 August presidential polls. Calling the Taliban a "very aggressive enemy", he added that the U.S. strategy in the months to come is to stop their momentum and focusing on protecting and safeguarding the Afghan civilians, while also calling it "hard work".

The Taliban's claim of disrupting 20 August elections is largely disputed, claiming over 135 incidents of violence; media was asked to not report on any violent incidents, however, causing many outlets to hail the elections as a success, even though some estimates give the voter turn out as much less than the expected 70 percent. In southern Afghanistan where the Taliban holds the most sway, there was a low voter turnout and sporadic violence directed at voters and security personnel. The chief observer of the European Union election mission, General Philippe Morillon, said the election was "generally fair" but "not free".

Western groups and election observers had difficulty accessing the southern regions of Afghanistan, where at least 9 Afghan civilians and 14 security forces were killed in attacks intended to intimidate voters. The Taliban released a video days after the elections, filming just up the road between Kabul and Kandahar, a major route in Afghanistan on election day, stopping buses, cars, and asking to see their fingers. The video went on to showing ten men who had voted, being talked to by a Taliban militant, they went on to say they may pardon the voters because of the Holy month of Ramadan The Taliban also attacked towns with rockets and other means of indirect fire. Amid claims of widespread fraud, both of the top contenders, Hamid Karzai and Abdullah Abdullah, claimed victory in the election. Reports also suggest that the turnout was lower than the last election, and there are fears that a results dispute can turn violent, even though both candidates vowed not to incite violence in case of a loss.

After Karzai's alleged win of 54 per cent, which would prevent a run off with his rival, Abdullah Abdullah, over 400,000 votes had to be discounted for Karzai, and many more with hundreds of thousands of votes and polling ballots being accused of fraud. Making the real turnout of the elections much lower than the official numbers, many nations criticizing the elections as "free but not fair". In December, an attack on Forward Operating Base Chapman, used by the Central Intelligence Agency to gather information and to coordinate drone attacks against Taliban leaders, killed at least six CIA officers and was a major setback for the agency's operations in the region.

2010: American/British offensive and Afghan peace initiative

In January 2010, American officials said privately that the Pakistanis are reluctant to go after the Afghan Taliban and the Haqqani network because they see them as a future proxy against Indian interests in Afghanistan when the Americans leave. In their public statements U.S. officials had previously praised Pakistan's military effort against the militants during its offensive in South Waziristan in November 2009. Afghan President Hamid Karzai also started peace talks with Haqqani network groups in March 2010. Pakistan's President Asif Ali Zardari said that Pakistan has lost over 35 billion U.S. dollars during the previous eight years as a result of the fight against militancy. According to the Afghan government, approximately 900 Taliban were killed in operations conducted during 2010. Due to increased use of IEDs by insurgents there was a significant increase in the number of injured coalition soldiers, mainly Americans, losing one limb or more or suffering major injury to their genital and pelvic areas.

Peace Initiatives

In October 2008 Defence Secretary Gates asserted that a political settlement with the Taliban was the endgame for the Afghan conflict. "There has to be ultimately – and I'll underscore ultimately – reconciliation as part of a political outcome to this," Gates stated.

By 2010 peace efforts began. In early January, Taliban commanders held secret exploratory talks with a United Nations special envoy to discuss peace terms. Regional commanders on the Taliban's leadership council, the Quetta Shura, sought a meeting with the UN special representative in Afghanistan, Kai Eide, and it took place in Dubai on January 8. It was the first such meeting between the UN and senior members of the Taliban.

On 26 January 2010, at a major conference in London which brought together some 70 countries and organizations, Afghan President Hamid Karzai told world leaders that he intends to reach out to the top echelons of the Taliban within a few weeks with a peace initiative. Karzai set the framework for dialogue with Taliban leaders when he called on the group's leadership to take part in a "loya jirga" – or large assembly of elders – to initiate peace talks. Karzai also asked for creation of a new peacemaking organization, to be called the National Council for Peace, Reconciliation and Reintegration. Karzai's top adviser on the reconciliation process with the insurgents said that the country must learn to forgive the Taliban.

In March 2010, the Karzai government held preliminary talks with Hezb-i-Islami, who presented a plan which included the withdrawal of all foreign troops by the end of 2010. The Taliban declined to participate, saying "The Islamic Emirate has a clear position. We have said this many, many times. There will be no talks when there are foreign troops on Afghanistan's soil killing innocent Afghans on daily basis."

In July 2010, *The Guardian* newspaper reported that the campaign to "win hearts and minds" of Afghan civilians by U.S.

troops has been proving more difficult than expected. One U.S. Army report read: "It seems to always be this way when we go there [to meet civilians]. No one wants anything to do with us." And a report on meeting up with school representatives mentioned students throwing rocks at soldiers and not welcoming their arrival, as has been reported on several occasions elsewhere.

In September 2010 General David Petraeus commented on the progress of peace talks to date, stating, "The prospect for reconciliation with senior Taliban leaders certainly looms out there...and there have been approaches at (a) very senior level that hold some promise."

Marja offensive

In early February Coalition and Afghan forces began highly visible plans for an offensive, codenamed Operation Moshtarak, on the Taliban stronghold near the village of Marja. It began on 13 February and, according to U.S. and Afghan officials, was the first operation where Afghan forces led the coalition. The offensive involves 15,000 US, British and Afghan troops. It is the biggest joint operation since the 2001 invasion that ousted the Taliban. The troops are fighting over an area of less than 100 square miles (260 km^2), with a population of 80,000.

Troop surge

Deployment of additional U.S. troops continued in early 2010, with 9,000 of the planned 30,000 in place before the end of March and another 18,000 expected by June, with the 101st Airborne Division as the main effort. The Pentagon anticipates that U.S. troops in Afghanistan will outnumber those in Iraq for the first time since 2003. The CIA, from a request by General McChrystal, the commander of NATO forces in Afghanistan, is planning to increase teams of operatives, including their elite paramilitary officers from Special Activities Division (SAD), with U.S. military special operations forces. This combination worked well in Iraq and is largely credited with the success of that surge. The CIA is also increasing its campaign using Hellfire missilestrikes on Al-Qaeda in Pakistan. The number of strikes in 2010, 115, more than doubled the 50 drone attacks that occurred in 2009.

The surge in troops also meant a sixfold increase in Special Forces operations. There were 700 air strikes in September 2010, alone versus 257 in all of 2009. From July 2010 to October 2010, 300 Taliban commanders and 800 foot soldiers were killed. Hundreds more insurgent leaders were killed or captured as 2010 came to a close. General David Petraeus characterized the damage Special Forces were inflicting on the insurgents this way: "We've got our teeth in the enemy's jugular now, and we're not going to let go."

The CIA created what would be called Counter-terrorism Pursuit Teams (CTPT) at the beginning of the war. This force grew to over 3,000 soldiers by 2010 and is considered one of the "best Afghan fighting forces". According to Woodward book *Obama's War*, Firebase Lilley as one of the nerve centers for the covert war conducted by the CIA's SAD. These units have not only been highly effective in operations against the Taliban and al-Qaeda forces in Afghanistan, but have expanded their operations into Pakistan. They were also important factors in both the "counterterrorism plus" and the full "counterinsurgency" options discussed by the Obama administration in the December 2010 review.

Taliban offensive

The Taliban announced an offensive for the spring and launched several attacks against ISAF and Afghan government forces. Attacks include a car bomb against a NATO convoy in Kabul which killed 18 people including six NATO soldiers and separate attacks against two of the largest ISAF bases in Afghanistan, Bagram and Kandahar Air Bases. Overall, 2010 saw the most insurgent attacks of any year since the war began, peaking in September at more than 1,500. Insurgent operations increased "dramatically" in two-thirds of Afghan provinces.

Wikileaks disclosure

On 25 July 2010, the release of 391,832 classified documents from the Wikileaks organization was made public. The documents cover U.S. military incident and intelligence reports from January 2004 to December 2009. Some of these documents included sanitised, and "covered up", accounts of civilian casualties caused by Coalition Forces. The reports also included many references to other incidents involving civilian casualties like the Kunduz airstrike and Nangar Khel incident.

The leaked documents also contain reports of Pakistan collusion with the Taliban. According to *Der Spiegel*, "the documents clearly show that the Pakistani intelligence agency Inter-Services Intelligence (usually known as the ISI) is the most important accomplice the Taliban has outside of Afghanistan."

The New York Times was especially alarmed by the level of collusion with the Taliban, having concluded that Pakistan "allows representatives of its spy service to meet directly with the Taliban in secret strategy sessions to organize networks of militant groups that fight against American soldiers in Afghanistan, and even hatch plots to assassinate Afghan leaders." *The Guardian*, however, did not think there was "a convincing smoking gun" for complicity between Pakistan intelligence services and the Taliban.

Kandahar offensive

A U.S. and Afghan military offensive, called Operation Hamkari, focusing on the Afghan province of Kandahar was launched soon after the Muslim holiday of Ramadan, which ended September 10. The Kandahar offensive was originally planned to be launched during July, but was delayed for further preparations. The offensive did not begin as one specific operation, but rather a series of operations in Kandahar City and its surrounding districts throughout the late summer and fall in 2010. Places where operations were conducted included Malajat, Zhari, Arghandab and the Horn of Panjwayi. Operations conducted in 2010 is credited with putting severe pressure on insurgent operations and increasing security in some key areas such as in Panjwayi. Unlike operations of previous years, Operation Hamkari featured the extensive use of Afghan National Security Forces, including the Afghan Border Police (ABP), led by Spin Boldak ABP Commander Gen. Abdul Razziq.

Operation Bawaar was the Canadian aspect of the 2010 Kandahar offensive. It involved the hold and build in the district of Zangabad as well as the Ground Line of Communication (GLOC) project to Mushan – all in an area known as the Horn of Panjwai.

Pakistan and U.S. tensions

Tensions between Pakistan and the U.S. were heightened in late September after several Pakistan Frontier Corps soldiers were killed and wounded. The troops were attacked by a U.S. piloted aircraft that was pursuing Taliban forces near the Afghan-Pakistan border but for unknown reasons opened fire on two different Pakistan border posts. In retaliation for the strike, Pakistan closed the Torkham ground border crossing to NATO supply convoys for an unspecified period. This incident followed the recent release of a video allegedly showing uniformed Pakistan soldiers executing unarmed civilians. After the Torkham border closing, the Pakistani Taliban attacked the NATO convoys carrying supplies, killing several of the drivers and destroying around 100 tankers.

Raids on Taliban leaders

Beginning in May 2010 NATO special forces began to concentrate on surgical operations to capture or kill specific Taliban leaders. As of March 2011, according to the U.S. military, the operations had resulted in the capture or killing of more than 900 low and mid-level Taliban commanders. The effectiveness of the operations in defeating the Taliban was not yet known.

THE TALIBAN STAKES OF PAKISTAN

As Ahmad Rashid has described so well, the Taliban (Islamic student) movement sprang from Pushtun refugees in Pakistan, concentrated in temporary camps in western Pakistan. Pushtun young men who had grown up in these camps were drawn back to the Afghan homeland after the Soviet exit, but under civil war conditions in their country. These youths had been trained in the use of small arms (carrying weapons was a natural legacy of their culture) and taught to believe they could impose a peaceful, Islamic moral order on their country. Most had no deep memory of traditional social life in Afghanistan itself, many had lost their parents and, being displaced, few were accustomed to the valued roles women played in Afghan society. The Taliban religious outlook was a product of the free, but largely Quranic, obscurantist education available to boys in the austere camp environments. Their teachers themselves typically were religious leaders (*maulvis* or *mullahs*) from Deobandi or Wahabi brands of fundamentalist Islam who ran traditional religious schools (*madrassas*) with hostels, frequently using them as recruiting grounds for political ends.

When the Soviet forces withdrew from Afghanistan in 1989, the United States essentially washed its hands of responsibility for the future of that debilitated country. Having defeated Soviet power and installed a weak Islamic republic under Tajik cleric Burhanuddin Rabbani in Kabul, Afghan mujahideen groups increasingly quarreled among themselves on ethnic and tribal lines and most of Afghanistan succumbed to internal warfare. Pakistan's elected, bureaucratic and armed leaders could not so easily ignore this turbulence and groped for a strategy that would restore civil order beyond Pakistan's borders in Afghanistan.

Under liberal Prime Minister and Interior Minister in 1993, the government of Pakistan worked out a two-fold strategy toward Afghanistan: (a) to support the revival of traditional Pushtun rule in the hope of extinguishing inter-tribal war, suppressing banditry, reopening roads, reviving trade with Iran and Central Asia, and securing Afghanistan for Western-financed pipeline projects that could provide Afghanistan revenue while transporting natural gas from Turkmenistan to Pakistan and on to India; and (b) to preempt Pushtun revival of the demand for a separate Pushtun state (Pakhtunistan) that had threatened Pakistan's integrity in the northwest tribal belt for many years after Independence, by ensuring the primacy of Pushtun stakes in Afghanistan's future.

The Taliban association emerging from the refugee settlements provided a natural political vehicle for this Pakistani strategy. It depended on the cooperation of the Islamist political parties that sponsored the Taliban in the camps. The task merely involved lightly arming and training Taliban cadres, and negotiating their entry through Quetta to join those Pushtun militia leaders inside Afghanistan who deplored the country's internal disintegration and aspired, however crudely, to pacify, reunify and rebuild Afghanistan.

The Pakistani armed intelligence arm, the Inter-Services Intelligence agency (ISI)—which had served as the main American and Saudi conduit for training, financial support, and transferring arms to the Afghan mujahideen—became the overseers and managers of Pakistan's assistance to the Taliban. This ISI role was secretive, but it was no rogue operation—as some in Pakistan and the United States may now wish to believe. Rather, it was the policy of Pakistan's elected governments from 1993, including that of the Harvard- and Oxford-educated Benazir Bhutto, Pakistan's first female prime minister.

The Taliban gained a local foothold around Kandahar in 1994 and then rapidly spread within southern and eastern Afghanistan, seizing Kabul and asserting a claim to govern Afghanistan in 1996, with all but a northeastern tenth of the country falling under their sway by 1998. Some financial support for the Taliban came from Saudi Arabia and other Gulf states. The Taliban regime was formally recognized by Saudi Arabia, Pakistan, and United Arab Emirates as the government of Afghanistan. Other governments and the United Nations either continued to recognize the first mujahideen (Rabbani) government even after it fled Kabul, or declined to recognize the Taliban regime, hoping that diplomacy and United Nations relief could patch together a workable, coalition government more representative of the country as a whole.

Almost imperceptible to Westerners at the start, the Taliban project at first was not considered objectionable in Washington. The Taliban became anathema only later, after word of its brutality spread. Having seized power in Kabul, the Taliban's inhumane governing practices undercut its once positive reputation for disarming warlord factions and bringing peace in one locality after another. From Kabul, the new regime imposed uniquely harsh judicial procedures and tried to force the surviving remnants of Afghanistan's battered urban society to give up music and entertainment. On pain of beating or even execution, men were forced to grow beards and wear traditional clothes, and women to leave jobs and whenever outdoors to wear the head-to-toe covering known as *burqas*. Western revulsion was aroused by media reports of the Taliban's draconian interpretation of Islamic law, confinement of women, suppression of female education, arbitrary arrests, mutilation or execution as punishments, and intolerance of non-Muslim religious minorities.

However a great deal the Taliban was eventually despised in the West, it was not the offspring of, nor originally associated with, al-Qaeda. Osama bin Laden apparently left Sudan in 1996 and moved back to Afghanistan some time in 1997. Thereafter, al-Qaeda gradually extended influence over the Taliban by spending its own resources to win the favour of senior Taliban leaders. Al-Qaeda also provided armed support and guidance to Taliban fighters who were fighting the Northern Alliance forces and other autonomous factions elsewhere in the country. The United States focused only on the significance of the Taliban's grant of sanctuary to al-Qaeda after its bombing of U.S. Embassies in East Africa in 1998.

Toward the end of its tenure, the Clinton administration put considerable pressure on Pakistan to arrange communication with Taliban officials, hoping to persuade them to expel Osama bin Laden and his associates. But the Taliban's counter demand was that it be recognized as Afghanistan's de jure government. This price the United States was unwilling to pay. How deeply the Taliban depended on al-Qaeda for armed operations against the Northern Alliance was not apparent to ordinary observers until after 9/11. What was clear, however, was that Pakistan had a major stake in the Taliban's claim to govern Afghanistan, was opposed to the Northern Alliance, and could not disengage from those positions in Afghanistan, short of a world-shaking crisis. September 11 brought just that crisis.

This analysis indicates that Pakistan's stakes in the Taliban were not based on a ordinary religion or on matters or Islamic principle, per se. Pakistan was interested in geopolitical objectives, not in the religious aims of the Taliban or its parochial justification of a strict Islamic discipline. Pakistan hoped to foster order through a client regime in a war-torn country on its borders. In doing so, it aimed to promote the revival of trade, to link Central Asian energy resources with the subcontinent, and to extinguish any Pushtun impulse to tear part of Pakistan away as a separate Pushtun state.

Exploiting reservoirs of Afghan Islamic fervor was useful to Pakistan (as well as to the United States) against the Soviet forces in Afghanistan, and useful again to Pakistan in helping the Taliban come to power, but the Taliban movement's Islamic fundamentalist orientation was never for Pakistan's government an end in itself. Only a smattering of individual Pakistanis and fundamentalist groups—mainly Pushtun tribes and Islamic political parties with roots in the Pushtun tribal regions—identified with the Taliban cause emotionally or ideologically. For the Pakistani authorities, the Taliban's religious appeal was only a tool.

Far more basic for Pakistan's government, and painful to abandon, was the aim of Pushtun dominance within Afghanistan as a means of resolving the civil war and opening the way to the trans-Afghanistan energy project. In achieving this aim, to cut off the Taliban even after George W. Bush threw down the gauntlet was tantamount to sacrificing Pushtun interests in Afghan politics and undermining Pakistan's interests in Afghanistan's stability and its own security. Pakistan's view of the power of the Northern Alliance, perhaps mistakenly, was that it jeopardized stability in Afghanistan. Thus, when Pakistani chief Pervez Musharraf turned against the Taliban under U.S. pressure, the decision was acutely difficult. Because Pakistan's strategy toward Afghanistan—and its own security on its western borders—was based on a successful Taliban campaign for power, it required accepting a fundamentally different calculation of Pakistan's national interests.

The new calculation was that Pakistan could not afford to be stigmatized by the West as a terrorist state. Once the Taliban refused to dissociate itself from al-Qaeda, Islamabad recognized that the United States would regard the Taliban as a de facto "terrorist" regime, and a legitimate object of armed attack. For Pakistan to be associated with the Taliban political cause after that would not only put Pakistan on a slippery slope toward international ostracism but could be used, potentially, to justify armed attack on Pakistan itself. Indeed, it was exactly this sensitivity that India latched onto when it initiated a armed confrontation with Pakistan after the attack on parliament in December 2001. But before we examine that crisis, the dramatic progress of the U.S.

war in Afghanistan and the potential effects on the Kashmir side of Pakistan's Afghanistan-related entanglement need separate discussion.

ARMED MOVEMENT AGAINST THE TALIBAN AND AL-QAEDA

Pakistan had to make a decision very quickly whether it would support the U.S. armed effort in Afghanistan. Senior Pakistani officials announced on September 15, *within four days* of the 9/11 terrorist attacks on the United States, that they had agreed to give "full support" to U.S. efforts to combat international terrorism. President Musharraf 's address in Urdu to the nation three days later informed his people that the United States had demanded armed overflight rights, logistical support, and intelligence cooperation against three targets—Osama bin Laden, the Taliban, and international terrorism. Musharraf noted that the United States had won United Nations support and confided to the nation that neighbouring India had offered its armed facilities to the United States in the hopes of isolating Pakistan and getting it declared a terrorist state. Musharraf made it clear to his countrymen that Pakistan had to assist the United States; otherwise four vital interests of Pakistan would be in jeopardy—its sovereignty, its economy, its strategic (nuclear and missile) assets, and its cause in Kashmir. Musharraf and his advisors apparently drew the line, however, at inserting Pakistani armed forces into Afghanistan.

Despite concerns about a violent domestic backlash from political parties and groups that had links with the Taliban as well as the threat of al-Qaeda or Taliban attacks across the border, Pakistan thus committed itself almost overnight to give the United States valuable flight corridors over its territory and access to stage U.S. search and rescue forces at facilities near Karachi in the south and closer to Afghanistan at the Pakistani armed airfield near Jacobabad.

Pakistani forces also provided backstopping for U.S. operations against al-Qaeda and the Taliban later, by attempting to seal the mountainous borders so as to prevent hostile units fleeing across the border into Pakistan. Pakistani intelligence and security forces also cooperated with covert U.S. forces in efforts to hunt down those al-Qaeda and Taliban elements that succeeded in entering Pakistan to take refuge, or to slip out of the country.

Operation Enduring Freedom against al-Qaeda and Taliban forces in Afghanistan began with air strikes on October 7, 2001. Saudi Arabia had vetoed U.S. use of amenities on its soil for the attack and Iran denied access through its airspace. This put a much greater burden on U.S. aircraft carriers and other naval forces that assembled in the Arabian Sea, on bombers that had been flown to Diego Garcia and some that flew all the way from the United States, and on the prodigious use of aircraft refueling capabilities. But to the surprise of most observers, Russian President Putin gave his blessing to the U.S. counterterrorist effort and the leaders of three post-Soviet Central Asian states neighbouring Afghanistan—Uzbekistan, Tajikistan, and Kyrgizstan—provided the United States air access and staging facilities near Afghanistan in the north and west. Use of these facilities greatly eased U.S. cooperation with the Afghan Northern Alliance and the Uzbek elements that had reestablished a presence under General Rashid Dostum and that would retake Mazar-i-Sharif.

As a result, not merely was the United States able to use its own infiltrated ground spotters and air strikes to destroy exposed Taliban armed assets and installations—there were relatively few big targets— but it was also able to use airborne firepower to break down the front lines of the Taliban forces opposite the Northern Alliance, enabling the alliance and the other anti-Taliban forces that reemerged to advance, taking Mazar-i-Sharif, Kabul, Herat and Konduz in succession. Mazar-i-Sharif fell on November 9. Kabul was retaken on November 12, and Herat fell the same day. Konduz, where a combined force of about twenty thousand al-Qaeda and Taliban forces put up a fierce resistance, fell on November 24.

A thousand U.S. marines were airlifted on November 26 into a remote landing strip (dubbed Camp Rhino) fifteen miles southeast of Kandahar to provide protection for a buildup of helicopters, armored personnel carriers, and the entry of additional special operations units. This also provided the United States with a staging area inside Afghanistan to pursue operations in the Pushtun areas to the north and east, including near the border with Pakistan. Coupled with well-targeted air raids, the ground presence of U.S.

combat forces helped break the main, residual Taliban resistance in the south, stimulated defections, and forced the hard core to disperse into hiding. Kandahar fell on December 7.

Aided by the Rome political process of negotiating a new Afghan government, Hamid Karzai's leadership had begun by this time to make significant headway among Pushtun elements in the south and east that could absorb defectors and accommodate the Northern Alliance in forming a new government in Kabul. The U.S.-assisted Afghan meetings in Rome helped negotiate agreed steps to constitute a new, representative government in stages—and made the level of international commitment to rehabilitating Afghanistan clearer.

Special combat operations shifted once Kandahar had fallen to the White Mountains, near Khost, adjoining Pakistan, where al-Qaeda and Taliban forces had taken refuge in fortified and well-provisioned mountain caves and bunkers. The Tora Bora operations heavily bombed the cave complexes and ground units then cleared most of them on the ground by early January 2002. Several hundred al-Qaeda and Taliban prisoners were taken, with many shipped to Guantanamo Bay in Cuba for interrogation. A significant number of the al-Qaeda Arabs at Tora Bora evidently slipped through into Pakistan, however. In March, U.S. and allied forces gathered in Operation Anaconda to attack a well-dug-in al-Qaeda/Taliban force of about 1,500 fighters in the Shah-e-Kot Mountains south of Gardez in northeastern Afghanistan. Anaconda produced the largest number of U.S. casualties in a single Afghan operation, but apparently took a heavy toll on the enemy, killing an estimated four hundred to eight hundred opponents. Again, some of the fighters melted away into Pakistan, although in this case Pakistani forces intercepted and fought small units, capturing and turning over a number of al-Qaeda members to the United States for interrogation.

In roughly six months U.S. and allied armed intervention, coupled with the residual anti-Taliban forces in Afghanistan, had radically transformed the situation. Momentum increasingly favored the formation of a new Afghan government—although it was clear that such a government would be hard put to establish order throughout the country and develop the capacity, even with international assistance, to conduct a far-reaching economic and social rehabilitation program. Pockets of Taliban and al-Qaeda resistance remained, with a capacity to harass the emerging Karzai government and foment perceptions of disorder, but by summer 2002, these isolated elements no longer held the capacity to counter-attack the U.S. and allied presence in any major way.

During that armed campaign, the radical Islamic backlash that the Musharraf government had feared would erupt within Pakistan launched a handful of demonstrations but then largely subsided during the remainder of 2001. Considerable anti-American feeling and anger with Musharraf 's decisions percolated below the surface but potentially massive, violent agitation was contained. Meanwhile, the level of violence in Kashmir rose to a degree. Then on December 13, 2001, halfway through the armed campaign, terrorists struck the Indian parliament and precipitated a full Indian armed mobilization against Pakistan.

8

Iran's Influence in Pakistan

Iran, activated by the revolution in 1979, was also wary of the situation in Pakistan, which, in the 1980s, was turning into a stronghold of Saudi Arabia.

In Pakistan, Shias boldly claimed their rights and representation, believing that Iran's Khomeini would support them; that their model of political activism would succeed in challenging authority. Khomeini, once, sent a message to Pakistan's General Ziaul Haq, telling him if he mistreated the Shia, "he (Khomeini) would do to him what he had done to the Shah." In 1979, when tens of thousands of Pakistan's Shias travelled to Islamabad demanding exemption from Islamic taxes based on Sunni law, the Pakistani government had no choice but to concede.

Since 1979, the Islamic Republic of Iran has spent blood and ample treasure to make its influence felt all the way to the shores of the Mediterranean. Iran's attempts were resisted by Arabs, through Sunni sectarianism (Nasr, 2014).

IRAN AND PAKISTAN – IT'S COMPLICATED

The recent kidnapping of 5 Iranian soldiers serving along Iran's border with Pakistan, and their subsequent alleged captivity in Pakistani territory has shed light on the complex relationship between the two states. With western media analysis firmly focused on continued negotiations over Iran's nuclear programme and Pakistan's internal troubles, there is little written about the relations between the two neighbours who share a 900km border running through the heart of the Baluchi cultural region. This is a relationship that contains myriad complexities and the potential for conflict and cooperation, ranging from tackling Baluchi separatism and drug trafficking to pipeline politics, Afghanistan and the ever present spectre of US and Saudi interests in the Middle East and beyond.

Despite the complexities, relations have been good up until now, showing the pragmatism of both states and the importance both place on the relationship. However, the recent comments of Iranian Interior Minister Abdolreza Rahmani Fazli, who has threatened unilateral action inside Pakistani territory as a means of maintaining Iran's security and that of its soldiers serving along the border, demonstrate the potential for a rupture and the necessity for pragmatism to prevail.

Historical backdrop

Iran and Pakistan have maintained formal diplomatic relations since the latter's independence, with Iran being the first state to recognise Pakistan's independence in 1947. Relations remained positive throughout the 50s and 60s with both states falling under the US defence umbrella as signatories to the Baghdad Pact and subsequent creation of CENTO.

The Iranian revolution in 1979 coincided with the strengthening of the nominally Islamist Zia ul-Haq regime in Pakistan and the two sides maintained a practical working relationship despite the anti-US stance of the new government in the Islamic Republic. Both states cooperate in shared multi-lateral initiatives, such as the Economic Cooperation Organisation, Non-Aligned Movement and D8 group of developing nations, and share a number of joint regional concerns as highlighted below.

Baluchi separatists

The issue of Baluchi separatism is a good starting point in light of recent events in the region. The Baluchi ethnic group are split between Iran, Afghanistan and Pakistan, and there has been separatist agitation resulting in open conflict several times in Pakistan's history since independence. In Iran, Baluchi separatists have been less prominent historically, but armed groups have stepped up attacks in the last 10 years. The armed group Junduallah carried out several attacks on Iranian forces stationed in Iran's Sistan-Baluchistan province from 2004, prior to their leader Abdolmalek Rigi being captured and executed by Iran in 2010.

The capture of Iranian border guards earlier this month, along with the killing of 14 Iranian soldiers in November, was claimed by the hitherto little known group Jaish ul-Adl, formed in January 2012. In keeping with the previous statements of Jundullah, their actions are framed within the wider sectarian divide that is resurgent across the Middle East. Claims of discrimination against Sunni groups within Iran are often given as a pretext for the actions of groups such as Jaish ul-Adl as a means of garnering wider support.

Iran has frequently raised concerns with harbouring of Jundullah and Jaish ul-Adl militants on Pakistani territory, and it is within this context that recent Iranian comments regarding unilateral actions across the border to maintain its security have been made. Despite the potential for conflict, the subsequent talks held between Iranian and Pakistani representatives since the kidnappings have been largely cordial, with a focus on joint measures aimed at securing the hostages' release and further cooperation in enhancing the security of the border region. Iranian unilateral action will most likely be held off providing they receive assurances from Pakistan that they are taking the matter seriously. At this time, the Iranian government has been assured by its Pakistani counterparts that they are taking the matter seriously and that troops will be sent by Pakistan to Baluchistan to search for the hostages.

Sectarianism

This brings us to the sensitive issue of sectarianism and its place in relations between Iran and Pakistan. The Islamic Republic has historically favoured a pragmatic quiescence on sectarian tensions within Pakistan, seeing it as a domestic issue. This should come as no great surprise to Iran watchers, as despite the media focus on its patronage of Hezbollah in Lebanon and attempts to depict the avowedly secular Assad regime in Syria as 'co-religionists,' Iran has displayed pragmatism on a number of issues that defy its image as a revolutionary actor supporting its Shi'i brethren. Its support for Christian Armenia over predominantly Shi'i Azerbaijan in their conflict over the disputed Nagorno-Karabakh region (in part an outcome of the need to dampen potential separatist agitation amongst its own Azeri population) is a case in point.

Furthermore, Pakistan's Shi'i community is not involved in any notable separatist agitation, and thus Iran has been able to build on its confessional linkages in a more benign manner, primarily through its cultural centres and the work of the Islamic Culture and Research Organisation (ICRO). The ICRO runs Iran's cultural bureaus abroad, and is directly accountable to the Supreme Leader, thus providing a useful diplomatic tool and an extension of Iranian soft power right from the most important centre of power in the Iranian political system.

It's worth noting that Pakistan is home to the largest number of Iranian cultural bureaus in the world, with 8 centres in total run by the ICRO, providing cultural activities such as Persian language classes, religious commemorations and joint activities with Pakistani cultural organisations. Persian culture, particularly in art and literature, has a strong tradition in Pakistan, and the cultural links between the nations are an oft-repeated theme returned to time and again in official meetings between the two states.

Afghanistan

On Afghanistan, there has long been potential for disagreement as both sides have supported different sides in that state's protracted internal conflict.

Iran has long provided material support to the often persecuted Shi'i Hazara minority in Afghanistan, and was a key ally, along with Russia, of the Northern Alliance in its fight against the Pakistan-backed Taliban prior to the arrival of coalition forces in 2001.

Despite this, there is not any sense of any kind of war by proxy being fought here and both states are served far better by a stable Afghanistan, particularly in light of the huge number of refugees that they have both absorbed over the last 35 years.

Although they have historically backed different sides, the arrival of coalition forces and Pakistan's ongoing internal struggle with its own Taliban wing in the form of the TTP has necessitated a shift in its direct patronage of the Afghan Taliban.

Since the Taliban's ouster in Afghanistan, the Islamic Republic has gradually increased its influence in the country, particularly in the East and North which are culturally and linguistically proximate to Iran. Furthermore, while Iran-Afghan relations have been broadly positive, the Karzai government has had a tricky relationship with Pakistan in light of its links with the Taliban regime. Thus, any incorporation of moderate Taliban elements in a future Afghan government may well serve Pakistan's interests. To this end, accommodation through recognition of informal spheres of influence could serve relations between Iran and Pakistan well, with the latter extending its influence to Afghanistan's Pashtun heartlands as a means of enhancing control over its porous frontier with that country.

PIPELINE POLITICS

A further feature of Iran-Pakistan relations has been the long-running negotiations taking place over Iran's supplying of natural gas to Pakistan. The pipeline was initially billed as the 'peace pipeline' as it was due to transport Iranian natural gas to India, via Pakistan. However, negotiations predictably floundered, and Iran has focused instead on pursuing bi-lateral initiatives with each state in terms of providing access to its hydrocarbon resources. The Iran-Pakistan pipeline was signed off in 2009, with construction on the Iranian side now largely complete; however, the project has been beset by delays on the Pakistani side. A key concern is that this would mean Pakistani circumvention of the US-led sanctions regime against Iran, which would further complicate its already difficult current relationship with the United States. Keen to increase its export market, Iran had also offered to provide funding for the construction of the pipeline in Pakistan but had to withdraw this offer due to its own financial problems.

Both sides had recently been looking at ways to revive the stalled project, but Pakistan has now stated that it cannot continue with its side of the deal due to the sanctions currently in place against the Islamic Republic. For the time being, Pakistan has decided that the likely penalties for not complying with the sanctions regime outweigh access to Iran's natural gas. The current PML-N government in Pakistan also has particularly close relations with Saudi Arabia, which many feel has exerted pressure on Pakistan to abandon the project. This is where the current nuclear negotiations between Iran and the P5+1 become influential – if a deal is struck whereby sanctions are lifted, then Pakistan will have greater freedom to act, and may be less inclined to follow the advice of its Saudi allies.

Wider geopolitics

The last point takes us to the wider geopolitical currents that also have a bearing on relations between Iran and Pakistan, particularly in light of the US and Saudi positions. Although there was a noticeable détente in Iran's relations with Saudi Arabia under Rafsanjani and into the Khatami era, relations between the two states have dipped considerably in recent years. This is not only due to the recent entrenchment of the sectarian divide in the Middle East, and subsequent proxy battles for control among competing belligerents in its myriad conflicts, but also a result of increased Iranian confidence in its position in the region following the fall of two hostile neighbouring regimes in the form of Saddam's Iraq and Taliban Afghanistan. Pakistan-Saudi relations have been traditionally close, however, this has not significantly hampered relations thus far with Iran (the pipeline issue notwithstanding).

Indeed, Pakistan sees itself as something of a mediator between the two, and has given Iran assurances that it will not assist in Saudi nuclear arms development. Similarly, Iran's good relations with India are not a hugely destabilising force in the Iran-Pakistan relationship. Iran has trod a careful line on Kashmir, offering rhetorical support for the Muslim population there but little more as it desires good relations with India. Both sides therefore have potential bargaining chips, but pragmatism has prevailed.

Pakistan's at times troubled relationship with US, while a significant influence as noted above vis-à-vis the pipeline issue, has also been largely put to one side in dealings between the two states, with the focus being primarily on bi-lateral and regional concerns. Interestingly, the domestic unpopularity of Pakistan's historical alignment with US foreign policy objectives is borne out by the high esteem with which the Pakistani population holds the Islamic Republic. A 2013 global attitudes survey conducted by Pew saw 69% of Pakistanis surveyed as viewing Iran favourably, with Indonesia the only other country to record a majority holding a favourable view of the Islamic Republic with 55%.

A complex relationship where common-sense prevails

The above points to a relationship that is fraught with potential difficulties and open to manipulation of competing agendas. Both states are, perhaps sometimes unfairly, painted as problem cases in the international system with powerful internal tendencies (be they official or unofficial) that seek to challenge the international status-quo. This, along with the above external and internal pressures makes the continued common-sense approach of both governments laudable at a time when opposing views, be they religious/sectarian in nature, or security-driven are sustaining some of the world's bitterest conflicts.

The relationship between the two states is founded on a pragmatic need to maintain a working relationship despite differing security alignments, more pressing concerns within their own 'regions,' and a lack of ideological confluence. Yes, there will always be competing pressures but the relationship has been largely characterised by tactful diplomacy when bellicosity could easily prevail. Despite the firm statements coming from Iran with regards to the recent kidnappings and Pakistan's responsibility for ensuring the soldiers' safe return, both sides have sought to work together on this issue. Furthermore, the recent upturn in the trajectory of Iran's relations with the West, although still dependent on a mutually agreeable outcome of the nuclear talks, will also help keep ties on a sound footing.

Pakistan-Iran Foreign Relations

In June 2009, the Pakistani government officially congratulated Iranian President Mahmoud Ahmadinejad on his re-election.

Pakistani President Asif Ali Zardari stated that the electoral victory was a "an acknowledgment of [Ahmadinejad's] outstanding services." Allama Sajid Naqvi, the head of Tehrik-e-Islami, said that the results of the election demonstrate that Ahmadinejad enjoys the trust and support of the Iranian people and expressed hope that Iran and Pakistan will enjoy an increasingly strong bond in the future. Tehri-e-Islami is a Shia political party in Pakistan that the former Pakistani President Pervez Musharraf twice banned for ties to terrorism.

Nuclear

Pakistan has publicly defended Iran's right to nuclear technology. Some American analysts also suspect Pakistani scientists employed by the Pakistani military of helping Iran acquire nuclear technology, although Pakistan officially denies any involvement. Henry Sokolski, former deputy for nonproliferation policy in the Office of the Secretary of Defense, explained in 2003 that "the notion that Pakistan wasn't involved is getting less and less tenable." Since then, inspectors have found in Iran's possession documents from Pakistani scientist Dr. A.Q. Khan detailing how to shape uranium for nuclear warheads, while in 2004 then-Pakistani President Pervez Musharraf officially pardoned Dr. Khan for his sale of nuclear technology. According to a report by the Congressional Research Service published in 2005, Dr. Khan "could not have functioned without some level of cooperation by Pakistani military personnel, who maintained tight security around the key nuclear facilities, and possibly civilian officials as well." On March 15, 2010, Pakistan rejected a US media report asserting that Khan provided nuclear related information and material, including drawings, centrifuge components, and a list of suppliers, to Iran. Abdul Basit, a spokesman for the Pakistani Foreign Office, described the claims, published by the Washington Post, as "yet another repackaging of fiction, which surface occasionally for purposes that are self-evident."

Over the past several years, Pakistan has increasingly called for peaceful reconciliation on the international nuclear standoff, despite increasing concern from the UN and Washington.

In a February 2010 meeting with her Iranian counterpart, Pakistani National Assembly Speaker Fahmida Mirza said that "Pakistan is against any kinds of sanctions against Iran and believes that Iran's nuclear disputes should be resolved peacefully and through dialogue." In a separate meeting with Iranian President Mahmoud Ahmadinejad, Mirza reiterated her earlier remarks and assured him that Pakistan supports Iran's independence and progress in all the areas, especially in utilizing peaceful nuclear energy. She also highlighted Iranian-Pakistani commonalities in religion, history, and culture, and added that extremism and terrorism is a common threat to the stability and progress of the entire region.

Economic Relationship

The two countries initiated significant cooperation in the energy sector in 1991, when Iran began negotiating an oil deal with Pakistan and Qatar. This initial collaboration, however, was limited and did not progress meaningfully. Iran again attempted negotiating with Qatar regarding the construction of gas pipelines to Pakistan in 1995, however was unsuccessful. Cooperation regarding energy has nonetheless increased since the 1990s and helped provide the foundation for a more thorough bilateral trade network between Iran and Pakistan in recent years. By 2005, Pakistan was actively seeking Iranian investment in bilateral trade and energy cooperation. Pakistan and Iran have deepened their economic partnership to such an extent that, in a joint statement issued in May 2010, the two countries expressed satisfaction with an increase in bilateral trade, which surpassed $1.2 billion in the previous financial year. In 2009, Pakistan increased its non-oil exports to Iran by 80 percent, reaching $279 million. Similarly, Iranian non-oil exports to Pakistan increased by 11 percent, totaling $278 million for the year. Despite this growth, Karachi Chambeer of Commerce and Industry President Abdul Majid Haji Mohammad said the lack of a banking system remains a major obstacle to Iran-Pakistan trade.

Since 2005, Islamabad has increasingly turned to Tehran to supply Pakistan's growing energy needs. In August 2008, Iran agreed to finance a robust energy project that would allow Pakistan to import 1,000 megawatts of electricity to overcome its power shortage. The project, a $60 million endeavor, consists of running a 100-kilometer electric line to help augment the 40 megawatts of electricity Pakistan already receives daily from Iran. In April 2010, Iranian Ambassador to Pakistan Mashallah Shakeri spoke before the Rawalpindi Chamber of Commerce and Industry, stressing Iran's commitment to economic relations with Pakistan. According to the envoy, Iran intends to supply the 1,000 megawatts to Pakistan at a discounted rate.

Iran and Pakistan have long discussed the construction of a 2,600-kilometer, $7.5 billion Iran-Pakistan-India gas pipeline (IPI) that would pump gas from Iran's South Pars field to Pakistan and India. Tentative talks on the pipeline began in 1994, however tense political relations between India and Pakistan frustrated realization of the project. International concern over Iran's nuclear program further delayed agreement and in November 2007 Iran and Pakistan accused India of hesitating because of pressure from the United States. In February 2010, Iranian Foreign Minister Manouchehr Mottaki accused the US of interfering with the planned pipeline by attempting to sway New Delhi away from the IPI. Indeed, Washington has repeatedly urged India not to follow through with the deal while Iran faces sanctions for its nuclear enrichment program. Both Russia and China have taken significant interest in the pipeline, with Russia's Gazprom offering to help supply oil and China holding talks with Iran and Pakistan in 2008 to replace India in case New Delhi chose to reject the partnership.

In May 2009, Iran and Pakistan signed a purchase agreement stipulating that Iran will initially transfer 30 million cubic meters of gas to Pakistan per day, with the volume eventually increasing to 60 million. The deal, to which India was not a party, ensures gas supplies to Pakistan for a period of 25 years. On June 13, 2010, the two sides formally concluded the $7.5 billion agreement over the objections of US Special Representative for Pakistan and Afghanistan Richard Holbrooke, who cautioned that although the "US understands that Pakistan faces [a] major energy crisis... new sanctions on Iran can impact Pakistan." According to a previous Pakistani Petroleum Ministry statement in May 2010, "the capital cost for the Pakistan section is estimated at 1.65 billion dollars…[and] the first gas flow is targeted by end 2014" with Iran completing the project ahead of schedule.

During a July 30, 2009 interview with the Iranian Islamic Republic News Agency, Dr. Ashfaq Hassan Khan, a former economic advisor in Pakistan, insisted that while economic ties between Iran and Pakistan should expand at all levels, cooperation in the energy sector is vital for Pakistan. Khan further expressed his view that the planned Iran-Pakistan pipeline would likely greatly benefit both countries.

Iran-Pakistan cooperation on transportation issues expanded greatly in August 2009, when the two inaugurated an international freight rail line from Islamabad to Istanbul via Tehran. The line is a "pilot project" of the Economic Cooperation Organization (ECO), a Central Asian trade bloc. Although Iran and Turkey already enjoy extensive rail cooperation, transportation ties with Pakistan are weaker. According to Director of Pakistan Railways Shafiqullah Khan, Islamabad and Tehran are seeking outside credit to resolve differences in rail gauge in order to regularize rail service between the two. Officials expect to begin regular freight service along the 6,500 km line in August 2010.

In February 2010, Punjab Chief Minister Muhammad Shahbaz Sharif called for the creation of an economic free-trade zone among Pakistan, Iran, Turkey and other Islamic countries. During a celebration of the 31st Revolution Day of Iran, Sharif noted that "deep, friendly relations exist between Pakistan and Iran and it is the need of the hour that socio-economic cooperation should be promoted."

Iranian and Pakistani officials, in February 2010, signed the first memorandum of understanding (MoU) between the two countries on cross border trade. The MoU was penned during the two countries' first joint committee meeting on border trade in Iran's southeastern Sistan and Balouchestan province. Iraj Hassanpour, the head of Sistan and Balouchestan's trade organization, stated that "[b]ased on [the] MoU, [the] two countries are bound to hold public and specialized fairs at their common borders and in [the] capital of Sistan & Balouchestan province,

Zahedan, and Quetta in Pakistan." Both sides also decided to establish large storehouses to facilitate the storage of trade commodities at their border customs.

Sardar Muhammad Latif Khan Khosa, a Pakistani advisor to the prime minister on information technology, has called for increased collaboration between Iran and Pakistan in telecommunications. During a June 2010 conversation with Iran's ambassador to Pakistan, Mashallah Shakeri, Khosa expressed his belief that increased bilateral activity in the sector has the potential to increase regional economic development and security.

POST TALIBAN AFGHANISTAN AND PAK-IRAN RELATIONS

The scenario in Afghanistan took a dramatic turn after 9/11, when US declared war against Al Qaida and Taliban in Afghanistan, which resulted in the fall of Taliban rule in Afghanistan. Mullah Omer and Osama Bin Laden, most wanted to USA, succeeded in fleeing the country, and thus, the Pro-US Government of Northern Alliance was installed in Afghanistan. The fall of Taliban (anti-Iranian) removed a major irritant in Pak-Iran relations. The new trends in the regional strategic dynamics necessitated Pak-Iran relations. But, more than, it was change in Pakistani policy towards Taliban in the wake of US led attack against Afghanistan that paved the way for new upward trends in Pak-Iran relations.Pakistan sided with the international coalition against Taliban, who were soon removed from the government in Kabul. The Taliban retreat led Pakistan and Iran to end their decade old strained relations and work for accommodating each other's strategic and economic interests in Afghanistan.

Soon after the fall of Taliban in Afghanistan, the Iranian Foreign Minister, Kamal Kharazi, paid a to day visit to Islamabad, during which he confirmed that both the countries had come to close to each other's point of view on Afghan issue. Both agreed to help to each other for the establishment of broad based multi-ethnic government in Afghanistan under the auspices of United Nations. He said "we have removed our differences in our talks as we observe that Pakistan has changed its policy and agreed to play collective role in the reconstruction of Afghanistan." The fall of Taliban ushered a new era of cordiality, goodwill and cooperation in Pak-Iran relations. A statement of the then Foreign Minister of Pakistan, Abdul Sattar, in November 2001, "That the clouds are over and the sun is shinning over the skies of Pakistan and Iran" was meaningful and reflective of the new political development between them. Earlier, Iran has seriously objected to not only the political and diplomatic support of Pakistan to Taliban but also on the reports of the presence of Pakistani troops within Taliban militia.

Pakistan and Iran promised to forget their past differences in Afghanistan if any one and resolved to work jointly for the establishment of stable and durable government in Afghanistan, which would not only served the best interests of these countries, but, the interests of all the ethnic communities living inside Afghanistan. According to the Iranian scholar; "the 9/11 terrorist attack and the subsequent fall of Taliban in Afghanistan paved the way for mending of bilateral relations." Both the countries are against the US bombardment in Afghanistan and resolved that the same should come to an end. Both the countries desire for peaceful, prosperous and harmonious Afghanistan. Such an understanding suits both the nations and helps greatly to ensure a complete stability in Afghanistan as well. They also retreated to respect the sovereignty, territorial integrity and their full support for Hamid Karzai's interim government and Bonn Peace Process.

Pakistan and Iran are geo-politically important to the peace and stability in Afghanistan, a fact recognized not only by both countries but also by the extra-regional players. Thus, Pakistan and Iran in the context of new Afghan set up under Hamid Karzai can work together to be the real guarantors of Afghanistan's reconstruction and security, which itself is very important for peace and prosperity for these countries. In fact, the convergence of interests and the policies of these two countries on Afghanistan could serve a strong basis for their future bilateral relationship. However, the US-Iran rivalry, the presence of the American forces in Afghanistan and Central Asia, Pakistan support to the US policies in Afghanistan and the bases and ports facilities provided by

Pakistan, still casts doubts on the prospects of any long tem strong relations between Pakistan and Iran.

Conclusion

The triangular relationship of Pakistan, Iran and Afghanistan was disrupted since the inception of Pakistan, when Iran became Pakistan's close friend and Afghanistan as its worse rival. The convergence of interests, common security concerns and policies, similar approaches and mutual understanding were the numerous factors which led Iran and Pakistan an enduring friends and allies. Moreover, Iranian help and full support to Pakistan on the issue of Kashmir and its two Indo-Pak wars proved a great source of courage, consolation, and satisfaction to Pakistan.

Friendship with Iran proved time-tested which greatly enhance Pakistan's international dignity and prestige against its over-ambitious rival, India. On the other hand, Pakistan's relation with Afghanistan became strain on the issue of Pakhtunistan. This issue proved an irritating factor in Pak-Afghan relations which caused a deep mistrust, misunderstanding, discontent, disruption and dissatisfaction in their bilateral relationship. However, the Iran's mediating role and its constructive and meaningful effort proved a significant factor in bringing these countries (Pakistan and Afghanistan), close to each other.

The situation took a different turn in the wake of the Soviet intervention in Afghanistan. The intervention produced the homogeneity of interests between Pakistan and Iran as both countries were facing equally the political, social and the economic consequences of the Afghan problem. Generally speaking, the policies of the two countries (Pakistan and Iran) regarding Afghanistan were similar and cooperative despite of Iran's strong objective Pakistan's close association with USA (Iran's staunch enemy) and its role as a frontline state on the other side, Iran did not play a major role in the Afghan's conflict due to its preoccupation with its inter problems arising out Islamic Revolution and its long eight years war with Iraq. But after the conclusion of Iran-Iraq War which coincided with the signing of Geneva Accord in 1988 that stipulated the withdrawal of Soviet

Union from Afghanistan, Iran began to play an effective role inside Afghanistan.

The Iranian activism vis-à-vis Afghanistan became a serious source of friction, which in the time transformed into active rivalry. The representation of the rival Afghan factions in the formation of future government in Afghanistan became the bone of contention between Pakistan and Iran. More important, the emergence of Taliban in Afghanistan witnessed contradiction, confrontation, competition, disruption and dissatisfaction in Pak-Iran relations. Their divergent policies, different approaches on the issue of Taliban in Afghanistan made them a virtual rivals and strong competitors. Friendship with Iran is a cornerstone of Pakistan's foreign policy. But the warmth in their relations; unfortunately, gave way to active antagonism following Pakistan's overt backing for Taliban. Thus, their confrontationist stance in Afghanistan blocked all the chances of their good relationship. Their support for respective ethnic groups (Pakistan supported the cause of Taliban while Iran supported the anti-Taliban Northern Alliance) further widened the gulf between the two countries. The occupation of Kabul and Herat by Taliban in 1996 and 1997 respectively added fuel to fire to already strained relations. Furthermore, the Mazar-e-Sharif incident and the assassination of nine Iranian diplomats gave a final blow to Pak-Iran relations.

The killing of Iranian citizens and diplomats in Pakistan adversely affected their relations. And above all, the intensification of the sectarian strife and the failure of Pakistan's judicial process to comply with contributed negatively in Pak-Iran relations. The sectarian disharmony gave the feeling of insecurity to the Iranian nationals and officials in Pakistan. Effort on the part of the government of Pakistan to eradicate this menace from society did not materialize. Similarly, the Indian media campaign against Pakistan was yet, another factor, which led the two neighbours, and friends continued to draft apart on the sectarian issue.

The ouster of Taliban from Afghanistan removed a major irritant which provided both the countries with the opportunity to work jointly as the real guarantor of Afghanistan's peace, progress, prosperity and reconstruction. Above all, the statement of Pakistan's Foreign Minister Abdul Sattar in November-2002, further clarifies the situation that, "the clouds were over and the Sun is shinning over the skies of Pakistan and Iran was meaningful and reflective of the new political development between these two countries."

PAK-IRAN RELATIONS UNDER THE SHADOW OF TALIBAN IN AFGHANISTAN

The relations between the two countries entered into rough and abnormal phase when an unknown faction, Taliban, emerged in Afghanistan, and within a short span of two years, became a leading political and military power of the country. According to Professor Dani, "the Taliban received their early education at Deeni Madrasas in Pakistan and were being supported by the religious elements in Pakistan. Dani claimed that the young students were being prepared for Jihad against whom; it was observed were not adhering to the moral code of Islam.

Regarding the origin of Taliban, two points of view are widely circulated. The first is 'the Islamic point of view', which highlights the rise of Islamic fundamentalism, and the second, is the 'the US point of view'. According to the Islamic point of view, Taliban had first come into force under the leadership of Mullah Umer, a well-known and respected Mujahid leader of the area, who successfully fought against the Soviet Union. After the fall of Najib, he got much popularity and assumed the religious role as the head of Madarsa. What followed than is better explained by Ralph Magnus and Eden Naby, in these words, "the chaos and lawlessness of the local lords, bandits, and drug dealers disrupted Mullah Umer and a number of like minded Mullahs and former Mujahideen.In July, 1994, a particular highway robbery and assault on women made Mullah Umer to assemble a force of his own group Taliban and former Afghan Mujahideen to punish criminals who were responsible for this inhume action. The effect of his action was electrifying public opinion, and other local commanders rallied round Taliban. They captured the Afghan border town Spin Boldak in October and Qandahar in November 1994, respectively after been invited by the local residents.

As for as the US point of view, it is generally believed the United States was a master-minded the creation of Taliban for serving its own interests in Afghanistan, most, on the similar pattern which it followed in organizing and training of Afghan Mujahideen to fight against Soviet Union in Afghanistan. This point of view, is however, credibly substantiate by Richard Mackenzie, Editor in Chief of Global News Services and a regular visitor of Afghanistan, who in his paper "the United States and Taliban" has successfully pointed out many realities behind the scene of US policy regarding Taliban. He asserted that "long before the Taliban began their thrust towards Kabul, the US officials had high aspirations." They hoped that Taliban would serve the US supreme interest in Afghanistan.

The ideological difference between Iran and Taliban made them a natural rivals and strong competitors in Afghanistan. The Taliban was highly orthodox Sunni Islamic Movement while Iran is a Shia majority country. Hence, the emergence of Taliban is Afghanistan was mentally and psychologically unacceptable to Iran, and tried its best to crush and to root out their lasting influence from Afghanistan once for all. The emergence of Taliban in Afghanistan led a major divergence in Pak-Iran relations. Both (Pakistan and Iran) had different policies, perceptions, and approaches, with regard to Afghanistan. Pakistan was supporting the cause of Taliban, while Iran was a staunch supporter of Anti-Taliban Northern Alliance. Their support for apposite factions made them natural rivals in the affairs of Afghanistan.

Pakistan was supporting Taliban in hope that they would have become a strong military force and their determination to establish their control over the major parts of Afghanistan. Pakistan's policy of supporting Taliban, however, was based more on the anger and antagonism as they felt against Rabbani, who was instrumental in sacking Pakistan's embassy in Kabul, than the genuine love for Taliban whose doctrine of interpretation of Shariah did not coincide with Islamabad. Pakistan's moral, diplomatic, and material support to Taliban was based partly on the desire to protect and promote its own national interest. According to C. Plano and Roy Olton, "National interest is the fundamental objective and the ultimate determinant that guide the decision makers of the state, is typically a highly generalize conception of these elements that constitutes the state's most vital needs."

Dr. Goga an advisor to Foreign Minister of Uzbekistan remarked during a Press Conference in Peshawar in February, 1996, that Pakistan foreign policy was not very passive, implying that Pakistan was involved in the supply of arms and armaments to its favorite in Afghanistan. The main objective of Pakistan's Foreign policy vis-à-vis Taliban have been;

a. Durable peace in a war-ravaged land;
b. A friendly government across its western border;
c. Repatriation of Afghan refuges;
d. Access to Central Asian markets;
e. A safe route for oil and gas pipeline from Turkmenistan to Arabian Sea.

Dr. Iffat Malik is of the view, that Iran has a several reasons of opposing Taliban. Apart from the ideological factor, the Iranian concern for Shia living in Afghanistan, of whom the largest group was Hazaras. Taliban have been accused of targeting Hazaras, even carrying out massacres against them. The obvious example was the murder of a prominent Hizb-e-Wahdat leader, Abdul Ali Mazari, while in their custody. Iran has also been accused that the drug-trafficking increased with the emergence of Taliban. According to General Zaeri, the Iranian Police Chief, around 147 tons of drugs being smuggled by Taliban has been seized in March, 1996.

More important than this essentially 'human' reason for Iran's opposition to Taliban are geo-politics and economics. For Iran, Afghanistan is a gateway to Central Asia, while it would not wish to rule the country. Iran wanted the establishment of Pro-Iranian Government in Afghanistan, which allow it an easy and assured access to Central Asia. Hence, Iran did not recognize Taliban's supreme control over most parts of Afghanistan. The geo-political reason for Iranian opposition to Taliban is linked to the Caspian Sea region and will be considered in movement. According to Iran, a counter informal alliance of USA, Saudi Arab, and Pakistan was emerged which support Taliban in Afghanistan. Iran was apprehended that in case of Taliban's victory, they would defeat the pro-Iran Afghan factions, unify the country, and thus made Afghanistan an alternative gateway for Pakistan to Central Asia. This was the part of general policy of US to contain Iran. Hence Iran's initial reaction to Taliban victory was to condemn it as the handiwork of Pak-US-Saudi.

Pak-Iran differences were increased when Taliban occupied the city of Heart in early 1995, and expelled pro-Iranian commander Ismail Khan from Heart and forced him to take refugee in Iran. This was realized by Tehran as Pakistan's backed move to take over the area, which was traditionally within Iran's sphere of influence. Afterwards, Iran and Pakistan supported the rival parties in their struggles for power. Moreover, Taliban's success to capture of Kabul in September 1996, further strained Pak-Iran relations. After the capture of Kabul most parts of Afghanistan (about 90%) adjoining Pakistani border; came under their control. The government in Islamabad had no option but to give de-facto recognition to Taliban Government in Afghanistan. However, Iran continued to support the so-called Northern Alliance consisting the faction of Rabbani, Dostum and Shia Hizb-e-Wahdat, which had it's headquarter at Mazar-i-Sharif.

The gulf between the two countries widened with the victories of Taliban and the defeat of pro-Iranian faction, Northern Alliance. The Iranian government and media openly criticized Pakistan for creating Taliban and stressing for the establishment of broad based multi-ethnic government in Afghanistan. Pakistan not only recognized the government of Taliban, but also pleaded for international community's recognition of Taliban government in Afghanistan on the basis of ground realities. While Iran continued to support and recognize the Rabbani Government. On October 23, 1996, the Iranian Foreign Minister, Ali Akbar Velayati at a Press Conference in Tehran made it absolutely clear that his country continued to recognize only the Rabbani Government. It also emphasized the need for the establishment of broad-based government upholding the sovereignty, and territorial integrity and political independence of Afghanistan.

THE TRAGEDY OF MAZAR-E-SHARIF AND PAK-IRAN RELATIONS

The differences between Iran and Pakistan touched their lowest ebb, in 1998, when the Taliban captured the Afghan city of Mazar-e-Sharif (the Stronghold and the Headquarter of Northern Alliance), and killed a scores of Iranian diplomats allegedly supporting the cause of the Northern Alliance. The Iranian reaction became harsh and severe and this led to the open confrontation between Iran and Taliban controlled Afghanistan. Pakistan was condemned by Iran for supporting Taliban. Iran blamed Pakistan for its considerable influence over Taliban in Afghanistan. However, Pakistani analysts were of the view that Pakistan's influence over Taliban in Afghanistan was exaggerated by Indian propaganda, whose objective was to project Pakistan as fundamentalist State by linking it with Taliban. The two armies (The Iranian and Taliban) stood eyeball to eyeball and there was grave possibility of conflict between them. What makes the situation so critical for Pakistan, is the opening warming of the Iranian Supreme leader Ayatollah Khamaini, asking Islamabad to stop backing the Taliban militia which has been told "to abandon its action which had led to catastrophe" In his statement from Radio Tehran, the Iranian Supreme leader said, "I have — so far prevented the lightening of fire in the region which would be hard to extinguish. But all should not that a very great and wide danger is quite near." It was really a strong reaction by the Iranian leader towards Pakistan. He called upon the people of Pakistan what he had said, was interference in Afghanistan by the segments of Pakistani Army.

M.S. Johari in his book, "the Taliban; Assent to Power" writes "that earlier the Iranian had seriously objected to not only to the political and diplomatic support to Taliban but also on the reports of the presence of Pakistani troops within Taliban militia. For instance, refugees from Mazar-e-Sharif reported that the Taliban were occupied by Pakistani fighter identifiable by their language and flag of the Muslim fundamentalist party aligned with Taliban." The Mazar-e-Sharif incident led dire consequences for Pak-Iran relations. The Iranian turned hostile against Pakistan. The Iranian anger and hostility was obvious from several demonstrations which occurred in Tehran and other major Iranian cities, in which thousand of people took part and raised a slogans "death to America, death to Taliban, and death to Taliban's backers."

It is something discouraging and disappointing that, in October 1998, the security forces prompted Iran to pull sixty of its diplomats out of Pakistan. The Iranian press had a great misgiving about Taliban. They considered Taliban as the offspring of ISI, puppet and stooge of Pakistan.The Iranian Foreign Minister, Kamal Kharazi told on Radio Tehran on his return from UN General Assembly that: "it is entirely natural to cut down the number of one diplomat in a country when their security is not assured."

In the words of Syed Abdul Hassan Raeissassadat, the Former Director General of Khan-e-Farhang, Peshawar, "the Taliban factor in Pak-Iran relations proved suicidal for the geo-strategic and the economic interests of both the countries (Iran and Pakistan). It was a serious challenge and a root cause of divergence in Pak-Iran relations, which in turn, gave birth to other problems, confusion and tensions in their mutual bilateral relationship. Of these, the sectarian conflicts in Pakistan, Pak-Iran tussle and competition in Central Asia, and Iran's growing and meaningful relations with India were outstanding. Of course Pakistan denied all the charges particularly its involvement of problem of some elements of its security agencies and official militia. The disagreement on Afghanistan was just one of the many jagged edges of a bilateral relationship that had been smooth more in 'myth than in reality; on this particular issue between Pakistan and Iran. But from the real political point of view, Pakistan support to Taliban was not because of its competition with Iran but primarily because of the India against which Pakistan, as a matter of defense policy, had always tried to avoid two front threats in its northeast and northwest. Thus, it was the compulsion of Pakistan to recognize a friendly regime in the shape of Taliban in Afghanistan which was more a geo-political rather than the ideological requirement for Pakistan.

Not only had this, but the government of Nawaz Sharif tried its best to diffuse the tension between Kabul and Tehran, and persuade them for negotiation. For this purpose, the Prime Minister sent his Foreign Minister, Sartaj Aziz, on a special mission to Tehran to resume the Iranian government that Pakistan would use all its influences with Taliban to obtain satisfaction of the Iranian demand for the return of its nationals and, the punishment of those guilty of the killing of Iranian diplomats in Mazar-e-Sharif. The Prime Minister Nawaz Sharif met President Khatami in New York a few days later, and their talks brought about a significant breakthrough in ending the tension between them. They agreed that brotherly relations between the two countries are "precious" and precondition for maintaining a complete regional peace and stability. The main points of agreement between the two countries were discussed. The external forces were shaping the situation in Afghanistan, and it was agreed that the efforts should be made under the UN auspices to promote durable peace. As the two sides agreed to build on positive signals, and to maintain mutual friendship and trust.

The developments since the historic meeting have witnessed the continuation of positive trends. During this period, Pakistan also coordinated closely with the neighbouring Iran with which it launched a joint mission to promote an Afghan peace process in June-July, 1998. Pakistan's Foreign Secretary Shamshad, accordingly, visited Tehran in the first week of January 1999, for bilateral consultation with his Iranian counterpart; during his meeting he was also received by Foreign Minister and President. But unfortunately, the Iranian response to our earnest desires and patient efforts to improve bilateral relations had been rather luck-warm. Apart from this, the eliciting reaffirmation of Tehran's support for UN Resolutions on Kashmir and reference to Afghan historical reality that discounts the utility of outside pressure in the evolution of government in Kabul, no convergence of views on Afghanistan seem to have emerged during these visits.

9

The Pakistani Army: Order of Battle

The Pakistani army is organized into nine Corps and Force Command Northern Area. These contain 22 divisions, 15 independent brigades (6 armoured and 9 infantry), 9 Corps artillery brigades, 7 engineering brigades and 15 army aviation squadrons - including two of attack helicopters. In addition, the Pakistani army has 8 air defence brigades. It must be pointed out, however, that Pakistani brigades and divisions are somewhat smaller than their Indian counterparts. Again, this order of battle differs to a certain extent from that normally quoted. The order of battle is as follows:

Pakistan's two principal fighting formations are Army Reserve North (ARN) and Army Reserve South (ARS). These are an approximate equivalent to the Indian Strike Corps in terms of size and composition. These have, as in the case of their Indian counterparts, a nucleus of a single armoured division and up to two infantry divisions with numerous brigades:

STATUS OF COMBAT ARMS

Armour

As in the case of the Indian army, the Pakistani army possesses three armoured division and a number of armoured brigades. These operate almost 2,500 Main Battle Tanks of a bewildering variety and from various generations. The most recent acquisitions are 320 T-80 UD MBTs from the Ukraine. This deal has been mired in controversy because of Russia's refusal to supply spares, including gun barrels, and doubts over Ukraine's ability to provide spares and support.

The T-80UD is a major improvement over the existing Pakistani tank fleet. The most modern units, until the arrival of the T-80UDs, were license made Chinese T-85 II tanks. An indigenous MBT - the Al-Khalid - has failed to materialise. The rest of the fleet consists of over a thousand T-69/-59 tanks of Chinese origin, which have been upgraded with 105mm guns. The rest of the fleet is a mixture of 1950s & 1960s vintage M-47/-48A5 tanks. These, while serviceable, are not really a match for even older Indian armour. The Pakistani tank fleet lacks modern fire control equipment and advanced night-fighting capabilities. It can be expected that Pakistan will attempt to rectify this in the near future.

Artillery

As in the case of its Indian counterpart, Pakistan's Regiment of Artillery has undergone a tremendous re-organization and modernization programme. While substantial quantities of new equipment have been inducted, large numbers of completely obsolete artillery pieces - long since relegated to reserve/storage status in the Indian army - remain in service.

Pakistan created the subcontinent's first artillery division using a core component of two artillery brigades and an air defence unit. While Pakistan has far fewer artillery tubes than the massive Indian artillery park, it is interesting to note that it was responsible for this major organizational innovation. The most noteworthy feature of Pakistan's artillery is the number of 155 and 203mm self-propelled guns. This gives Pakistani armour an integral artillery capability that is currently lacking in Indian armoured units. Moreover, these guns are more easily operated in an NBC environment than towed guns.

Pakistan's artillery also comprises an assortment of older pieces, including some Second World War vintage 25 pounders. As in the case of the Indian artillery, considerable progress has been made in the introduction of fire control computers and other surveillance and target acquisition equipment. This, of course, dramatically enhances the efficacy of artillery - no matter how old the guns are.

Infantry

There is not much difference between Pakistani and Indian army infantry formations. Pakistan has not developed an organization equivalent to the Indian RAPIDS and has not attempted the massive modernization programme - in terms of modern night vision, target finding and anti-tank weaponry - that the Indian army has recently undertaken. The only really noteworthy aspect of the Pakistani infantry is the fact that it was the first to introduce mechanized units to the subcontinent. These mechanized infantry units are provided with over eight hundred M-113 armoured personnel carriers. While not as capable as India's BMP-2 units, these older APCs provide Pakistan's infantry with a reasonable degree of battlefield mobility. However, as far as NBC warfare is concerned, these older APCs offer somewhat less protection than the BMPs.

Air Defense

Unlike the Indian army, Pakistan lacks any medium self-propelled surface-to-air missiles and modern self-propelled air-defence guns. Pakistan's six air defence brigades are equipped with a wide variety of shoulder-launched SAMs and thousands of towed air defence guns. These are used with both Western and Chinese fire-control radar. It is not known if Pakistan intends to obtain any more advanced radar and target acquisition equipment. The Pakistani army air defence units remain constrained in their ability to obtain advanced self-propelled air-defence assets since Russia, the principal producer of these items, will not sell these items to Pakistan. Strangely enough, Pakistan does not seem to be making particularly vigorous efforts to rectify this shortcoming in their army air defences.

NBC Warfare

Both the Indian and Pakistani armies are extremely well trained. This is especially true up to brigade level. Both armies possess a high degree of tactical skill and pride themselves on their ability to perform their assigned tasks. Using a mixture of traditional methods and modern techniques and equipment, both armies are extremely capable. In the area of NBC warfare, however, a rather confusing picture emerges. Both countries frequently made mention of their ability to fight in NBC conditions, but little hard information is available on the degree of NBC readiness.

In the 1980s, the Indian army began some tentative preparations for NBC warfare. In the early part of that decade, a limited quantity of S6 respirators and No.1Mk.3 NBC suits - both of British origin - was purchased. A quantity of NBC equipment was imported from the USSR, but proved to be useless in Indian environmental conditions. Moreover, India's defence research organization, in 1987, produced prototypes of NBC suits, decontamination suits, facelets, overboots and NBC tents. This equipment has entered production and service with the Indian armed forces.

As regards training, from 1987 onwards, the Indian army, through its College of Military Engineering, began running familiarization courses in NBC warfare, while scientist conducted courses at brigade level. Moreover, a series of studies were undertaken to provide for both active and passive defence against nuclear attack for army combat formations.

As regards equipment, the Indian Ministry of Defence has obviously allocated high priority to the indigenous production of NBC gear.

This has also involved the participation of the private sector for the manufacture of both NBC suits and respirators. In addition, the Indian army has retained its old Second World War respirators - these are old, but would still offer significant protection. India would not find it particularly difficult to produce enough NBC personal gear - respirators and NBC suits - for its armed forces in a relatively short period of time - though this equipment might be placed in storage. Mention should also be made of the fact that a new decontamination vehicle has entered production.

While it is abundantly clear that NBC warfare has been accorded a much higher priority in the Indian army, it remains unclear as to the exact status of NBC preparedness and training in the Indian army. Attempts to contact senior military officers on this subject proved unsuccessful, though some retired officers offered some vague information that leads to the conclusion that some training is in progress.

It has become clear that India's Army Training Command has conducted detailed studies into NBC warfare. Indeed, given India's perception of its nuclear threat, it is not surprising that the Indian army schools of instruction and combat include NBC scenarios. Moreover, the publisher of the prestigious Indian Defence Review stated that the forces earmarked for use against Pakistan are well equipped to deal with NBC warfare.

It would be natural for India's Strike Corps to be the first to be fully equipped and prepared for NBC warfare and there are some indications of this beginning to occur. It is highly probable that at least one Corps is fully prepared - trained and equipped for NBC warfare. The other formations would probably receive personal NBC gear - but will be allocated a lower priority for receiving decontamination and monitoring equipment. It should be pointed out that the RAPIDS require virtually no modifications for deployment in an NBC environment.

It can probably be assumed that the state of NBC warfare in Pakistan is in a similar state to that of India, except that Pakistan's industry is not yet capable of meeting all NBC needs and that the country lacks the massive R & D infrastructure of India. Indian sources assume that Pakistan has a nucleus of NBC trained personnel - with Chinese NBC gear.

One thing is clear, however, both countries have now made NBC warfare something of a priority and are making efforts - covertly - to train and equip themselves. Nonetheless, there may be a large gap between what the military wants and reality.

While there is some reference to NBC warfare and the necessity to fight under such conditions in both armies, there have never been any major NBC exercises conducted by either side. It is therefore not inconceivable that the principal focus of NBC training and equipment programs in both countries is more geared towards meeting an emergency that might arise after one side uses such weapons. This would involve stockpiling equipment and drafting rapid training instructions - aimed at rapidly familiarizing troops who have to enter an NBC contaminated area. It does not seem that either country intends to develop a tactical nuclear warfare doctrine.

One of the reasons for the lack of NBC exercises could be the extremely severe environmental conditions prevailing on the South Asian battlefield. These conditions range from the intense cold of the Siachen glacier to the blistering heat of the Thar desert. Under normal peacetime conditions these climates pose great difficulties for human endurance, if the troops were clad in full NBC gear and armoured vehicles 'buttoned-up', there would be more casualties from heat-stroke than from exposure.

This brings us to the other issue that needs to be considered - where on the South Asian battlefield could tactical nuclear weapons possibly be used ? The answer to this question will determine whether or not there is any battlefield use for nuclear weapons.

PAKISTAN ARMY MOVED INTO THE POLITICAL ARENA

Pakistan Army, throughout its 54 years of existence, has been involved in the administration of the country – often in augmentation of bureaucracy in purely civil jobs, occasionally in aid of civil power for maintenance of law and order and off and on in governing the country under Martial Law regimes. It has earned kudos and criticism depending on its aims and achievements in the assigned or assumed tasks. Escorting caravans of refugees, fighting floods, checking illegal trade, running steamers and trains, building roads or killing wild boars were all people friendly activities. Number of times troops were called out in aid of civil power for maintenance of public peace and imposition of the will of the government. Lahore (1953), Kalat (1958), Dir-Bajaur (1961), Balochistan (1974) are examples that fall in this category. These operations were constitutional and executed with efficiency and elan.

Three times 1958, 1969 and 1977 the whole country was placed under Martial Law. In 1999 when the mismanagement of a ruthless dictator had reached a new zenith the Army moved in and replaced the civilian government. Martial Law was not declared. The regime received its legitimacy from the Supreme Court. In all these cases, the purists have vehemently argued against assumption of civil power by the army.

According to them, problems of political adjustment and consensus could have been sorted out through the political process had it been allowed the time. Others make vigorous case in favour of the army leaders' actions and credit them with having saved the country at relevant times.

However, even by the standards of pro-military elements the glaring failure of army leadership to keep the country together in 1971, prevent estrangement of Balochistan in the wake of 1974 Marri-Bugti operations and thwart understated hostility in Sindh during the MRD movement (1983) are exceptions that cannot be glossed over lightly.

It must also be admitted that differences did exist in the perceptions of junior ranks and the leadership component on the role of the army in situations that were purely political. It goes to the credit of the institution and its leadership that the essential unity of the force has remained rock solid. For this compliments are due to the moral and mental prowess of the army commanders who at relevant times were able to convince the rank and file and indeed the whole country that army's actions were indeed in the defence and extension of supreme national interest. Part of credit must go to army's recruitment and training policies that emphasise loyalty under stress and willing subordination of the individual to the collective will of the institution.

Now back to history. The departing British rulers had initially not contemplated the division of the Indian Army. The Chiefs of Staff in London had 'hoped for a political settlement'. When the Quaid made it clear that he meant to see Pakistan a fully independent country with no binds on its sovereignty, the directive for the bifurcation of the Indian Army was issued. Liaquat Ali Khan echoed the Quaid and said that Pakistan without an army would collapse like a 'house of cards'. Muslim League was resolved to take over only when the incipient government of Pakistan had its army and under its own control.

A degree of emphasis is detectable. Why such a stance? Was it solely due to the external dangers that undoubtedly loomed large? Or did their concerns have an internal dimension also? Wasn't there an element of doubt in the mind of the two leaders about the capability of political institutions to control and ensure cohesion in the newly acquired state?

'Moth-eaten,' lamented the Quaid-e-Azam when he first saw the map of Pakistan. Implied was a cause to worry and a reason for speedy acquisition of strength to offset the diminished capability. Machinations of the Hindu bureaucracy in the Ministry of Defence ensured that Pakistan's Armed Forces are denied their rightful share of defence equipment.

The new state with no government machinery and infrastructure faced danger from two sides. An influx of refugees and a war in Kashmir in the east and claims to the Frontier province by Afghanistan in the west put Pakistan in a bind. However, despite meagreness in men and material, the Army proved to be the most effective, reliable and stable among the instruments of state power.

Colossal problems and chaos on one hand and proven effectiveness of the army on the other persuaded the early rulers to quickly 'starch the limp security apparatus' they had inherited. The Army claimed and received special patronage from the government. In view of what it could be asked to do in a situation of extreme uncertainty allocation of resources was perfectly justified.

Says Stephen Cohen in his treatise on Pakistan Army, 'There are armies that guard the nation's borders, there are those that are concerned with protecting their own position in the society, and there are those that defend a cause or an idea. The Pakistan Army does all three.' This is a tall order. Its successful fulfilment demands equal in size resources implying a position of pre-eminence in the financial and hence political scheme of things.

The task of maintenance of national unity and cohesion also fell to the lot of the army by default. Pakistan's political leadership was land based and parochial in make-up, approach and outlook. The top rung was always prone to suggestions, allurements and intimidation. In the absence of strong political programmes, parties aspiring for power made no appeal to the people. National politics was confined to the drawing rooms of the elite. Inevitably a permanent climate of instability, like that of monsoon weather alternating regularly between the fair and the cloudy was created.

Pakistan Peoples Party of 1967-71 was an exception but soon after its assumption of power it also became like any other grouping of the established classes. In good time the PPP became to be identified more as a disturber of social harmony and tranquillity than a proponent of a new social order.

Now go back in time again and witness displacements and degradations of governments. At provincial level changes started from the first day of independence. Dismissal of Dr. Khan Sahib ministry in the Frontier on the morrow of independence was followed sometime later by Khurro in Sindh and Mamdot in the Punjab. This points out to early fissures between the centres of power. In East Pakistan Mr. Nur ul Amin was defeated in elections by a student that went to highlight the gulf between the ruling party and popular sentiment.

At the centre a game of musical chairs started after the assassination of Liaquat Ali Khan in 1951. In such a scenario everything had to come to a stand still. After 9 years of impasse, a constitution was finally promulgated only to be abrogated two years later. By then, the politics of Pakistan had entered a dark phase. Sectarianism and parochialism had taken root. Occasionally riots were choreographed for show of force and intimidation. Leaders of political establishment, instead of focussing on the national level crises concentrated on games of power and pelf. The main political party, the Muslim League split up under such pressures.

The vacuum had to be filled in consonance with the laws of nature. The Army moved in on a very good logic. Political instability was affecting the integrity of the Army and hence the defence of the nation was jeopardised. The situation had to be put right. General Ayub Khan, first the Chief Martial Law Administrator, a little later the President, eagerly and competently filled the top leadership slot. He was a military man and had a clear mind but an authoritarian style. He had the Constitution of 1962 tailor made to his requirements. However, he ruled well and laid the foundations for the industrialisation of the country. He also laid the foundations of break up of Quaid-e-Azam's Pakistan.

He authorised a war over Kashmir soon after his victory against Miss Fatima Jinnah in the presidential election. Pakistan Army failed in its objectives in Kashmir (1965) but did succeed in defending the country against Indian invasion across international borders. The pointless war disillusioned people particularly in East Pakistan where they felt insecure, unprotected and exploited. By 1968 movement against Ayub government gathered tremendous momentum and in March 1969 he stepped aside handing over power to the Commander-in-Chief of the Army. Some observers point out that around that time the establishment led by Ayub Khan took the decision to let East Pakistan go its separate way. They point out that it was in conformity with that bias that General Ayub Khan handed over power to the Commander-in-Chief rather than to the Speaker of the National Assembly as was laid down in his own constitution. Theories that General Yahya Khan forced Ayub out are not convincing and are certainly not held out either by the character of Yahya Khan or by the events that followed.

Under General Yahya Khan came the East Pakistan tragedy. Thousands of innocent citizens were killed and the ensuing war resulted in the break of Quaid-e-Azam's Pakistan and emergence of Bangladesh. But was the Army as an institution to blame? Had not the political establishment coaxed, cajoled and encouraged the Army in its actions. Read again the first comment on the army action in Dacca on 26th March 1971 'Thank God, Pakistan has been saved'. It came from a political leader, Mr. Bhutto.

Mr. Bhutto, became the CMLA and the President before he became the first elected Prime Minister of Pakistan. Such was the influence of the military on a 'champion of democracy'. To remove a counterpoise, he quickly forced out General Gul Hassan Khan the incumbent C-in-C who according to many was instrumental in Mr. Bhutto's accession to power. General Tikka Khan served loyally for four years. Then Mr. Bhutto in preference to a number of other equally competent officers selected General Zia-ul-Haq as the next Chief of Army Staff mainly because he believed the latter to be more reliable.

Events following the 1977 elections, created a crisis of huge proportions. The whole nation was in turmoil and the Army once again took over the administration of the country. True that the Army had intervened only when the country was on the verge of a civil war but equally true is the fact that there was a presence of highly ambitious officers among the top brass. Stephen Cohen mentions that Bhutto had been warned of the dangerous consequences of military crackdown in Balochistan as the middle ranks of Officer Corps were acquiring a taste for political power. Obviously, Mr. Bhutto ignored the warnings.

General Zia proceeded cautiously and read the whole situation carefully. He came up with a perfect solution. He realised that the Pakistani people could be easily rallied under the slogans of Islamisation. He promised Nizam-e-Mustafa leaving its definition in contemporary economic and political terms as vague. Under this scheme Zia acquired the brawn of the street in addition to the power of the state. With this intermixture of formal and informal power came a deeper penetration of the Army into politics. The army also assumed the role of the defender of the ideological borders of the state to the joy of a certain group.

Then in 1979 Soviet Union intervened in Afghanistan. Here the interests of Afghan Mujahideen, Pakistan, United States, China and other Muslim countries came to coincide. Pakistan supported Afghans and the Army trained Mujahideen guerrillas with American weapons. Mujahideen's success was a great plume in the hat of Pakistan Army but the country was left plagued with the fallout.

Zia's era ended in 1988. Some people draw a comparison between the regimes of Ayub and Zia. Although the two regimes lasted about the same number of years but Zia would have continued, had he not been killed in the air crash. Ayub Khan was a reformer who treaded on a number of toes in pursuit of a social agenda. Zia didn't commit that mistake. He brought about no reforms but preserved the status quo in the name of piety. As leader of the army also he was no patch on Ayub. Ayub's army was spick and span; straight, professional and exclusive. Zia transformed it beyond recognition to some of its old souls. It became 'awami' in culture, threw away its exclusivity, acquired hypocrisy, cultivated the art of compromise on standards and learnt the many unsavoury ways that were considered essential to ruling Pakistan.

After General Zia, came General Aslam Beg who now runs an NGO and a political party. He exercised political power through proxy. General Asif Nawaz, who was a little more forthright, created waves when he took on the MQM in Karachi although the party was a partner in the coalition at the centre. General Abdul Wahid was unobtrusive. However, when the occasion called, he exercised the power of his office in a most decisive manner and saw his constitutional bosses President Ghulam Ishaq Khan and Prime Minister Nawaz Sharif out of office. General Karamat was tolerable but towards the fag end of his tenure he was asked to resign over a non-issue. This highhandedness did not go well with the Army.

This was a period when a naval chief also had to go due to a corruption scandal. The overall image of the forces was badly smeared. Their former sheen and prestige had suffered. Their confidence and sharpness was reduced. They came to be treated like any other department of the Government of Pakistan and often assigned duties far removed from the business of warfare. Somewhere along the line they also picked up some of the tasteless peculiarities of their civilian counterparts and became poorer in self-regard.

In such a season of despair, General Pervez Musharraf took over as Chief of Army Staff. His first concern was restoration of the morale of the command. Kargil was an opportunity and he made the best of it. The soldiers found their mettle and were well on their way when the Prime Minister bungled. Victory won in the field was thrown away. Showing complete ignorance of the military system he began to conspire against his own Army Chief. A badly choreographed drama to sack the COAS rebounded with a force that knocked the Prime Minister from his perch.

Having taken over the country as a result of the consensual action by the army, General Pervez Musharraf is now striving for continuity. People have tentatively put their faith in the General and are hoping for results.

Mr.Nawaz Sharif like some of his predecessors had badly underestimated General Pervez Musharraf both as a leader of the army and leader of the country.

PAKISTAN AIR FORCE - MODERNIZATION

The US security assistance relationship with Pakistan resumed subsequent to September 11. Given its geo-strategic location and partnership in the Global War on Terrorism (GWOT), Pakistan is a vital ally of the United States, as reflected in the June 2004 designation of Pakistan as a Major Non-North Atlantic Treaty Organization Ally. By 2008 the United States had delivered a variety of equipment to Pakistan, including refurbished C-130E transports, refurbished P-3C surveillance aircraft, refurbished Cobra helicopters, new Bell 412 helicopters and a number of Harpoon missiles, Harris radios, AN/TPS-77 surveillance radars, night vision goggles and AIM-9M Sidewinder missiles. On 16 July 2002, the Defense Security Cooperation Agency notified Congress of a possible Foreign Military Sale to Pakistan of C-130E Cargo Aircraft and associated equipment and services. The total value, if all options are exercised, could be as high as $75 Million. The Government of Pakistan has requested a possible sale of six used C-130E aircraft with engines, one C-130E operational capabilities upgrade aircraft for cannibalization with engines, upgrade of engines to Allison 56-A-15 engines, modification kits, spare and repair parts, devices, support equipment, publications and technical documentation, personnel training and training equipment, U.S. Government and contractor engineering and logistics personnel services and other related elements of logistics support.

The estimated cost is $75 million. This proposed sale will contribute to the foreign policy and national security of the United States by helping to improve the security of a friendly country which has been and continues to be an important force for economic progress in South Asia. Pakistan needs these aircraft to support a current and long-term airlift shortfall, both for Pakistan Air Force internal requirements, and as it seeks to support the U.S. Government with Operation Enduring Freedom. These C-130E aircraft will be used for the purpose of providing airlift support. Pakistan can easily absorb and utilize these within its existing structure.

In August 2003 Pakistan agreed to receive from the US six ex-Australian Air Force Lockheed C-130E Hercules aircraft. The seven aircraft had been in storage in the USA for three years awaiting re-sale. A contract was signed in September 2004, for Lockheed to upgrade the six aircrafts, while the seventh example will be used as spares. The first of the six Lockheed C-130 Hercules military cargo airplanes ordered by PAF in 2003, left US on 31 October 2005, heading for Islamabad. *The disposition of these aircraf is unclear - logically, they would replace the older L-100 and C-130B in the PAF inventory, but this point is unresolved in the open literature.*

PAF ordered four Mi-171 helicopters in 2002 from Ukraine for its Special Services Group, which were delivered in 2004. A follow-on order of further 12 examples was also placed. The helicopters were intended for search and rescue duties at various PAF bases. The delivery of the follow on order also commenced in 2004.

The first of four CN-235 transport aircraft ordered by PAF was delivered three months late, in February 2004, due to labour dispute at the aircraft factory. PAF ordered these planes in 2002 in a $52 million deal. The second example was delivered in September 2004. The delivery of the third was due in October and the final was due in December 2004. The final of the four CN-235 ordered by PAF from Indonesia, was delivered in Jun 2005. This is a VIP aircraft, the interior of which has been designed and fitted by Avion-interiors of Italy.

In July 2004 PAF finalised a deal with Libya to buy its fleet of 50 Mirage IIIs and Vs, 150 sealed pack engines and a huge quantity of Mirage spares. Libya had purchased the Mirage jets in the 1970s, and they had been grounded for the previous decade following sanctions imposed after the Boeing 747 was blown up over Lockerbie. With these airframes, Pakistan operated more Mirages than the French Air Force. It is believed that jets would be cannibalized for spare parts to provide spares for the PAF fleet of Mirages for the next seven to ten years. As of 2009 the Mirage Rebuild Factory, which is a part of PAC, had been rebuilding 35 year old version of the Mirage aircraft which were bought as scrap from various countries.

Following the delivery of two JF-17 aircraft from China in 2007, PAF received delivery of a further six which were undergoing tests & evaluation at PAC Kamra as of April 2008. The assembly of JF-17 aircrafts in Pakistan was formally launched on 22 January 2008 at PAC Kamra. In the first year (2008), eight to ten aircrafts will be assembled for the Pakistan Air Force. The assembly will gradually increase to 25 aircraft per year by 2011. It is reported that around 60% of the frame of the aircraft and 80% of the avionics to be fitted in the aircraft will be manufactured in Pakistan by 2010. PAF have a requirement of 150 aircraft in phase-I. The first 40 to 50 examples would have the Chinese avionics, thereafter the aircraft would be fitted will indigenously developed avionics.

In June 2006, the PAF had signed a deal for the supply of six Saab 2000s. However, because of shortage of funds, the number of aircraft was revised to five. Another report suggests that the Erieye airborne surveillance system deal involves up to eight Saab 2000 aircraft. The first Saab 2000 AEWC aircraft ordered for the PAF was rolled out on 3 April 2008 at the SAAB factory in Sweden. The ERIEYE, developed by the Ericsson Microwave Systems, comprises fixed, dual-sided and electronically scanned phased-array pulse-Doppler radar mounted on top of the fuselage.

Pakistan Air Force received the delivery of a second Gulfstream 450 aircraft in November 2007. The first aircraft was delivered in December 2005.

In September 2008 it was reported that Pakistan was to receive 20 refurbished T-37 training aircrafts from the USA. The aircraft will be supplied to Pakistan free of charge, however Pakistan will bear the cost of shipment only. The delivery of the aircraft was due in two months time.

On 25 January 2009 Pakistan's defence minister informed the parliament that Pakistan has placed a $278 million order for the Chinese AWACS system ZDK-03 based on Chinese Y-8 aircraft.

In January 2009 PAF received delivery of two IL-78 tanker aircraft from Ukraine, out of the four ordered. Once the IL-78 tanker aircraft have been commissioned into service, it will enhance the long range capability of Pakistan air force.

Pakistan Air Force (PAF) Chief of Staff Tanveer Mehmud Ahmad gave an interview to AFM and was published in the September 2008 issue.

- By 2015, PAF would comprise 240 JF-17, 60 F-16's, 40 FC-20's (PAF version of J-10), 50 F-7PG's [for a total of 390 combat aircraft, versus 335 in 2008], along with 4 SAAB Erieye, 4 ZDK-03 (PAF version of Y-8), 4 IL-78 Midas. In 2015 the PAF will remain at its current strength of 15 Squadrons.
- The current order status comprised 150 JF-17's, 32 F-16's (variant unspecified), 4 Erieye's, and 4 IL-78.
- The Block 52 F-16's will be based at PAF Shahbaz to replace Mirage air defense aircraft.
- The Peshawar based 26 & 16 Squadrons will be the first to convert from A-5 to JF-17 in 2009. Delivery of JF-17 had started and once the assembly facility had been completed at AMF, the induction pace will pick-up to eventually allow delivery of 25-30 aircraft per year to achieve the final numbers by 2015 [this makes no sense, with a 30/year production rate only yielding about 150 aircraft by 2015, not the stated 240]. The 150 JF-17's are expected to equip 7 or 8 squadrons.
- The FC-20 order would be confirmed in 2009. The current J-10 technology was not up to PAF requirements, and PAF hoped to include western equipment in the J-10. This would create a different version than the PLAAF J-10, which would be known as FC-20 in PAF service. The FC-20 would not be required to have conformal fuel tanks, since it had sufficient internal fuel capacity as well as AAR by Il-78 Midas tankers. The FC-20 requirement was 2 squadrons of 36-40 single and dual seater aircraft.
- The IL-78 Midas tankers would provide aerial refueling for all PAF fighter aircraft excepttf the US manufactured

F-16s. The F-16s can only refuel with a boom system, and the Midas will be equipped with a probe and drogue underwing pods system. First Midas delivery will commence early 2009. PAF is holding out hope that a KC-135 could be acquired from the US in the near future.

- While the Erieye's will datalink the F-16's, they will not be able to do so with the Mirage fleet. The first Erieye will be delivered in 2009, followed by the remainder by 2011. The Chinese origin fighter aircraft will have AEW&C support from the planned acquisition of 4 ZDK-03 (Chinese Y-8 AWACS). The ZDK-03 contract was close to be being finalised for the required 4 aircraft.
- The PAF is acquiring 2 Squadrons of the Italian Falco UAV with coversion taking place for operations from PAF Mushaf and PAF Peshawar. Eventually, the PAF plans to field 5-6 UAV Sqn's.

On November 20, 2008 Air Chief Marshal Tanvir Mahmood Ahmad said 36 high-tech combat aircraft (CF-20) would be inducted into the PAF fleet by 2010. He said that modalities were being discussed to acquire two squadrons of the aircraft for the PAF. He said the FC-20 aircraft had been selected after hectic and lengthy deliberations besides considering a long list of the similar category aircraft of various origins. In December 2010 Pakistan Air Force received the final batch of the F-16 fighter jets from the United States. These new F-16 C/D Block 52+ fighter jets were part of the 18 aircrafts ordered by the Pakistan Air Force. These new F-16 C/D Block 52+ fighter jets are stationed at the Pakistan Air Force's Shahbaz airbase. Pakistani defense minister said that PAF is interested in purchasing the F-16 fighter jets from the Royal Norwegian Air Force which was looking to replace them with the low observable stealthy F-35 fighter jets.

The deliveries of the Block II JF-17 Thunder to Pakistan Air Force were scheduled to start from the second half of the 2012 and will continue till 2015. From 2016, JF-17 Thunder Block III would enter into production.

In August 2011 it was reported that the Chinese government had offered to provide its advance fourth generation J-10B fighter jets to the Pakistan air force to meet its requirements of high tech fourth generation frontline fighter aircraft.

The J-10B is an improved version of the basic J-10A powered by the Chinese WS-10 engine. Pakistan has total requirement of 150 front line fourth generation aircrafts which will be met with the induction of Chinese J-10B/FC-20, F-16AM/BM and F-16 C/D Block 52+ fighter aircraft. In September 2013 it was reported that Pakistan air force (PAF) would receive its first FC-20 / J-10B fighter jet in 2014.

In February 2014 the Pakistan Air Force acquired 13 F-16A/ B block 15 aircraft Fighter jets from Royal Jordanian Air Force (RJAF). Pakistan was to take the delivery of 12 F-16A and 1 F-16B fighter jets starting in March 2014. The Jordanian fighter jets would increase the F-16 total to 76. These fighter jets will serve PAF for another 20 years with almost 3,000 hours on average available to them for flying.

Pakistan Air Force achieved another significant milestone in its quest for modernization and expansion of fighter aircraft fleet, as the first batch of F-16s from Jordan landed at an operational Air Base 27 April 2014.

The aircraft were purchased from Royal Jordanian Air Force after series of negotiations held between concerned Ministries and the concerted efforts of Air Chief Marshal Tahir Rafique Butt, Chief of the Air Staff Pakistan Air Force. To avoid extra burden on the national exchequer, PAF opted for the used planes as they were acquired at nominal cost per bird and could serve for longer duration.

The Pakistan Air Force (PAF) showed interest in buying fourth generation stealth fighter aircraft FC-31 from China. Janes reported 12 November 2014 that the Pakistan Air Force (PAF) was in talks with China to buy 30 to 40 of the Shenyang FC-31 twin-engined stealth fighter displayed at Airshow China 2014 in Zhuhai.

Pakistani Defence Production minister Rana Tanveer Hussain said in late Novembe 2014 that the matter was being discussed with Chinese authorities. According to Dawn, it was for the first time that a senior government functionary had confirmed talks with China over purchase of the longer-range stealth aircraft.

2001–2011: WAR ON TERROR AND 'NEW DAWN'

Counter-insurgency operations

The Pakistan Army faced several problems during its 2009 offensive against the Taliban in north-west Pakistan. Hundreds of thousands of Pakistanis fled the area when the offensive was announced and, eventually, over 2 million had to be accommodated in refugee camps. The offensive was to be completed as quickly as possible to allow the refugees to return to their homes but the army's fleet attack helicopters were not sufficient to provide adequate support to the infantry. The PAF was sent into action against the Taliban to make up for the lack of helicopter gunships. Because the PAF was trained and equipped to fight a conventional war, a new "counter-terrorist doctrine" had to be improvised.

The PAF's *Saffron Bandit 2009/2010*exercise focused on extensive training of combat personnel to undertake COIN operations. New equipment was inducted to improve the PAF's joint intelligence, surveillance and reconnaissance (ISR) capabilities. A C-130 transport aircraft was indigenously modified for day/night ISR operations.

The PAF had been forced to use Google Earth for reconnaissance imagery until high resolution infra-red sensors were provided by the U.S. prior to the army's 2009 campaign in the Swat valley. These were installed on around 10 of the PAF's F-16 fighters and used to gather detailed reconnaissance imagery of the entire valley. Use of laser-guided bombs was increased to 80% of munitions used, as compared to 40% in the previous 2008 Bajaur campaign. A small corps of ground spotters were trained and used by the PAF, in addition to PA spotters, to identify high value targets.

Prior to the PA's offensive into South Waziristan the PAF attacked militant infrastructure with 500 lb and 2000 lb bombs.

After the Mumbai attacks and threats made by India PAF was put on high alert. Pakistani press reported an outstanding order to launch a counterattack in case of an air attack from India after Indian Foreign Minister Pranab Mukharjee threatened Pakistani President in rough tone. On the morning of 14 December Indian aircraft started moving towards Pakistan,PAF moved swiftly and intercepted them before they entered international borders. Two of the aircraft did cross the border but Indian aircraft managed to turn back. PAF was ordered to carry on the defensive combat patrols but avoid hostile action unless further hostile action was to take place.

A number of civilian deaths occurred during PAF air strikes on 10 April 2010 in the Khyber tribal region. According to a Pakistani military source, the first bombing was targeted at a gathering of militants in a compound. Local people, who had quickly moved onto the scene to recover the dead and wounded, were then killed during a second air strike. There was no confirmed death toll but at least 30 civilian deaths had occurred according to the military source, whereas a local official stated at least 73 locals, including women and children, were killed. A six-member committee of tribal elders from the area, tasked with finding the exact number of civilian casualties, reported that 61 civilians were killed and 21 wounded. This was not confirmed by military or political leaders but Pakistan's Chief of Army Staff, General Ashfaq Kayani, gave a public apology on 17 April. It is reported that BBC news and several other media correspondences were not allowed to take interviews from injured which makes the whole episode more mysterious.

On 22 May 2011 it was reported that the PAF had retaliated against attacks by Afghan mortar and machine gun positions on the Pakistani posts at Miskinai and Sangpura in the Bajaur area. It was stated that since 19 May, around 1000 Afghan Askaris had entered the Bajaur area at Sahi as well as Miskinai and Sankpura. The Afghan forces had been firing at the posts during night and, after reconnaissance sorties, PAF aircraft destroyed the Afghan positions.

Modernisation and acquisitions

In light of Pakistan's significant contribution to the War on Terror, the United States and Western European countries, namely Germany and France, lifted their defense related sanctions on Pakistan; enabling the country to once again seek advanced Western military hardware. Since the lifting of sanctions, the Pakistan Air Force (PAF) became heavily active in evaluating potential military hardware such as new fighter aircraft, radars and land based air-defense systems. However the urgent relief needed in Kashmir after the 2005 Kashmir earthquake forced the Pakistani military to stall its modernisation programme so it could divert its resources for fuel and operations during the rescue efforts.

The modernisation stall would end in April 2006 when the Pakistani cabinet approved the PAF's proposals to procure new aircraft and systems from several sources, including modern combat aircraft from the U.S. and China. The AFFDP 2019 (Armed Forces Development Programme 2019) would oversee the modernisation of the Pakistan Air Force from 2006 to 2019.

The Bush administration on 24 July 2008 informed the US Congress it plans to shift nearly $230 million of $300 million in aid from counterterrorism programs to upgrading Pakistan's aging F-16s. The Bush administration previously announced on 27 June 2008 it was proposing to sell Pakistan ITT Corporation's electronic warfare gear valued at up to $75 million to enhance Islamabad's existing F-16s. Pakistan has asked about buying as many as 21 AN/ALQ-211(V)9 Advanced Integrated Defensive Electronic Warfare Suite pods, or AIDEWS, and related equipment. The proposed sale will ensure that the existing fleet is "compatible" with new F-16 Block 50/52 fighters being purchased by Islamabad.

After the September 11 attacks in 2001, the U.S. and Pakistan began discussing the release of the embargoed F-16s and a purchase of new aircraft. Of the 28 F-16A/B built under the *Peace Gate III/IV* contracts and embargoed in 1990, 14 delivered as EDA (Excess Defense Articles) from 2005 to 2008., two of which were delivered on 10 July 2007.

Between 2005 and 2008, 14 F-16A/B Block 15 OCU fighters were delivered to the PAF under renewed post-9/11 ties between the U.S. and Pakistan. These had originally been built for Pakistan under the Peace Gate III/IV contracts but were never delivered due to the U.S. arms embargo imposed in 1990.

To upgrade the F-16A/B fleet, 32 Falcon STAR kits were purchased for the original *Peace Gate I* aircraft and 35 Mid-Life

Update (MLU) kits were ordered, with 11 more MLU kits optional, in. 4 F-16A/B being upgraded in the U.S. to F-16AM/BM, delivery expected December 2011. F-16A/B in PAF service to be upgraded starting October 2010 by Turkish Aerospace Industries, 1 per month.

The *Peace Drive I* contract for 12 F-16C and 6 F-16D Block 52+ (Advanced Block 52) aircraft, powered by F100-PW-229 engines was signed on 30 September 2006. The first F-16 to be completed, an F-16D, was rolled out on 13 October 2009 and began flight testing. The first batch of F-16C/D Block 52+, two F-16D and one F-16C, landed at PAF Base Shahbaz, Jacobabad, on 26 June 2010 and one more F-16C was received by 5 July 2010.

On 19 May 2006 the PAF inaugurated a refurbished Sector Operations Centre at PAF Base Mushaf (Sargodha) which had been installed with a Pakistani-developed air defence automation system for command and control. An old air defence system installed in the 1980s was replaced.

During talks with a delegation from the French Senate on Monday 28 September 2009, Prime Minister Yousuf Raza Gilani stated that the PAF had used most of its stockpile of laser-guided munitions against militants in the Malakand and FATA regions and that replacements for such types of equipment were urgently required.

In December 2009 the PAF's first Saab 2000 Erieye AEW&C was delivered from Sweden and Il-78MP Midas aerial refuelling tanker/military transport aircraft from Ukraine.

The PAF is reported to be considering purchasing the Hongdu L-15 advanced jet trainer to train pilots for high-tech fighters such as the FC-20. Extensive evaluations of the aircraft took place in Pakistan during December 2009.

On 26 June 2010 the first batch of 3 F-16C/D Block 52+ fighters were delivered to PAF Base Shahbaz, Jacobabad. According to Air Chief Marshal Rao Qamar Suleman the new fighters would eliminate the PAF's limitations in precision night-time strike operations, the existing capability being based on around 34 Dassault Mirage 5 fighters upgraded with new avionics for night-time precision strike missions under the Retrofit Of Strike Element (ROSE) programme during 1999-2004.

It was reported in 2010 that the R-Darter, an active radar homing beyond visual range air-to-air missile, is being operated by the Pakistan Air Force.

2008 air alert

On 13 December 2008, the Government of Pakistan stated that two Indian Air Force aircraft were intercepted by the PAF kilometres within Pakistani airspace. This charge was denied by the Indian government.

Introduction of female engineers and pilots

Previously, women had been employed by Pakistan's armed forces in non-combat roles only, such as the medical corps, and the PAF had remained all-male throughout its history. However, in 2003 women were allowed to enroll in the aerospace engineering and other programs of PAF Academy Risalpur, including fighter pilot training programmes. It was stated that standards would not be compromised for women and those who did not achieve the same performance as their male counterparts would be dropped from the course. A level of segregation between the genders is maintained. For example, early-morning parades are performed together but some parts of training, mainly physical exercises, are done with males and females separated. According to Squadron Leader Shazia Ahmed, the officer in charge of the first female cadets and a psychologist, this also improves confidence of the women.

In 2005 it was reported that two batches in the Air Force Academy's flying wing contained 10 women, with many more in the engineering and aerospace wings. Cadet Saba Khan, from Quetta in Balochistan, applied after reading a newspaper advertisement seeking female cadets. She was one of the first four women to pass the first stages of flying training on propeller-driven light aircraft and move onto faster jet-powered training aircraft.

In March 2006, the PAF inducted a batch of 34 fighter pilots which included the organisation's first four female fighter pilots. Three years of training had been completed by the pilots at PAF Academy Risalpur before they graduated and were awarded their

Flying Badges during the ceremony. Certificates of honour were handed to the successful cadets by a "delighted" General Ahsan Saleem Hayat, vice chief of the Pakistan Army, who acknowledged that the PAF was the first of the Pakistani armed forces to introduce women to its combat units. One of the women, Flying Officer Nadia Gul, was awarded a trophy for best academic achievement. The other female graduates were Mariam Khalil, Saira Batool and the above-mentioned Saba Khan. A second batch of pilots, including 3 female pilots, graduated from the 117th GD(P) course at PAF Academy Risalpur in September 2006. The Sword of Honour for best all-round performance was awarded to Aviation Cadet Saira Amin, the first female pilot to win the award. Aviation Cadet Saira Amin won the Asghar Hussain Trophy for best performance in academics. In September 2009 it was reported that seven women had qualified as operational fighter pilots on the Chengdu F-7, the first female combat pilots in the PAF's history, one of them being Ambreen Gull. Commanding Officer Tanvir Piracha emphasised that if the female pilots "are not good enough as per their male counterparts, we don't let them fly." It was noted that some of the female pilots wear the hijab while others do not.

Bibliography

Abdul Qadir : *Criminal Law of Islam,* Kitab Bhavan, New Delhi, 1999.

Akbar, M. K. : *Kargil Cross Border Terrorism.* South Asia Books, 1999.

Amitabh Sikdar: *India and China : Strategic Energy Management and Security,* Manas, Delhi, 2009.

Arend, A.: *International Law and the Use of Force,* London, Routledge, 1993.

Ayesha Siddiqa-Agha: *Military Inc.: Inside Pakistan's Military Economy,* London: Pluto, 2007.

Azad, Maulana Abul Kalam: *India Wins Freedom,* New Delhi, Orient Longman, 1959.

Bamzai, P. N. K.: A *History of Kashmir,* Delhi: Metropolitan, 1962.

Bhaskara Rao: *Military Conversion : Impact on Science and Technology,* Discovery, Delhi, 2003.

Chitkara, M.G. : *Indo-Pak Relations Challenges Before New Millennium,* APH, Delhi, 2001.

Choudhury, Golam W: *Pakistan: Transition from Military to Civilian Rule,* Scorpion, 1988.

Duscha, Julius. *Arms, Money and Politics.* New York, 1965.

Fatima, T. : *Islamic Law and Judiciary,* Deep & Deep Publications, New Delhi, 2001.

Gao, Mobo: *The Battle for China's Past: Mao and the Cultural Revolution,* London, Pluto Press, 2008.

Ghosh, Ajoy : *Indo-Pak Conflict : Threat to South Asian Security,* Reference Press, Delhi, 2003.

Heathcote, T. A.: *The Indian Army – The Garrison of British Imperial India, 1822–1922.* David & Charles. Newton Abbot, Devon. 1974.

Hoffman, Bruce, *Inside Terrorism,* New York: Columbia University Press, 1998.

Hussain Mushahid: *Pakistan: Problems of Governance,* Vanguard 1993.

Ikram, S.M. : *Muslim Civilization in India,* Oxford, New York, 1981.

Imtiaz, A.: *State and Foreign Policy: India's Role in South Asia*, New Delhi, Vikas, 1993.

Jha, Prem Shankar : *India and China : The Battle Between Soft and Hard Power*, Penguin Books India, Delhi, 2010.

Juvale, R.P. : *Military Strategy and Diplomacy*, Cyber Tech Publications, Delhi, 2010.

Keane J.: *Democracy and Civil Liberty in Afghanistan*, London, Verso, 1988.

Kilcullen, David: *Counterinsurgency*, Oxford University Press, 2010.

Lamb, Alastair: *Kashmir: a disputed legacy, 1846-1990*, Oxford University Press, 1991.

Laquer, Walter: *The New Terrorism: Fanaticism and the Arms of Mass Destruction*, Oxford: Oxford University Press, 1999.

Mohiuddin, Ahmad : *Saiyid Ahmad Shahid*, Modern Pub., Lucknow, 1975.

Nevile, P.: *Lahore: A Sentimental Journey*. New Delhi: Penguin, 1993.

Oudha, Abdul Qadir : *Criminal Law of Islam*, Kitab Bhavan, New Delhi, 1999.

Prasad, Lal Bahadur : *Indian Political System and Law*, New Delhi, Shree, 2005.

Rhodes, Richard, *The Making of the Atomic Bomb*, New York: Simon and Schuster, 1988.

Rosen, P.: *Societies and Military Power: India and its Armies*, Ithaca, Cornell University Press, 1996.

Shaun Narine, *Explaining ASEAN: Regionalism in Southeast Asia*, Boulder, CO: Lynne Rienner Publishers, 2002.

Singh, Amarinder : *A Ridge Too Far: War in the Kargil Heights 1999*. Motibagh Palace, Patiala. 2001.

Smith, W. C. : *Modern Islam in India : a Social Analysis*, Manohar Publishers, New Delhi, 1985.

Sumantra Bose, *The Challenge in Kashmir : democracy, self-determination and a just peace*, New Delhi: Sage, 1997.

Sutton, J., *Technology and Defence Market Structure*, MIT Press, Delhi, 1998.

Winkler, Allan M. *Life Under A Cloud: American Anxiety About the Atom*. New York: Oxford University Press, 1993.

Zafeeruddin, M.M. : *System of Modesty and Chastity in Islam*, Idara Ishaat-e-Diniyat Pvt. Ltd, New Delhi, 1995.

Index

R

S

T

W

❑❑❑